Black Success in the UK

Essays in Racial & Ethnic Studies

Edited by Doreen McCalla

First published 2003 by DMee: Vision Learning Ltd.
Lonsdale House, 52 Blucher Street, Birmingham, B1 1QU

Copyright © 2003 Doreen McCalla

First distributed 2003 by Cambridge University Press,
Shaftesbury Road, Cambridge, CB2 2BS

Typeset by Cambridge University Press,
Shaftesbury Road, Cambridge, CB2 2BS.
Printed and bound in England by Cambridge University Press
Shaftesbury Road, Cambridge, CB2 2BS

Cover design and illustration by Louis Wright

All rights reserved. No part of this book may be reprinted, reproduced, or utilised in any form or by electronic, mechanical, or other means, now known or hereafter invented, including photocopying, recording, information stored or retrieval system, or otherwise, without the prior permission in writing from the publisher.

The views expressed in each chapter are those of the individual authors and are not necessarily the views of the publisher.

British Library Cataloguing in Publication Data
A catalogue record for this book is available from the British Library

ISBN: 0-9545856-0-7

For my parents Galfymore and Dorothy

Contents

Foreword i
Trevor Phillips
Contributors ii
Acknowledgements iv
Introduction: Tracking the Terrain 1
Doreen McCalla

Part I Black Success and Society

1. Collective Action and Black Politics 9
   Harry Goulbourne
2. Media Representations: Continuity, ... 39
   Contradiction and Change
   Simon Cottle
3. 'We don't just make tea': Redefining Political 50
   Activism
   Julia Sudbury
4. The Success of our Mothers: Caribbean 85
   Mothering, Childrearing and Strategies
   in Resisting Racism
   Tracey Reynolds

Part II Education and Black Success

5. The Influence of Home, School and Community 101
   on African-Caribbean Success in the UK
   Susan Hallam and Jasmine Rhamie
6. Syble's Successful Children 125
   Doreen McCalla
7. Uncovering Genealogies of the Margins: 151
   Black Supplementary Schools
   Diane Reay & Heidi Safia Mirza

Index 175

—

Foreword

When we celebrated the Windrush anniversary Britain was reminded of the depth of its Caribbean roots. Black Britain is a vibrant and dynamic part of modern British life. But it is often seen through the prism of negative stereotypes, of difficulties with the police and of academic underachievement.

What a pleasure it is to be invited to write the foreword to this collection of essays which reminds us that not only is Black Britain a powerful presence in our society but that it can also be a highly successful one.

Perhaps it is Black Britain as much as the rest of society which needs to be reminded of the stories of success as well as the pain of discrimination and prejudice. Let's all take inspiration from the stories and the arguments laid out here but let's also learn the lessons and understand better how to turn Black exclusion into Black success.

Trevor Phillips,
Chair of the Commission for Racial Equality

Contributors

Professor Simon Cottle is Professor of Media and Communications and currently Director of the Media and Communications Program at the University of Melbourne, Australia. Prior to his previous appointment he has worked as an academic at University of Leicester, Bath Spa University College, University of East London and University of Coventry. His research publications address the mediation of diverse conflicts and the production of news and television programmes. His books include: *Television and Ethnic Minorities: Producers' Perspectives* (1997), and as editor *Ethnic Minorities and the Media: Changing Cultural Boundaries* (2000). He is currently series editing a new international collection of 'Media in Focus' books for Sage Publications and has written two books in the series *Media Production and Organization* (2003), and *News, Public Relations and Power* (2003). He is also currently writing *Media Performance and Public Transformation: The Case of Stephen Lawrence* (Praeger 2003) and conducting a major international comparative study of TV news and current affairs entitled 'TV News, Current Affairs and Deliberative Democracy'. In addition, Simon has written numerous commissioned reports as an academic consultant.

Professor Harry Goulbourne is Professor of Sociology and Director of the Race and Ethnicity Research Centre, South Bank University. He is presently researching into a large-scale Economic and Social Research Council (ESRC) funded Research project on Families and Social Capital programme of work. Harry is co-directing the Ethnicity strand of the project. He has written widely on ethnic studies and published several books including *Race Relations in Britain since 1945* (1998) and *Caribbean Transnational Experience* (Pluto, 2002).

Professor Susan Hallam pursued careers as both a professional musician and a music educator before joining the Department of Psychology and Special Educational Needs at the Institute of Education, University of London in 1991. In 1996 she took on the role of Co-ordinator for Promoting Excellence in Teaching and in 1997 became Assistant to the Dean of Professional Development. She joined Oxford Brookes as Professor of Education in January 2000 returning to the Institute of Education in January 2001. Her PhD was concerned with the development of expertise. Since then she has received research funding from many funding bodies including the Economic and Social Research Council (ESRC), Calouste Gulbenkian Foundation, Nuffield Foundation and several LEAs for a range of projects relating to attendance at school, exclusion from school, school-home links, ability grouping in primary and secondary schools and pedagogy in secondary and higher education.

Professor Heidi Mirza is Director of the Department of Ethnic and Racial Studies at Middlesex University, London. She has taught Afro-American Studies at Brown University USA and carried out research on gender issues in the Caribbean and Britain. She has published widely and is the author of *Young, Female and Black* (1992) and editor of *Black British Feminism: A Reader* (1997), both published by Routledge.

Dr Doreen McCalla is a Social and Educational Consultant and Director of Doreen McCalla Education Enterprise (DMee): Vision Learning Ltd. She is also an external academic to the University of Birmingham. Her research interests are race and gender studies, pre-school and out-of-school provision, research methods (mainly qualitative) and decision making in education. She has produced publications in each of these areas. She is co-author of *Local Nurseries for Local Communities* (2001), published by the National Children's Bureau. Doreen has taught education policy/sociology, social policy and comparative social policy in which racial studies was featured in all these areas at various UK universities such as, University of Manchester, Manchester Metropolitan University and Nottingham Trent University. In addition to her academic engagements Doreen has been involved in various charity and community activities for many years including Pentecostal Church engagements.

Dr Diane Reay is Senior Lecturer in Research Methods in the School of Social Sciences and Public Policy, King's College London, University of London. Diane is an education sociologist working in the area of social class and its intersections with gender and ethnicity. She has researched boys' underachievement, Black supplementary schooling, higher education access, female management in schools and pupil peer group cultures, parental involvement in education and children's relationships to space and place in the city. She is the author of *Classwork: Mothers' Involvement in their Children's Primary Schooling* (UCL, 1998). Diane is on the editorial boards of the *British Journal of Sociology of Education* and *Gender and Education*. She teaches Research Methods at post-graduate level.

Dr Tracey Reynolds is a Research Fellow in Faculty of Health and Social Studies (FHSS) at South Bank University, London where she completed her PhD. She is currently carrying out research on Mothering, Paid Work and Childcare. Tracey's research interests are Mothering in Britain and African Caribbean Women and has published academic articles from her PhD and current work such as 'Black mothering, paid work and identity, *Journal of Ethnic and Racial Studies*, 24, 6, pp. 1046-64.

Jasmine Rhamie is an experienced African Caribbean teacher who has worked in a range of educational settings in both primary and secondary phases of education. She graduated from Newman College, University of Birmingham in 1983 and is currently completing her Doctoral studies at the Institute of Education, University of London where she completed an MA in the Psychology of Education with distinction in 1998. In addition to teaching she has also worked in several voluntary projects with children and has recently published an article with Susan Hallam in *Race Ethnicity and Education*.

Professor Julia Sudbury is Rockefeller Humanities Residency Fellow in the Sex, Race and Globalization Project at the University of Arizona (2002-03) and Associate Professor of Ethnic Studies at Mills College, Oakland, CA. Before moving to the U.S. she was the Director of Sia: The National Development Agency for the Black Voluntary Sector, London, and Coordinator of Osaba Women's Centre for African Caribbean Women and Children in Coventry. Her book *Other Kinds of Dreams: Black Women's Organisations and the Politics of Transformation* (Routledge, 1998) is a best seller, having won various awards. It documents coalition building and contested identities in the black women's movement in Britain.

Acknowledgements

This book has been eighteen months in the making that is, from the inception of thought concerning an edited collection on Black achievement in the UK, to approaching prospective authors regarding submission of chapters, potential distributors and possible publishers, to the finished print. This edition of *Black Success in the UK* is finished but Black success in 'Black Britain' must be seen as an ongoing project that is ever evolving and transforming beyond the pages of this literary text. Many people have contributed to this book's making and ultimate completion without whom *Black Success in the UK* would not exist.

I would first wish to appreciate five people. Errol Williams, an author of several books himself, incited me to approach Cambridge University Press while thoughts of this book was still in its embryonic stage. He has remained a constant source of encouragement. Wilton Powell, thoughtful, considerate and pastoral, has allowed me both time and space to complete this work. Thanks to Louis Wright, a 'cool, calm, and collected all-rounder', for his professional approach, unceasing devotion, creative and technical insights who worked relentlessly on the cover design. Adrian Thorne and his team at Cambridge University Press have also worked alongside me and given their expert advice and constant support and inspiration. My appreciation goes to Sam Chen for his financial management and administrative direction.

The production of *Black Success in the UK* gained for me some new intellectual contacts, colleagues and friends, and reaffirmed existing ones. I gratefully acknowledge Simon Cottle, Harry Goulbourne, Susan Hallam, Heidi Safia Mirza, Diane Reay, Tracey Reynolds, Jasmine Rhamie and Julia Sudbury for contribution of chapters. Lesley Atkins has provided invaluable comments on revisions to chapters and, along with Tracey Jones, proofread the book. Both Lesley and Tracey are to be commended for their swift turnaround of suggestions to chapters.

Special thanks to copyright holders and authors for permission to reprint all or parts of existing publications. These publications are:

Goulbourne, H. (2002) *Caribbean Transnational Experience*. London, Pluto Press, chapters 4 and 6: pp. 79-101; 136-158. Kind permission granted by author and Pluto Press Ltd.

Reay, D. and Mirza, H.S. (1997) Uncovering Genealogies of the Margins: Black Supplementary Schooling, *British Journal of Sociology of Education*, 18, 4: pp. 477-499. Kind permission allowed by authors and Routledge Publications Ltd.

Rhamie, J. and Hallam, S. (2002) An Investigation into African Caribbean Academic Success in the UK, *Race, Ethnicity and Education*, 5, 2: pp. 151-170. Kind permission granted by authors and Carfax Publishing.

Sudbury, J. (1998) *Other Kinds of Dreams: Black Women's organisations and the politics of transformation.* London: Routledge, chapter 3: pp. 51-92; Appendix 1: pp. 238-243. Kind permission allowed by author and Routledge Publications Ltd.

A heart-felt acknowledgement to Trevor Phillips for agreeing to do the Foreword and for supporting colleagues at the Commission for Racial Equality, namely Chris Myatt, the CRE Press Officer.

Finally, every effort is made to acknowledge everyone who has directly or indirectly contributed to the success of this book, but if anyone has been inadvertently overlooked, I will be pleased to amend this at the first opportunity.

Introduction: Tracking the Terrain

Doreen McCalla

Black Light

Hopped into my car
Went down to Birmingham, Alabama
(There I) went to the museum of civil rights
And got a lesson in suffering
(There I) saw the likes of Rosa Parks,
Medgar Evers, Dr. Martin Luther King
And I got all emotional singing 'we shall overcome,'
'Let freedom ring'

I'm looking for a boy, looking for a girl
Who's got a dream inside to change the world
Give me a lady
Come on give me a man
Who's strong enough to take a stand (and be a)

Chorus

Black light, a candle in the darkness
Black light, courageous and strong
'Til there is no more bigotry and madness
All it takes is a spark, and the fire will burn on and on

I stood in front of the porch with all the lights out
Guess what I was seeing
There was a myriad of diamonds
flung out across a velvet sky
And it served to remind me of the
perseverance of those before me
'Cause the darker the night
the brighter the starlights are gonna shine

I'm looking for a boy, looking for a girl
Who's got a dream inside to change the world
Give me a lady
Come on give me a man
Who's strong enough to take a stand (and be a)...

Chorus

Nicole C. Mullen and David Mullen (2000)[1]

Introduction

Black Success in the UK paints a timely, historical and contemporary portrait of the successes and achievements (broadly defined) of people of Caribbean and African descent in the UK. The thrust of the argument is that despite the universal underachievement of people of African and Caribbean descent in the UK, with which the general public, British and World medias, professional and academic literature is constantly portraying, all is not doom and gloom.

As a people, Caribbeans and Africans have experienced mass, colonial slavery and international migration and its ensuing economic, social and cultural struggles. These struggles mainly relate to racial discrimination and a lack of cultural knowledge (culture capital) on the part of the indigenous people about the migrating population. Of course, the mistreatment meted out by the indigenous population on African and Caribbean people when they first arrived in the UK is not unique. Other ethnic groups who also migrated to Britain in the 1950s and 1960s share similar experiences and tell comparable stories. Nonetheless, unlike some non-White ethnic groups, who came to the UK as middle-class professionals, such as immigrants from India, for example, and therefore received a less hostile reception from the host nation, the majority of African and Caribbean migrants were, and still are in varying degrees, working-class and were invited to Britain as semi- and un-skilled labourers (Goulbourne, 1991; Layton Henry, 1992). Whilst the social and economic position of some working-class, unskilled ethnic groups, especially from the Southern Asian Continent, have largely remained unchanged since their arrival in the UK, my previous research project which investigated Black success (see chapter 6) not only demonstrated academic and employment achievement, but also upward social mobility of people of Caribbean descent. The findings from this study confirmed my prior inkling about social mobility and the success of a segment of Caribbeans. It also excited my interest and curiosity to further investigate this area and network with other practitioners and scholars who were also endorsing my interest. This book thus emanates from these two factors.

Success or what?

In order to fully appreciate and understand successes of Caribbean and African people residing in the UK, they must be viewed with and from retrospective, consecutive and prospective lenses. Retrospectively speaking, success is seen as experienced amidst difficulties, racial oppression, unexpected circumstances, in attempts to combat racism and/or challenge racial and cultural ignorance on the part of both Blacks and Whites. The 1950s and early 1960s produced limited effort and progress towards countering racial aggression through political and social activism. This was because Caribbean and African migrants were still coming to terms with their astounding welcome and mistreatment in the UK. However, the late 1960s and 1970s witnessed a wave of emergent political and social action with the promotion and development of Black projects/organisations primarily geared towards aims and outcomes of racial justice and equality. Both Harry Goulbourne and Julia Sudbury, in their chapters, discuss some of these social and political innovations.

In consecutive terms, progression from the 1970s to the present day has been an evolutionary one. In addition to attempts to champion the cause of racial equality and integration, success has taken on new meanings and is manifesting itself through numerous definitions such as, theories, policies and practices of racial diversity, greater tolerance and Black identities - common features of mainly the 1990s (Hall, 1992). As this book highlights, fifty years after the first immigration influx of African and Caribbean peoples, we are now able to speak of, demonstrate and produce conceptual knowledge about educational and/or employment achievement.

What of the future? Whilst it can be argued that some successful advancements have been made, there is definitely no room for complacency with regards to prospective developments. The year 2003 marks the tenth and second anniversaries of the murders of Stephen Lawrence and Damilola Taylor respectively in South London. Whereas the families of these two Black boys still grieve over their tremendous losses, the criminal justice system has failed to produce convictions and the prime suspects remain at large. Unfair police arrests and the deaths in custody of Black youths remain a prominent concern in British society. Racial stereotyping and racism still exist, albeit covertly expressed and thus more difficult to detect, in for example, social and public provision. More specifically, the educational and employment underachievement of Black males is particularly concerning.

Of course the deaths of Stephen and Damilola can never be condoned nor seen as acceptable, it is nevertheless the fact that the impact of their deaths in terms of theoretical and practical developments in racial studies and race relations, has been phenomenal. This phenomenon is not only evident from a British perspective but is also of immense interest to academics and practitioners of 'race' and ethnicity in western advanced societies, in particular, North America. Stephen's and Damilola's murders have advanced our understanding of the concept of 'institutional racism' (McPherson,1999), produced new insights into ways of tackling racism and, based on the lifestyles of Stephen's and Damilola's parents, has produced anecdotal evidence to suggest that a African and Caribbean middle-class is emerging in Britain (see McCalla,2002). In terms of educational and employment underachievement, constant talk of failure has the negative effect of 'self-fulfilling prophecy'. The aim of this book is now to focus on success in an attempt to reverse this trend of perpetuating failure and underachievement.

Although racial divisions and tensions have always been far more prominent in the U.S. than the U.K., America is, nonetheless, pioneering the recognition of Black successes within educational establishments and other public providers with regards to individuals' and groups' actions. In principle, its affirmative action programmes are designed to ensure that access to education and employment, at all levels and types, is maintained, although, in practice, this is questionable. Maybe now the time and climate has come for Britain to follow suit in terms of promoting Black British achievements beyond the remit of sport and music; starting with the State schooling system as part of the National Curriculum and to continue developments into the Citizenship Education Curriculum.

The Structure

The structure of this book is in two parts. Part I looks at Black success in society more generally whereas Part II focuses specifically on the relationship between education and Black success.

Part 1: Black Success and Society

> The past five years have witnessed a remarkable growth in documentation of the diverse histories that make up 'Black Britain'. No longer limited to the pages of the *Voice*, or the stage of the Hackney Empire, Black writers, playwrights, artists and television producers have brought the diverse voices of African and Caribbean communities to the forefront. ... from the world of haute couture to the House of Commons (Julie Sudbury's comments in email, November 2002).

Introduction

In chapters one and three, Harry Goulbourne and Julia Sudbury respectively, address themes of Black political and collective action in 'Black Britain'. Goulboune's essay examines the processes of political change and focuses on Black consciousness, group formation, Caribbean community participation and the Black ideologies underpinning these processes. He shows that Black people have utilised the medium of publications as a communicative voice for political change. From a Womenist perspective, on the other hand, Sudbury concentrates on the important role of women in political collectivism. Drawing on interviews with women activists, Sudbury explores the campaigns, debates and collective successes of Black women's organisations from the 1970s. She is careful to point out that women activists 'don't just make tea', but, from battles on the frontlines over Depo Provera, racist violence and school exclusions, to building alternative school and childcare programmes, Sudbury demonstrated that Black women's grassroots activism has broken new ground and redefined the Black experience in Britain.

Simon Cottle draws on research studies on the role of the media in addressing the problematics of race, racism and ethnicity. His essay argues that media representations are historically dynamic and conflicted, exhibit complexity and, increasingly, give expression to the surrounding politics of cultural diversity and changing identities. He points out that unlike yesteryear, we are better able to understand media representations. The reporting of the Stephen Lawrence affair and the 'public crisis' that this unleashed across the period 1993-2000 serves to exemplify both the changing terrain of 'race', racism and diversity in Britain as well as the complex articulations of the media within this.

Finally in part one, Tracey Reynolds' essay discusses Caribbean mothering success in childrearing which involves the mothers' adopting necessary strategies to teach their children how to combat racism which they are apt to encounter in 'Black Britain'.

Part 2: Black Success and Education

In Part II, all three essays discuss issues of Black attainment in education and employment. Susan Hallam and Jasmine Rhamie demonstrate two models impacting on the success of participants: a Home-School Model, which describes positive interaction between the home and school where both cultivate academic excellence, and a Home-Community Model which suggests that the family and community together create a 'sense of belonging' and foster achievement. My own essay touches on some of the issues raised in Hallam and Rhamie's account. However, it primarily celebrates the significant role played by a Black-mother figure, Syble Morgan, in the lives of Black achievers and discusses concepts of 'positive self-identity', 'citizenship', and 'high expectations'. Finally, the successful contribution of supplementary schooling in the education of Black children is the focal point of the discussion in Diane Reay's and Heidi Mirza's essay.

In his book, *Young, Gifted and Black*, where he focuses his study on English schools, Mac an Ghaill (1988) demonstrates educational success of children of Asian origin. The book does not examine educational success of children of African/Caribbean origin but instead, portrayed them as educationally lagging behind compared with other ethnic groups. Yvonne Channer's (1995) book *I am a Promise* makes some inroads in attempting to redress this unbalanced view concerning Caribbean children's education underachievement. However, her work is heavily criticised for not making a clear link between achievement and other social factors as intended. Nonetheless, some evidence of school academic accomplishment is demonstrated by Heidi Mirza (1992) in *Young, Female and Black*. Mirza's book focuses exclusively on education success and specifically on the academic achievement of girls. She fails to consider other areas of Caribbean achievement or boys/men. The three chapters in

Part II thus aim to bridge a gap in terms of African and Caribbean educational success in Black Britain.

Apart from references to educational achievement mentioned above, Stephen Small (1994) in *Racialised Barriers* briefly points out employment success of Caribbean peoples in sport and music and in fact Small demonstrates that they excel and dominate their White counterparts in specific fields. With these exceptions, however, Small's work is essentially about obstacles to Caribbean success in England and the USA rather than achievements. The recent appointment in 2002 of the first, Caribbean Cabinet Minister (Paul Boateng) by the current Labour Government is a prime example of employment success. In addition to Boateng, other politicians such as, Diane Abbott, have played prominent roles in British politics for many years. Sir Trevor McDonald, in news media coverage and factual TV presentations and Sir Bill Morris, leader of the Transport and General Workers Union (TGWU), demonstrate that there is some practical evidence of Black success in the UK.

The point to be made here is that although there is some success in areas other than in sport or music, it is rarely documented and seldom perceived as success. Part II therefore aims to show the employment success of groups as well as individuals.

Conclusion

The most important aspect of this edited book is the problematics of Black success that is, Black success amid the presence of struggle. Black struggle cannot, nor should not, be ruled out from our understanding of racial and ethnic relations in the UK. This is simply because for many Caribbean and African peoples, and other Black ethnic groups, such struggles exist. Whilst they do exist, it is possible to succeed without showing the struggles that accompany or accompanied achievement. From my interaction with some first- and second-generation Caribbean immigrants, this is a reality. Some of their well-furnished homes that are located in leafy suburbia disguise the overcrowded, rundown dwellings which they once occupied. It is only when conversing with them that their historical struggles are revealed. These Caribbeans have not forgotten their modest beginnings but simultaneously do not allow it to prevent them from basking in and enjoying their newfound accomplishments.

Whist many writings on race and ethnicity clearly demonstrate Black struggle, it should not be assumed that Black achievement is and must always be the result of struggles. It is possible for people of Black descent to succeed in the absence of opposition as seen in aspects of this book. As pointed out above, the US is historically ahead of the UK in terms of having produced and in promoting generations of 'Black Lights'. However, for Caribbeans and Africans to also follow in the steps of Black America, 'Black Britain as much as the rest of society ... needs to be reminded of the stories of success as well as the pain of discrimination and prejudice' (Trevor Phillips, the Foreword) and for our literary accounts to reflect both sides of the debate.

Introduction

Note

[1]*Black Light* is taken from Nicole C. Mullen's (2001) album *Talk About It* which is published by Word Entertainment, a division of *Word Music Group, Inc.* Nicole Mullen is a composer of modern, funky, pensively provocative, Christian music. The lyrics of most of her songs combine her faith with critical issues relating mainly to 'race' and gender and often recalls the memories of her own lived-experiences as a practising, African-American, female Christian in a racially divided society.

References

Channer, Y. (1995) *I am a Promise: The Schooling Achievement of British African Caribbeans.* Stoke-on-Trent: Trentham Books

Goulbourne, H. (1991) *Ethnicity and Nationalism in Post-Imperial Britain.* Cambridge: Cambridge University Press

Hall, S. (1992) New Ethnicities, in J. Donald, and A. Rattansi (Eds.) *Race, Culture and Difference.* London: Sage

Layton Henry, Z. (1992) *The Politics of Immigration.* Oxford: Blackwells

Mac an Ghaill, M. (1988) *Young, Gifted and Black.* Milton Keynes: Open University Press

McCalla, D. (2002) *The Academic and the Community Meet: Two Black Female Voices, International Journal of Inclusive Education, 6:2, pp.165-183.*

McPherson, W. (1999) *The Stephen Lawrence Inquiry, CM4262-1.* London: The Stationary Office

Mirza, H.S. (1992) *Young, Female and Black.* London: Routledge

Small, S. (1994) *Racialised Barriers.* London: Routledge

Part I

Black Success and Society

Chapter 1

Collective action and Black politics

Harry Goulbourne

Editor's Note

In this chapter Harry Goulbourne focuses on collective (and individual) social action in two related areas: (1) Black political coalitions and (2) professional publications by writers as a communicative voice. This chapter is a slightly modified version of two chapters in Goulbourne (2002) that is, chapter 4, 'Africa and the Caribbean in Caribbean consciousness and action in Britain in the 1970s' and chapter 6, 'Having a public voice: Caribbean publishers and diasporic communications.' In these chapters Goulbourne examines the processes of political change by focusing on Black consciousness, group formation, Caribbean community participation and ideologies. He demonstrates that the derivative of collection action in both these areas is the trademark of Caribbean accomplishment in Britain. Goulbourne points out that British Caribbeans have actively and successfully been engaged in social and political change and not merely passive spectators of social injustice.

This chapter aims to capture both areas mentioned above through two sections. Section one will focus on Black political coalitions and section two shall concentrate on professional publications. As this book is concerned with Black success in the UK much of the detailed material that relates to activities performed in the Caribbean and/or Africa shall be omitted from this account. Similarly, due to space, specific case studies of events will also not feature here. Instead, the reader is invited to consult Goulbourne (2002) for a comprehensive discussion.

Section 1: Black political coalitions

Of the various Caribbean groups in Britain which saw themselves as being essentially political in purpose, perhaps none was more consistently so in the formative years of the 1970s than the Black Unity and Freedom Party (BUFP). But, expectedly, the BUFP could not neatly separate political from welfare activities. However, with its radical agenda for change, it eschewed what it saw as cultural nationalist postures, but at the same time drew upon Caribbean and African heroes, icons and radical ideas, thereby playing a major part in the development of the consciousness of a wider Caribbean as well as reviewing the historic breach with Africa, themes that were to become fairly familiar by the 1980s.

This section analyses three aspects of the group's history in order to illustrate two important points: first, the sense of Africa and the Caribbean as parts of a general Atlantic diaspora; and second, the backdrop to active political participation of Caribbeans in mainstream British politics and society in the last decades of the last century and the beginning of the present one. The three aspects of the group's history are, first, the origins of the group; second, its beliefs or ideology, and third, the kinds of activities with which the group was involved in the emerging Caribbean communities of the 1970s. The account here draws on the group's publications including minutes, memoranda, leaflets and its newspaper, *Black Voice*, coverage in the local press, and personal observations at meetings. While subsequent developments are not neglected the emphasis here is on the early history of the group in the 1970s when not unlike other similar groups, BUFP was most active and relevant to the general articulation of radical politics in these new communities.

Origins, continuity and structure

On Saturday 27 July 1991, the BUFP celebrated its twenty-first anniversary with an afternoon programme around the theme of 'self-defence and community organisation'. Held at the premises of the Simba Project at 239 Uxbridge Road in West London, the programme included an address by founding member Danny Morrell who spoke on 'The first year - 1970' followed by open discussion. There were two sessions of poetry readings by young writers, messages of solidarity from other groups in Britain and abroad, and open discussion sessions. During the course of the afternoon there were long presentations by BUFP spokespersons on 'From Aseta Simms to Rolan Adams (1970-1991)',[1] and 'Self-defence and community organisation - the struggle for liberation today'. Creches for babies and small children were provided; a 'collection' was made, a donation of £1 requested and a small charge made for some food items - all in order to help with the costs of the day. Book selling, the playing of music, the exchange of a variety of information, 'reasoning', and good cheer and humour punctuated the day. The event was billed for the afternoon, and everything went on in a well-organised, orderly manner, with the programme being kept within schedule. At no point did it appear that there might be police interference, as would have been the case in the 1970s, when one or more comrades would be tasked to keep an eye open for either agents provocateurs and/ or the raiding police. Participants appeared to be perfectly at ease with themselves and their surroundings and many appeared to be conscious of the fact that the BUFP had played an important role in the development of Black consciousness in Britain.

Indeed, there was something here of a happy family affair. True enough, Comrade Danny, Comrade Jerry and myself were present, but missing were most of the original founding members of the BUFP, and a different membership had command of affairs. George Joseph, the premier figure in the founding of the group, had returned to Trinidad in 1973, worked as a civil servant and came to an untimely death in the mid-1980s. His widow, Sonia Chang (from Jamaica) had accompanied him to Trinidad, but returned first to Jamaica and then to London with their son Che (named after Ernesto Che Guevara, the Argentinian turned Cuban revolutionary). Busy working in London with the Hackney West Indian Neighbourhood Association and caring for her son, Sonia was also absent at the BUFP meeting on 27 July. Also absent were Emil Chang (a cousin of Sonia's), who had come to Britain to play cricket in the 1940s, returned to Jamaica in the 1970s and then returned to live in north-east London (where he died in the mid-1990s). There was a noticeable absence of the kinds of young, critical, intellectuals who would have been present in the early years.

Typical of this last group was Alrick (Ricky) Xavier Cambridge, undoubtedly the second moving spirit behind the formation of the group in the summer of 1970; he was also absent at the twenty-first anniversary celebrations. He and the BUFP had parted company in late 1971. A dynamic and creative personality, Ricky had gone on to found the Black Liberator journal which sought to pull together a number of themes about revolution and change in the Caribbean and in Britain. Indeed, for the few years of its existence the Black Liberator became the leading Black and Caribbean journal in Britain, but apart from Hall et al. (1978), the work of this publication has attracted no attention in the academic literature. With the demise of the journal Cambridge went on to realise a long ambition of completing a degree. Following well-established middle-class West Indian tradition, he went to Oxford, where he later registered for a doctorate in philosophy, studying the Trinidadian historian and intellectual, C.L.R. James, and publishing on issues such as identity and belongingness.

George Joseph on the other hand, of a less intellectual bent than Cambridge but with perhaps a more practical mind, had studied sociology at university and held an MA. The first years of the BUFP were very much a credit to him, moving between south-east and north-east London and Manchester (Moss Side and Oldham) in the north-west of England. He exuded quiet confidence and optimism among both the majority younger, as well as the older, members of the group. Of the generation of middle-class West Indians who came to Britain primarily to study, he was one of the first of the relatively few who established a meaningful and practical relationship with working-class West Indian immigrants and their offspring. The fact that he ended up teaching/training the Trinidad police is part of the irony of class, race and the migration process. The story for a number of the group's members was to be similar, that is to say, some would end up in professional (medicine, law, academic work, etc.) or semi-professional (teaching, social and youth work, etc.) occupations in Britain or elsewhere.

The family atmosphere of the twenty-first anniversary celebrations was also reflected in the sense of forgiveness, the irrelevance of past differences and quarrels. Danny Morrell, for example, had for a while been regarded as 'Daft Danny', due to his enthusiasm over some now forgotten matters. Two decades on, he proved to be one of the most faithful and consistent of the group of 1970-71, and he clearly appreciated the respect the younger people were paying him. Comrade Jerry had gone on to establish a happy family, with children doing well at school and one about to go to university (the bourgeois institution he would have condemned in the early 1970s). He looked as young as he did in 1971, but he was now a great deal more tolerant and appeared a wiser man.

In many respects, the agenda in 1991 was not very different from what it would have been in the early 1970s. There would have been much the same mix of social provision and care, entertainment and general social mixing reminiscent of the church, the family and the social club in Caribbean communities in Britain. Political discussion, however, formed the central concern of the day. Earlier, there would have been a stronger emphasis on constitutionality, and procedures would have been more formal; dogmatism and certainty, verbal intolerance and adherence to purity of doctrine, with frequent references to Marx and Engels, Lenin, Stalin, Mao and Fanon would have been stronger, or at least less subtle in 1970 than in 1991.

But perhaps the noticeable difference between the founding members of the BUFP in 1970 and those who met to celebrate its twenty-first anniversary in 1991 was the gender dimension of the leadership. In 1970 all the leading speakers were men, with women aplenty playing supportive but less prominent roles. On 27 July 1991 the main players were women. Now, a number of men played supporting roles, and thereby reflected one of the major social shifts in Caribbean communities in the UK, that is, the greater prominence of women in the public sphere.

Thus, whilst the invitation to the occasion went under the signature of a male, Kimathi (name of a Kenyan Mau Mau leader who fought against settler colonialism), the chairperson for the day was Julietta Joseph (no relation to George), and women dominated the occasion. It was as if the men had come to recognise or accept their broader subordinate role to the women (where active participation and responsibilities are concerned), but there was no sign of resentment, disrespect or competition. The situation seemed natural enough to all present. Nor was there any reference to gender issues in order to justify the situation. The group had obviously either achieved something important here or was reflecting the sad state in the community whereby the absence of men or their less than active leadership roles are becoming more pronounced.

In terms of age distribution, the membership of the group appeared to be much the same as in 1970. In general, the BUFP had been an organisation of young people in their late teens or early adulthood to their thirties. The re-migration of many of its members in the 1970s, and the moving on of some to other concerns, had helped to keep the age profile of the group more or less constant. Spawned by the protest of youths in the 1970s, the BUFP in the 1990s sought to renew its original inspiration; it appeared as if one generation was passing on responsibility for the organisation to the next. This youthful profile did not conform to the general description of most groups where there is usually the tendency for the membership either to remain constant or decline, the membership ageing with the organisation. This is certainly a major problem for what may still be the main Caribbean umbrella organisation in the country, the West Indian Standing Conference (WISC) which has been both a broker and a protest group from its inception in 1957 following the Notting Hill white riots (Editor's Note: see Goulbourne, 1990).

The constantly renewing membership of the BUFP did, however, have its weakness. If older members were inaccessible, then the accumulation of useful experience could disappear all too rapidly, and younger people were then forced to start afresh the process of learning. The continued existence of the BUFP beyond the early 1990s was therefore in question. One mitigating factor was the prospect of there being more elderly Caribbean folks spending their retirement years in Britain instead of returning to the Caribbean or re-migrating to North America. Another mitigating factor was the fact that the organisation had relatively clear ideas about its work: it kept records, published, and members were deeply committed to what they saw as their work. The group was also rooted within local communities. The ups and downs of state and other forms of public funding did not affect the group, because it did not depend on such resources, but on its own membership.

It was not surprising, therefore, that the publications announcing the group's activities in 1991 would appear familiar to anyone from a meeting in 1970. One poster called upon supporters to celebrate the two-hundredth anniversary of the emergence of Toussaint L'Ouverture, the Haitian liberator, who led the only successful slave rebellion in history; the Haitian Revolution was being interpreted as 'Black history for action' in the 1990s. Another leaflet called for support of the family while others protested against the racist killing of Rolan Adams on 21 February 1991 in Thamesmead, and was to trigger a London-wide protest with the famous Revd Al Sharpton of New York participating at one point, thereby continuing to make links between Black struggles and concerns across the Atlantic. The group called for support at the Old Bailey on 7 October 1991, when the case would be heard, and at the British National Party headquarters in Welling (East London) on 2 November 1991. Not surprisingly, another pamphlet was concerned with the 'Black community against women's oppression'. There was information about developments in the Asian communities in Britain, events in the Caribbean, Africa and elsewhere. The group reaffirmed its basic principles, which were first set out in 1970, and although modified over the years, remained consistent.

It may be useful, therefore, to consider the circumstances which brought the group about, circumstances which would have, to one degree or another, most likely informed the formation of similar groups in and around London and a number of large cities in Britain such as Birmingham, Bristol, Liverpool, Manchester and Southampton. London was, however, the centre of these activities not only by virtue of being the nation's capital, but more importantly because the vast majority of people from the Caribbean between 1948 and 1962 had settled in one or the other of the inner boroughs such as Lambeth, Haringey and Southwark.

Three closely related sets of developments may be said to contribute to, and set the context for, the emergence of the BUFP and similar groups such as the Croydon Collective, the Black Liberation Front, the Black Panther Movement, and the South East London Black People's Organisation, which sprang up throughout the city in the early 1970s.

Black consciousness and group formation

Perhaps the first development which formed the backdrop for the emergence of these community-based groups was the breakup of the Universal Coloured Peoples' Alliance (UCPA). This had been formed by the Nigerian playwright Ebi Egbuna in 1967 (Egbuna, 1971), and some leading lights included the Guyanese Ron Phillips who later played a major role in community politics in Manchester,[2] and Roy Sawh, later of Black Rights UK. As the UCPA explained in one of its leaflets in 1970, the word 'coloured' was widely accepted at the time, and the name also reflected that of Marcus Mosiah Garvey's Universal Negro Improvement Organisation of the 1920s (see Lewis and Warner, 1986; Lewis and Bryan, 1988). The formation of the UCPA followed the dramatic visit of Kwame Toure (at the time, Stokeley Carmichael) to London and his talk at the Roundhouse in Chalk Farm.[3] Just as the earlier visit in 1964 by Martin Luther King - en route from Stockholm after receiving the Nobel Peace Prize – had stimulated the founding of the Campaign Against Racial Discrimination (CARD), so Kwame Toure's visit stimulated the birth of a new body. CARD had become an umbrella organisation, bringing together existing Asian groups – such as the Federation of Pakistani Organisations, the Indian Workers Association and Caribbean groups such as WISC themselves umbrella bodies – under its aegis. CARD sought to influence government to legislate against racial discrimination in housing, employment and public places such as clubs and restaurants, much as civil rights groups in the US had done, resulting in Lyndon Johnson's momentous 1963 Civil Rights Act (see Heineman, 1972).

It would appear that just as CARD broke up into its previous constituent parts and in the process stimulated the birth of new groups – such as the Joint Council for the Welfare of Immigrants (JCWI)[4] and the Runnymede Trust and the UCPA itself – so too the collapse of the UCPA spawned new groups in Black communities in England's inner cities. With respect to Caribbean groups, the two main organisations which emerged during these years were the Black Panther Movement (BPM) and the BUFP.[5] The BMP was initially led by David Udah, a Church of England clergyman, who later went on to play an important role in opening the established church to issues of colour and inequality in the Diocese of Southwark. Another leader was Darcus Howe, a nephew of the late C. L. R. James and a then collaborator with John Larose or New Beacon Publishers. Howe later went on to lead the Race Today Collective with Leila Hussain (originally from Zanzibar and a former member of the BUFP) and the poet Linton Kwesi Johnson, who became, and has remained a fusion of Black poetry and music movement in Britain. Later still, Howe became a programme producer and journalist with the television network Channel 4, working closely with the former student radical, the Trotskyist Tariq Ali, and Channel 4's programme commissioner, Farouk Dhondi, who was himself a former member of the BPM. Others included Eddie Leconte and Althea Jones (later Leconte), who was at the centre of the famous Mangrove Nine trials in 1970-71 in Notting Hill.[6]

The BUFP founders claimed that they were the legitimate inheritors of the UCPA. Indeed, the build-up to the formation of the BUCP occurred under the umbrella of the UCPA, and the pre-launch documents as well as early BUCP letters, were written on UCPA headed paper, and the UCPA addresses in London and Manchester were taken over by the BUFP. One of the earliest BUFP letterheads read 'Black Unity and Freedom Party (Formerly the UCPA)', and two addresses were given: 45 Fairmount Road, London SW2, and 22 Monton

Street, Moss Side, Manchester 14. One of the major documents prepared for the launch of the BUFP with 'confidential' written at the top and the bottom of the front page reads, 'UCPA for members only, draft reorganisation document'. This document, almost certainly written by Cambridge and Joseph, sets out the group's reasons for the need of a new organisation which would pursue both short- and long-term goals in the interest of the 'masses', or 'Black humanity'; it hailed 'Marxism-Leninism-Mao Tse Tung Thought' as the relevant ideology which would guide the new organisation, whilst practical examples would be drawn from the Chinese and Cuban revolutions. But it proclaimed that the 'best example today' of how to avoid slipping into a totally reformist ideology and programme was declared to be 'the breakfast programme being carried out by the Black Panther Party, while at the same time revolution is on the agenda' (BUFP, p. 4, n.d., but presumably 1970).

The founders of the BUFP, principally led by George Joseph and Alrick Cambridge, saw the BPM and themselves to be divided along fundamental ideological lines. In brief, these lines of difference involved their understanding of the notion or concept of Black Power and the place of the class struggle in the fight for equality in Britain and elsewhere. It would appear that the BPM placed the emphasis on cultural awareness and the unity of all Blacks, and were therefore regarded - using the American term popular at the time - as 'cultural nationalists'. This meant that African history, culture, dress, hairstyle and so on were of predominant importance to them. So too were events in the Caribbean and elsewhere in the Third World. These were also important for the BUFP, but as will be noted, the BUFP tended to place the class struggle at the forefront of their concerns, and cultural matters as relatively less important. Indeed, for the BUFP, events in Britain, the Caribbean, Africa and elsewhere were properly to be understood in class terms. The group condemned the Black bourgeoisie as 'Uncle Toms'[7] as vehemently as it condemned capitalism and imperialism. The BUFP also sought more actively to work with white radical groups than most Black groups did, not because they were white but because these groups shared or had similar ideological orientations as the group, that is to say, they placed the emphasis on class, not colour/race or gender. The ideological hegemony of feminism and cultural studies as well as the demise of collective politics in the 1980s and 1990s were to vindicate the position taken by the BPM and marginalise the BUFP's more uncompromising political position.[8]

Yet, in several ways the BUFP and the BPM were not so very different from each other as their members thought. Their differences might have been as much about personality as about ideology although both groups would have denied this. They were physically located close to each other in the Peckham, New Cross and Brixton areas in South London, and again in North London in Hackney King's Cross and the Angel. To a degree they both drew upon local communities for their memberships. For example, Linton Kwesi Johnson was a pupil at Tulse Hill Comprehensive School a mile or so from Shakespeare Road in Brixton where the BPM had its South London headquarters. Probably half of the BUFP membership in Peckham, New Cross (such as Garfield James, Philip Murphy,[9] Joan Roger Lofters[10] and several others) had been at comprehensive schools in the area such as the then Peckham Manor, Peckham Girls', Dick Shepherd's and so forth. Members of the groups knew each other, and shared similar experiences. George Joseph, Althea Jones and a number of the BPM members were from Trinidad and had come to England to attend university. Memberships were, however spread across the continents for both groups, because Black (a crucial criterion for membership in both groups) was understood to mean any person who hailed from Africa, Asia, the Caribbean or South America; Black or Blackness pointed as much to a person's experience as to his or her pigmentation. The largest membership was in both cases , because these were primarily Caribbean groups responding to and also shaping the radical challenge of young Black people to their status in English society.

The second factor which influenced the formation of the BUFP the BPM, and other groups was the coming of age of a relatively small number of individuals who were neither part of what are usually called the 'first' nor the 'second' generations of immigrants by migration scholars. Typically, the leaders of these groups, such as Joseph, Cambridge, Howe, Leconte and others were individuals born and brought up in the Caribbean. Some, like Howe, had had direct experience of political life before coming to Britain, and were close to individuals such as C.L.R. James and John LaRose who, between them, had considerable Caribbean, North and Latin American experiences. Most members, however, were individuals born in the Caribbean but almost entirely brought up in Britain in the late 1950s and early 1960s. Some had graduated from colleges and universities, others had just left school and were entering the world of work. Here was a mix of factors which spawned a radical questioning of the socioeconomic structures of a Britain which was barely beginning to adjust to its post-imperial position in the world.

The memberships of these groups represented, therefore, a creative cross-fertilisation of youthful aspirations, and these young people were able to draw upon British as well as wider international experience. Perhaps for the first time a dynamic link was being forged between immigrant communities and those who had come to Britain primarily to study. In these years, Caribbean communities in Britain lacked a recognisable elite; middle-class migration had been relatively small, and in any event the relatively few who had come from that class did not necessarily share the experiences of the majority of Black workers and their offspring. The progressive Caribbean Artists Movement (CAM) - documented by Anne Walmsley (1992), one of its English participants - was the major outlet for the Caribbean intellectual elite in Britain but was coming to an end in 1970. This was just at the point when new groups, new voices representing different experiences, were about to begin to articulate new demands and new issues bred largely of the immigrant workers' experience as well as the exclusionary experiences of their disaffected children in the school system and the employment market. CAM was not, however, an elite with particularly strong connections with the immigrant communities; it was a Caribbean elite of young scholars and artists temporarily away from the Caribbean - or in 'exile' as some were wont to say.[11] Their production was important in portraying and structuring the Caribbean across the Atlantic, but the vast majority of its members returned to the region rather than become intellectuals in Britain.

This was a time for the coming of age of a neglected group in the migration process - those who had accompanied immigrant parents to Britain and were not prepared to face the prospects of replacing their parents in lowly, marginal, jobs. It was the loss of innocence about the nature of British society on the part of older folks who had been schooled in the Caribbean about fair play and equality in the 'Mother Country' (see, for example, Carter, 1986). The new assertion also marked the decline of groups such as WISC, which had carried the banner for Caribbean protest in Britain since 1957.

The third aspect of the period which provided the general context for the emergence of radical and Black Caribbean groups was, of course, the prevailing social and political situation of the years 1968-71. Enoch Powell, MP for Wolverhampton and member of the Conservative shadow cabinet, had given his infamous 'rivers of blood' speech in Birmingham in 1968, at a time when US cities were in flames as Black America protested on the streets about their centuries-old repressed and marginalised conditions. These scenes were on television for everyone to see. Also, in the summer of 1970 the Tories under Edward Heath unexpectedly won the general election, and although Powell had been sacked from the shadow cabinet in 1968, his influence in the country and indeed within the Conservative Party was paradoxically on the increase, not in decline (Goulbourne, 1991a).

Moreover, the new government soon made clear where it stood on domestic and international issues pertaining to Africa and Britain's new Black minorities. The foreign secretary, Sir Alec Douglas-Home, the former prime minister who had accompanied Halifax to appease Hitler in the late 1930s, visited South Africa and agreed the sale of arms from Britain to the apartheid regime at a time when all South Africa's neighbours were prosecuting wars of liberation against Salazar's Portuguese colonies and South Africa itself. Nothing significant would be done about the illegal white minority regime of Ian Smith in the then colony of Southern Rhodesia (now Zimbabwe). Not that Labour, in office when UDI was declared in 1964-65, had demonstrated any greater willingness to bring the regime to heel. Indeed, whilst Harold Wilson's government had been quick to dispatch Metropolitan police officers to the tiny islet of Anguilla to squash Webster's attempt at self-government, Smith was made to understand that the British would not use troops against kith and kin in the colony of Rhodesia.

To Britain's Black population these clear signals of support for whites at home and abroad seemed to fit perfectly into a more general pattern of international affairs. From North America to the Caribbean to Southern Africa (including South Africa, Zimbabwe, Mozambique, Angola, Namibia), using NATO, multinational corporations and police forces, white power appeared to be mobilised against the very existence of Black populations in Africa and its diaspora.

Discussions in Britain over control of immigrants soon led to the Immigration Bill which in 1971 became an Act virtually barring Black immigration into Britain by resurrecting from Reconstruction America the 'grandfather clause' as the 'patrial clause'. Individuals with no personal connections with the country but whose grandfathers had been born in Britain could gain entry, but individuals with origins outside Britain currently living in the UK would be restricted in their rights to invite members of their families to join them. Coupled with the policy of repatriation which Powell and the Tory right-wing Monday Club were trying to get their party to adopt, these measures amounted to a very nasty signal from the government to people from Asia, Africa and the Caribbean that they were unwelcome in Britain. Moreover, these were years when the US under Richard Nixon and Henry Kissinger was making a desperate attempt to defeat by any means necessary the Vietnamese people, and expected Britain's political support. In Britain, the anti-Vietnam war movement was petering out after the dramatic demonstrations outside the American Embassy in Grosvenor Square in 1969, and the Vietnam Solidarity Campaign appeared to be at a loss over what should be done to assist the peoples of East Asia in their struggles against imperialism.

Of these developments none seemed more relevant to a settling British Black population than those in Black America. The slogan of Black Power, the news about the Black Panther Party in Oakland, California founded and led by Bobby Seale and Huey P. Newton, ex-prisoner and celebrated essayist Eldridge Cleaver and others, the militancy and fluency of Stokeley Carmichael, the flamboyance of H. Rap Brown, the bravery of Angela Davis, the courage of the Soledad Brothers[12] and a number of similar developments throughout the US (in politics, the arts, sports, etc.) fired the imagination of radicals throughout Britain's new minority ethnic communities. The Americans' books and popular publications, particularly the *Black Panthers Speak*, were avidly read. The fact that the youth of Caribbean backgrounds shared a common history of slavery and a diasporic African culture with Black America meant that their activities would be more immediately received by this section of the new communities in Britain. Moreover, in the late 1960s and early 1970s, before Idi Amin's expulsion of British Asians from Uganda, Black youths with a Caribbean background constituted the majority of young people in the ethnic minority communities. It is a mistake however to assume - as it has become fashionable to do since the mid-1980s (see Modood, 1988) - that the Black explosion in America did not affect people in the British Asian communities; it did (see Sivanandan, 1986). And it was also to have a major impact on most areas of community life in Britain for the next two decades, thereby forming - for better or for worse - part of the link between British and American race relations issues and perspectives (see Hiro, 1971).

The militant radicalism of the American Black Panthers was also to influence the formal structure of the BUFP. The Panthers had deliberately set themselves up as an organisation mirroring the governmental structure of a state, even though they did not formally demand territorial separation and the establishment of a Black state in North America. There was a prime minister (Stokeley Carmichael), a minister of information (Eldridge Cleaver), a minister of defence (Huey Newton), and as in Mao's China, a chairman (Bobby Seale), and a chief of staff. These titles demonstrated the group's seriousness and the main problems they faced. The BUFP did not seek to import wholesale this structure to the British context, but the general tone could be felt within the organisation as reflected in the emphases the group gave to the functions these 'ministers' would be expected to perform in the US. Information and propaganda were important, but of greater significance was the role of the general secretary.

The influence here came from an entirely different source - Leninism. The BUFP's proclaimed adherence to Marxism-Leninism meant that many of the titles used by the American Panthers had to be subordinated to those of the Leninist theory of organisation. This not only involved having a general secretary of the party, but also a commitment to what Lenin called democratic-centralism, the fusing of the dual or contradictory principles of democracy and central control. In practice, central control has proven to be the stronger principle in Leninist organisations, as Rosa Luxemburg had foreseen in the states where such parties came to achieve control of power - the former state socialist systems of East Europe and the former USSR. In the BUFP, Joseph and his successor general secretaries never came to exercise the power or control expected of a Marxist-Leninist group. For several years discussion took place over the appointment of a full-time national organiser, but this was never achieved. Instead, the work of the organisation was conducted by members themselves, with their own internal resources. Unlike the BPM the BUFP never came to own their own premises, but used rented accommodation. This meant that the group did not go through lengthy disputes over ownership of property when some members left the organisation, due to differences, or remigration or return to the Caribbean. However, again, this difference between the groups was to be reflected in later developments, with the BPM being vindicated; the more idealistically orientated BUFP, which eschewed private ownership of property, was proven to be mistaken.

There would be several reasons for this, for instance, the BUFP had never been the clandestine, underground organisation Lenin had in mind; nor was it really a political party as its name would suggest - it never contested elected seats either at national or local levels of the state. The principal reasons for the failure or irrelevance of the Leninist principle, however, are that membership (entry and exit) had been voluntary, and the socio-political culture of members was deeply rooted in the liberal individualism that was characteristic of the social and political ideologies and values of the Commonwealth Caribbean. As I have suggested elsewhere (Goulbourne, 1991, 1998) and have implied in the discussion so far, this is one of the most important underlying principles within the value system of English-speaking Caribbeans; it is in sharp contradiction with the extreme collectivism the Leninist principle takes for granted.

Aims, objectives and ideology

What then were the aims and objectives of the BUFP in 1970, which were still considered to be relevant in the significantly different early years of the 1990s? These were clearly set out in the group's manifesto dated 26 July 1970 (the precise date of the BUFP's founding[13]) repeated in one form or another in the group's newspaper, *Black Voice*, and in various documents. The manifesto is divided into two parts.

The first is a general statement of BUFP's ideological predisposition. It proffers a radical prognosis of British society, and the international context of imperialism and capitalism, and in 1970 its central principles were set out in six points (seven in later years). The differences between the original and the revised later statements are perhaps more significant in this part of the manifesto than in the second part about demands. There is a shift here in ideological tone away from the Maoism of the early years. These principles also set out more forcefully the aims and objectives of the group. It is interesting that the first principle stated by the 1970 document is that it recognised 'the class nature' of British society; the second point was the recognition of the usual Marxist consequence of class and class struggle, resulting in the Leninist commitment to 'the seisure of state power by the working class and the bringing about of socialism'. The later document commences with the 'aim to build a unified and principled organisation capable of serving the needs of Black people'; the statement about socialism and class struggle comes second. Both documents are clear about the class nature of British society, the need to unite against capitalism and imperialism, and bringing an end to the exploitation of 'man by man' (changed to -people by people' in the later version). In 1970, however, the group's leaders drew heavily upon Mao's essay 'On contradiction' in stating these points. The contradiction, following Mao, between the working class and the capitalists is fundamental (of 'primary importance' in the later version), whilst the contradiction between the white and Black working classes is a contradiction among the people (and therefore presumably, in Mao's terms, non-antagonistic). The later statement does not employ Maoist thought.[14]

On the other hand, racism continued to be seen as a major factor in the lives of Britain's Black population. Additionally, in line with the changing times, the manifesto firmly addresses the need to overcome misconceptions among 'oppressed peoples of different cultures' and to promote good understanding among them. Clearly, the multiculturalist theme had worked its way into the group's thinking about British society, because the major ideology embraced by both left and right along the political spectrum had become multiculturalism. Even so, the later statement, like that of 1970 ended with a commitment to the complete overthrow of capitalism/imperialism', bringing to an end exploitation and forging unity with all who share common goals against inequality and are committed to equality and social justice for all.

The second part of the manifesto is a list of immediate demands patterned on the platform of the US Black Panther Party. This part of the manifesto later came to be called the group's 'short term demands', and later still they were condensed from eleven to nine points. The demands were modified, in most cases, to meet British conditions. The first of these remained over the years an end to police brutality against Black people, and a call for a public enquiry into the activities of the police against this section of the community.[15] Official racist hostility at ports of entry into the country; abolition of the Race Relations Acts of 1967 and later 1976 the Race Relations Board and later the Commission for Racial Equality because these measures and bodies were perceived to be used against Black people or were tools 'for the purpose of maintaining the status quo', not changing it. The demands included, further, full employment, trial by peers, an end to racist education of children, representation of Black people on school boards, and 'decent housing, bread, peace and social justice for all people', following the Panthers of Oakland, California.

Whilst the list of demands had remained consistent over 21 years, they had also undergone subtle modifications, reflecting change as well as closer engagement and knowledge of the situation. For example, the fifth demand of 1970 which spoke about returning superannuation and national insurance contributions to Black people who return to their homelands was later omitted, no doubt because it was recognised that people returning to the Caribbean were indeed able to repatriate their contributions. Again, the later version of the demand to be tried by peers does not specify as the 1970 statement does that this means trial by Black magistrates, judges and jurists. It is not clear whether this was because by the 1980s the point had been well made and partly accepted, or because the group's leaders had come to recognise that having Black magistrates did not necessarily alleviate injustice and that their own emphasis on class as the major determinant factor was indeed the more powerful and relevant consideration in such matters. The later statement is also concerned about 'the discrepancy of sentences passed on Black/White "offenders"', reflecting how the debate over the judicial system had moved on. By the 1990s the demand for full employment was no longer the bland, abstract statement it had been; the group now called for an 'end to all forms of discriminatory practices in employment', thereby reflecting change and development in its understanding of the complex employment market situation for Black workers (see Modood and Berthoud, 1997).

The later statement contains two new important demands: first, 'an immediate repeal of the Immigration Act 1971, the repeal of the 1988 [sic] British Nationality Act'. The second new demand is for an 'end to all types of sexual discrimination and the ending of the exploitation of women by men'. These clearly reflected crucial developments since 1970, for although the group was deeply concerned about the status of women from its very beginning, the gender question was less sharply focused upon in British society in the early 1970s than it came to be in the late 1980s and the 1990s. From its very first issue the *Black Voice* carried specific articles on Black women; some were about Black women of historical significance in America and the Caribbean, such as Harriet Tubman who organised the underground escape route for runaway slaves to Canada, and Nanny of the Maroons in seventeenth-century Jamaica. Contemporary women in sports, such as Marilyn Neufville, the Jamaican Olympic gold medalist, and political figures, such as Angela Davis who was being prosecuted by the US authorities for her part in the Black movement in that country, were also featured. The paper also carried pieces on women in Vietnam, and other places where wars of liberation were being waged.

Apart from its formal statement of aims, objectives and broad principles, the BUFP articulated its ideology at its discussions, through its publications and in the causes it espoused. The next section considers some examples of the last of these. But for the remainder of this section I want to look at some of the main questions which the BUFP addressed and in doing so elaborate more generally its beliefs and principles.

The first of these was the question of the revolutionary potential of the working classes in advanced capitalism. This was, of course a long-standing question within Marxism. Marx had argued that the world proletarian revolution would first occur in the advanced capitalist West where the proletariat was being transformed from a class-in-itself into a class-for-itself through class consciousness. In later life he became less certain of this by admitting that the revolution could start in Russia where German capital was making rapid progress in capitalising production and relations of production. It was the debate between Lenin's Bolsheviks and the Mensheviks, leading to the breakup of the Russian Social Democratic and Labour Party at the end of the nineteenth century, which clarified this issue. Lenin and his supporters held that capitalism had reached a new stage where it needed to export capital in order to continue to create surplus, and to defeat capitalism in the present age it was easier to break it at its weakest link. This would be in the periphery of capitalism, in the imperial hinterlands, not in the centres of capitalism. The revolution's success would, however, depend on the eventual revolution in these heartlands by the Proletariat. The Bolshevik Revolution of 1917-18 came, but with the defeat of the Spartacists in Germany, Syndicalism in France, and Fabianism in England no revolution occurred in the West.

But revolution occurred in China, a farther hinterland from the centre of capital in Western Europe and North America. Moreover, the Chinese Communist Party, whilst preaching Marxism, had come to hold state power in 1949 after abandoning the cities following the debacle of 1927 at the hands of the nationalist Koumintang, two decades of fighting in the rural areas and eventually taking the cities. Fidel Castro's successful seisure of state power in Cuba in 1958 further demonstrated the seeming validity of the Leninist-Maoist principle of organised insurrection from outside the advanced centres of capitalism.

BUFP leaders were convinced that contemporary history revealed that revolutionary change could not be realistically expected to come from the workers of Europe and America. Lenin's thesis of the 'labour aristocracy'[16] in the West seemed to be about right with respect to the behaviour of workers, particularly their leaders. Moreover, the working classes had imbibed the racism of the capitalists; workers, organised or otherwise, had allowed themselves to become divided, seeing colour or race or culture as being more important than objective class interests. In Maoist terms, they had allowed secondary, non –antagonistic contradictions to override the fundamental contradiction between capital and labour. This fundamental basis for organised opposition to, and resistance of, exploitation and the divide-and-rule tactics of capitalists, was seen to be frustrated, and revolutionary action by white workers and their organisations was not to be expected in the foreseeable future.

With migration, however Black workers from the neo-colonial world had come to the centre of capitalism. Racism had become a further tool of divide-and-rule. Whiteness united white workers with their capitalist bosses against Black workers. There were few Black capitalists to speak of; and the Black *petite bourgeoisie* (intellectuals, bureaucrats, small capitalists, etc) would vacillate between support for the working classes and support for the capitalists and the oppressors of Black people. In these circumstances, Black workers were placed at the forefront of revolutionary politics in Britain. They constituted the most exploited, the most marginalised and therefore the most class-conscious element within the wider working classes. A particular historical responsibility, therefore, fell to the Black worker. This position pitched the BUFP against those who held firmly to a Eurocentric view derived from Marx, the Mensheviks and particularly Trotsky whose followers felt that they were carrying forward the authentic principles against heretics such as Stalin, Mao, Castro and others.

A second question over which the BUFP's position was very clear, if unorthodox amongst Black groups, was colonial wars of liberation. The group agreed that these must be situated within the context of class struggles, and not be seen as essentially a struggle between Black and white people. This was particularly relevant and important with respect to Africa. In the contention for supremacy between different radical groups in Angola, Mozambique, Zimbabwe and South Africa, the BUFP sought to support those groups which presented a class position coupled with the notion of 'people's' struggle for national liberation as the first step towards emancipation from capitalism and imperialism. Thus, the BUFP supported the ANC in South Africa, SWAPO in Namibia and MPLA in Angola, because these were groups which sought to organise the 'whole people' irrespective of class, colour or creed against the common enemy of colonialism. But these were also groups which sought to see things in class, not racial, terms; imperialism was being opposed, not the colour of the oppressors.

Third, the BUFP sought to impress on its members and the Black community that the just hunger for a closer knowledge of the history of Blacks in Africa and the West and the promotion of Black culture was not enough to put an end to capitalist and racist oppression and exploitation. At the same time, it was important for the BUFP to emphasise that given the history of white working-class organisations which marginalised Black workers' interests, it was important for Blacks to organise themselves autonomously. This view was also supported by the observation that where white liberals joined Black organisations their superior resources usually result in whites controlling the agenda. Additionally, to maintain its independence of thought and action, the BUFP was consistent in refusing to accept funding from national or local government departments, or foundations. Although it supported the socialist bloc of countries, it maintained its independent political position from them by not aligning itself to any national or international group, and therefore unwittingly, reflected the healthy scepticism of radical Third World leaders such as Abdul Nasser of Egypt, Jawaharlal Nehru of India and Kwame Nkrumah of Ghana who, with other radicals, founded the Non-Aligned Movement in response to the Cold War.

Community aspects of the group's activities

Whilst it is important to look at a group's stated aims and objectives, and to take into consideration their ideological orientation, it is their activities which best help us to define them. This may be particularly true with respect to Commonwealth Caribbean groups, which are prone to establish elaborate constitutional devices without doing the necessary practical work to make their organisations the living and dynamic bodies they sometimes appear to be from the outside. It should be noted that most of the activities in which the BUFP engaged were essentially of a community welfare nature. This does not negate the fact that the intended purpose was mainly to raise political consciousness in order to better struggle against what the group saw as exploitation and oppression.

From its very beginning, the group engaged itself in a number of social or community welfare activities. Such activities varied from the organising and running of a summer and alternative school for Black children, to defending Black youngsters against attacks on the streets. Activities ranged from defending Black workers, to critically assessing women's roles in the workplace and the household. These issues were raised at meetings and discussion groups, and in publications such as leaflets and the *Black Voice*. The group adopted a tough line against what was described as 'male chauvinism' and drug taking; for these offences members could be suspended or expelled. Like most Marxist-Leninist groups, the BUFP advocated what amounted to a late Victorian bourgeois morality which eschewed excess of any kind such as heavy drinking, promoted the strict utilisation of time, and displayed what Max Weber described as the Calvinist Protestant ethic of hard work, discipline and accountability for individual action underpinned by a this-worldy asceticism (see Weber 1930). 'Good manners', exemplary and orderly behaviour, cleanliness were all virtues to adhere to, particularly when out on the streets selling newspapers, distributing leaflets, and at public demonstrations.

Although not the first to raise the question, the BUFP was perhaps the first group in the country to organise alternative schooling for Black children who had been marginalise by local education authorities and schools.[17] The publication of Bernard Coard's (1971) *How the British education system underdeveloped the Black child* by New Beacon Books had an immediate impact on the founders of the BUFP. In 1971, the group organised a summer school for Black children who were placed in educationally subnormal schools. These children were drawn from the boroughs of Southward, Lambeth and Lewisham. The school was held mainly in Deptford, on premises provided by the Church of England, when a number of local schools refused to help with what was then perceived by many as a subversive action by hotheads. Again, in 1972 the BUFP organised another summer school for these children, and with the help of Sybil Phoenix, the veteran Guyanese community worker, premises were provided at 77 Pagnell Street, New Cross. During the year classes in maths, English and history were conducted in members' homes for a smaller group of children. The summer schools had about fifty children, and outings to zoos and other places of interests were organised as well as a one-week holiday by the sea in 1972. The subjects offered were deliberately limited to English, history (Black, Caribbean, US and African), and maths, (subjects neglected in their schooling), art and drama. Table-tennis, badminton, football, chess, draughts and swimming were also offered at break times and for specific periods, with teachers and helpers actively participating.

The teaching and summer school experiences were intended to achieve three principal aims and objectives: first, developing the children's skills in the traditional 'three Rs' of reading, writing and arithmetic. In several cases the children had to be taught these rudimentary skills which their schools had claimed these children could not be taught because they were educationally subnormal. It was important to teach English in a manner that would properly situate, and not ignore or marginalise, the Creole the children spoke at home with their parents and spoke in groups at school. The second aim was to redress the imbalance in the regular school curriculum by teaching the children about their own neglected backgrounds in Africa and the Caribbean; to acquaint them with names, events places and achievements of Black people; to help develop a framework within which they would understand their own and their parents' presence and position in British society and how they, like others before, could help to change the situation. These helped, thirdly, to develop their confidence in themselves as young Black people in a world almost entirely owned, controlled and defined by the white majority society in which they lived. In the wider Black world the Afro hairstyle, the musicians, sportsmen and sportswomen, politicians and artists of Black America were recreating an environment of Black worth and value to which British Blacks could relate across the Atlantic. The teaching of specific subjects could help to fill in the details missing in the collective knowledge of a people experiencing the loss of their illusions (see Carter, 1986; Cross and Entzinger, 1988).

It was hoped that the total experience would result in the children not only having a stronger sense of self and history or background, but that they would also develop a deep commitment to their own communities. It was therefore important that the children gained confidence in their teachers, experienced the caring environment their parents would have enjoyed at schools in the Caribbean and for them to realise that although nearly all their schoolteachers were white people, Black people were also capable of imparting the knowledge they would need for forging their own individual paths through life in a competitive society.

Thus, whilst small grants and support were secured from public bodies in order to help with this specific project, the initiative organisation, work, teaching and so on were conducted by Black schoolteachers, sixth-formers and undergraduates as well as other BUFP members with relevant experience.

In 1972 the BUFP was joined by the Croydon Collective in mounting the summer project. The alternative school experience was a challenge not only for the children, but also for the teachers and helpers, because they themselves had to learn some of what they were teaching. Whilst they were able to draw on Black American experience, there was nothing comparable in Britain from which to learn. This was because Caribbean groups in Britain had not yet developed the institutions they required for survival in a society based on (white) ethnicity which automatically excluded the Black 'other'. The Black-led churches were both an exception to this and also partly a symptom of British exclusivity. Paradoxically, however the Black churches' proximity to white churches and the sharing of a common faith by Black and white practising Christians, prevented the Black churches being active participants in the youths' radical protest against marginalisation. The churches' message seemed too quietist in the face of massive police brutality and state repression; to the churches, the radicalism of Black youths was simply bewildering. Yet, in the longer view, the different forms of social action in which Black radicalism and the conservative churches were respectively involved, were largely responses to more general processes of exclusion in British society. Both responses - of conservative quietism and militant radicalism - were also deeply rooted in Caribbean social and political traditions and these were being established in the emergent Caribbean diaspora in England.

The BUFP's concern with the young in the Black community in South London and elsewhere brought them into conflict not only with the education authorities (which were initially hostile to the alternative school initiative because they did not control it), but also with the police and the courts. There were several dramatic instances of such confrontations throughout the period which was marked by community activism. Demonstrations against legislation such as the 1971 Immigration Act in specific localities with significant Black settlement involved sharp confrontation with the police, and were covered in the *South London Press*. Attacks on members of the group by the police in the early 1970s led to several confrontations and locally celebrated court cases. The group's support, for example, of the struggles of others such as the Irish against the 1971 Internment Act, or the trades unions' demonstrations against the 1971 Industrial Relations Act, again led the BUFP into confrontation with the authorities. As the decade drew to a close, the group became deeply involved with what came to be known as the New Cross Massacre on its doorsteps. With respect to the Black community and the police and the courts, two well-documented events will suffice to make this general point: the Peckham Rye Confrontation of 1971 and the Joshua Francis Case (Editor's Note: See Goulbourne, 2002, pp. 101-110).

Section 2: African Caribbean publications

This section advances the analysis of the Caribbean transnational experience by focusing on the work of two Black publishing houses, and the major contributions they have made to the emergence and development of Caribbean publishing presence in Britain from the late 1960s. These are the New Beacon Books (NBB) situated in North London, founded by John LaRose from Trinidad and run with his partner Sarah White from Wales, and Bogle L'Ouverture Publications (BLP) in West London, founded by Jessica and Eric Huntley from Guyana. Both NBB and BLP have been far more than publishing concerns, and have been involved with British as well as world events. Moreover, they have been intricately wrapped up with specific forms of community action and have reflected as well as developed the Caribbean transnational experience in their practices. Before, however, exploring these aspects of the groups' activities, it is useful to make a broad observation about the publications scene in Britain and how they relate to the intellectual and community life of Caribbeans in Britain and relate to the wider Caribbean and African diasporas.

Caribbean communities and publishing

Publishing is important in its own right in all communities, but it has been particularly so in the process of Caribbean communities being established in Britain. However, comparatively little is known about this dimension of Caribbean life in Britain although it is generally taken for granted within the diaspora.

First, the weekly newspapers have played the crucial role of keeping people informed about events 'back home', introducing readers in Britain to a wider perspective of the Caribbean and African diaspora, and Africa itself than is the case 'back home' in the Caribbean where, in general, middle-class hegemony is still in a kind of colonial time warp regarding Africa and the Caribbean diaspora in Europe. Of course, there have been different kinds of newspapers over the years. For example in the 1970s papers such as *Black Voice and The Panther* were published by particular community-based groups in specific localities in the urban centres of Caribbean settlement. Earlier, in the 1960s, there was the far more professionally managed and produced *West Indian Gazette* run by Claudia Jones, one of the major figures who linked the Caribbean where she was born, the US where she was brought up and commenced her radical work, and Britain where she spent her last years and stimulated the birth of radical Black journalism within the community (see Sherwood, 1999; Boyce Davis, 2001). What these publications shared was an emphasis on public concern over problems that faced the new Caribbean communities, and they were parts of a wider British activist agitprop (radical agitation and propaganda) literature characteristic of the years from the late 1960s to the early 1980s. Whilst Claudia Jones brought to Brixton and the emerging Caribbean communities springing up in England her immense experience from the US, the other publications were largely experimental, produced on extraordinarily messy Gestetner printing machines in often damp and unhealthy basements and terraced houses both north and south of the Thames.

With the consolidation of Caribbean communities in Britain, new popular publications emerged to meet a number of easily identified needs. *The Weekly Gleaner*, its headquarters in the Elephant and Castle, and offices in Brixton and Birmingham, established a recognisable place for itself in the UK market; it resonates particularly with Jamaicans, some of whom will still have memories of the legendary *Gleaner* in Jamaica. Regarded as one of the oldest newspapers in the English-speaking world after *The Times*, Jamaicans have long perceived the *Gleaner* as their eponymous newspaper. Clearly, the *Gleaner* company in Kingston, Jamaica, recognised the potential of a British market, and it is now well over 2,500 volumes in publication. The weekly paper, around 35 pages in length, carries news about Jamaica and the wider English-speaking Caribbean that may be of interest to communities in Britain; it also carries specific items about Africa that may be relevant to Caribbeans, and the same with respect to North America. Not surprisingly, music, general culture, activities by the region's leaders and sportspeople feature prominently, as does the Commonwealth Caribbean preoccupation with the ritual of ceremonies around all kinds of celebrity figures and trivia around fashion, gossip, and mediocre non-achievements by sons and daughters of relatively unknown individuals in the region whom few in Britain would know or particularly care about.

Of course, the same is true for the other papers that sprung up over the years since the 1960s. Such was the *West Indian World* edited by Aubrey Baines, which is no longer in existence, but helped to blaze a path. Such is the *Voice*, which at the turn of the millennium was nearing its second decade and was becoming more available in regular newsagents in some of the main cities of England where Caribbeans have settled. Where the *Weekly Gleaner* claims to be 'the top Caribbean newspaper', the *Voice*, with offices in Brixton, Birmingham and Bristol, asserts that it is 'Britain's best Black paper'. Certainly, the latter is almost twice the length of the former, although their contents are not dissimilar.

Perhaps more than the *Weekly Gleaner*, the *Voice* and the *New Nation* - which started later in East London and boasts that it is 'Britain's no. 1 Black newspaper' - would appear to cover more news of the kind found in any local newspaper in England: crime, injustice, racism, sometimes overlooked achievements by Black individuals, and so on, and perhaps less coverage about the Caribbean, Africa and the US. Items which are apparently of considerable concern to people of Caribbean backgrounds in Britain feature significantly in both papers, and they all carry advertisements about hair and skin care, music and cosmetics, food and beverage, and holidays in the Caribbean - all are apparently items of considerable interests to Caribbeans. Nostalgia or concern to maintain close links with consumer aspects of culture appear to combine with an obsession over appearance and keeping up with style to provide a basis for such advertisements. As more Caribbean companies - banks, insurance, real estate agencies, legal firms dealing with such matters as immigration law, forwarding companies - became active in England offering services to nationals and their offspring, the papers have also carried advertisements reflecting the varied needs of members who live within a transnational Atlantic world.

Increasingly too these papers carry advertisements and general coverage about the activities of the various Christian denominations, particularly evangelical gatherings such as American preachers visiting the UK in search of souls for Jesus and money for their pockets. As in the Caribbean, these papers have all performed the task of what may be seen as admonition to improvement: education, achievement in private and public life, telling the story of individual achievement as well as group attainment. These papers, therefore, provide for the Caribbean communities in London, Birmingham and other English cities where the majority national and local papers do not. Of course, these functions or services are also provided by niche newspapers in Britain's other new minority ethnic communities and therefore Caribbean newspapers are not unique.

A second kind of publication that was vitally important in the process of establishing a Caribbean presence in Britain was, of course, books about the region and its people's experiences which were closely linked to England's past, but also distinctive. This was to occur at two levels. First, the decades of immigration from the region and steady settlement in Britain coincided with the great strides in Caribbean creative writing. Edgar Mittleholzer, Wilson Harris, V.S. Naipaul, Eddie Brathwaite, E.E. Braithwaite, Andrew Salkey, Sam Selvon and others became familiar names amongst those in the majority national and the new minority communities attuned with literary creativity. While, however, these writers may have been familiar to many readers, they sometimes tended to merge into a wider collectivity of writers from the former colonial world, and had little to do with the new Caribbean communities with children born and/or brought up in England. Much of what writers from the Caribbean expressed was primarily of concern to people in the Caribbean experiencing the transition from colonialism to self-recognition. There was clearly therefore a need for writers who shared the new experiences of emergent Caribbean communities in Britain. It was in this context that the new publishers in these communities were to make a definite contribution by introducing new writers such as Linton Kwesi Johnson to the British community and encouraging established writers, such as Salkey, to make more easily accessible his novels for children in the Caribbean relevant to a wider Caribbean diasporic readership.

The remainder of the discussion here focuses on the work of two key contributors to this important enterprise in the Caribbean communities, which is too often overlooked. The focus on New Beacon Books and Bogle L'Ouverture Publications in no way belittles similar contributions rendered by small bookshops and publishing enterprises in several English cities. In the first place, it is important to recognise that there have been other publishers, such as Saba Sakana's Karnak House, Buzz Johnson's Karia Press, Rudolph Kiserman's Blackbird Books and Len Garrison's Black Star Publisher. These ventures performed valuable services to the Caribbean communities, but for one reason or another folded after a few years and a limited number of new titles or re-publications.

Second, the Caribbean communities owe much to those many individuals who have long and consistently ensured that they find themselves at a range of public meetings with their suitcase of books and pamphlets from the US, the Caribbean, Africa and Britain about the perceptions and experiences of life in the Atlantic world. Veteran observers such as the Huntleys have noted that the presence of such individuals diminished in the late 1980s and early 1990s. However, by the turn of the century a return to the habits of the radical 1970s appeared to be on the increase, and here and there outside London small bookshops emerged. Whatever the reasons for such fluctuation in publishing and in the number of men and women with their suitcase of literature over the last three decades or so, it may be suggested that together these activities constitute an area of Caribbean enterprise in Britain that deserves more attention in much the same way as Caribbean participation in business enterprises and the management and ownership of companies which benefit from Caribbean sporting, musical and other artistic creativity deserve critical inquiry, assessment and advancement. After all, much of the access that many Caribbean intellectuals enjoy with major commercial publishers has come about subsequent to the early and dynamic contributions by unrecognised entrepreneurs in their communities.

Bogle L'Ouverture Publications

As suggested earlier, both BLP and NBB had their origins in developments which took place in the Caribbean, but which had direct relevance to the emerging Caribbean communities in Britain. Perhaps the more dramatic, and at the same time less deliberate, was the founding of the Bogle L'Ouverture Publications in 1969 at 110 Windermere Road, South Ealing, which was the home of Eric and Jessica Huntley, who moved there from North London earlier in the 1960s. While the founding of BLP may be well known to the small group of individuals who were involved and who may now live in Britain, the US and the Caribbean, the story is far less well known to the wider community and the academic world. This story deserves telling as part of the process of the Caribbean communities' articulation of a public voice in print.

BLP and Walter Rodney

The dramatic occasion or catalyst of the founding of BLP was the banning by the Jamaican government in October, 1968 of a 26-year-old Guyanese historian, the late Walter Rodney, from returning to Jamaica (see Payne, 1994, ch. 1; Lewis, 1998, ch. 5). In 1963, Rodney had graduated with a brilliant first-class honours in history from the University of the West Indies, and gone on successfully to submit a doctoral thesis on the slave trade in West Africa[18] for London University's School of Oriental and African Studies in 1966. He had lectured at the University of Dar es Salaam, Tanzania for two years before returning to the Mona campus of the regional University of the West Indies in 1968 as a lecturer in his *alma mater* department of history. But Rodney soon attracted the attention of the government through his public social activism and intellectual concerns with the relevance of African history to the Black majority of Jamaica. This simple activity in an overwhelmingly Black country was perceived to be subversive and highly dangerous for the status quo taken wholesale from the colonial past.

But Rodney's history lectures touched a very raw nerve in post-colonial Jamaica's national psyche. While the majority of Jamaicans were Black, the wealth of the country was almost entirely owned by minorities such as the white Europeans, the Chinese and the Lebanese; political office was held mainly by the mulattos, even though they had to gain legitimacy from a Black electorate (Editor's Note: see Goulbourne, 2002, pp. 141-143).

The Rodney affair in Kingston had an immediate and powerful impact on Black communities in Britain. And it is surprising that the emerging scholarship around Rodney is failing or refusing to recognise this aspect of his influence. Perhaps the best example of this neglect or refusal is to be found in Rupert Lewis's (1998) otherwise widely researched and interesting treatment of Rodney's intellectual life in the Caribbean and Africa. Lewis correctly pinpoints Rodney's Dar es Salaam days as perhaps his most important in an all-too-short career; Rodney was only 38 years old when he was killed in a car bomb in his native Georgetown, Guyana - both the region and the world lost an intellectual and activist whom C. L. R. James (1982) later described as 'the brightest spark' to have been produced in the post-Second World War Caribbean. Lewis's work is the latest and perhaps the most serious treatment of Rodney's life and work, but while Lewis touches upon Rodney's London years (1963-66) little or nothing is said about the pivotal importance of his London connections. It was in London that Rodney's most influential books, *The Grounding With My Brothers* and *How Europe Underdeveloped Africa* were first published. But London is more important than for just the publication of Rodney's books. And it is this story that needs to be told alongside the story of Rodney's overall place within the Caribbean and African diasporas.

Whilst a student at SOAS, Rodney had been close to a wide range of Caribbean fellow-students and intellectuals, but he was particularly close to his compatriots Jessica and Eric Huntley - a fact which is curiously ignored by a scholar as thorough as Lewis, and this weakens his account and analysis of Rodney's life and work. Rodney had sought out the Huntleys and often stayed at their home. He knew of their uncompromising non-racist principles and active participation in Guyanese politics during the 1950s, when the joint leadership of Cheddi Jagan and Forbes Burnham in the People's Progressive Party (PPP) appeared to be on the path to forge a prosperous future for both the African and East Indian populations in the physically largest English-speaking country in the region. Developments in Guyana (then British Guiana) - race riots, suspension of the 1950 Constitution, suspicions about US involvement, etc. –were of general interest to all Caribbean communities in Britain, and intellectuals, students and activists sought to make their views known to the Labour government of Harold Wilson as well as to inform the general public. Meetings were organised by the Huntleys, John LaRose, Richard Small and others and Rodney was a major voice and presence in these activities. In October 1965, Rodney presented a paper on the situation in Guyana at a symposium organised by LaRose and the Huntleys at the then centre of Caribbean attraction, the West Indian Students Centre in Earls Court. In the process, Rodney and the Huntleys became socially close, Jessica sometimes typing his work and also helping to find a typist for Walter's doctoral thesis; with others they frequented weekend dancing parties, for which he had a legendary liking.

It was not surprising, therefore, that on having news of Rodney's banning from Jamaica, the Huntleys, LaRose and others picketed the Jamaica Tourist Board (the Jamaica High Commission had not yet been established for them to target), where a number of protesters were arrested. Rodney, passing through London en route to Dar es Salaam, where he had worked and was again offered a post at the history department, expectedly called on the Huntleys. As Eric Huntley later recalled 'so then when he went to Jamaica and he was banned, it was the natural place for him to come back to Jessica', the central figure in the group he had known in London (interview with Eric and Jessica Huntley, 22 October 1992). A meeting was arranged and on leaving for Dar es Salaam, Rodney left with Jessica for safe-keeping the notes of a set of lectures he gave in Jamaica. Jessica in turn showed these to other individuals concerned about developments in Jamaica as well as the wider Atlantic world, including Earl Greenwood, Fitzroy Griffiths, Barbara Joseph, Chris LeMaitre, Dale Saunders, Richard Small and Ewart Thomas. With Jessica and Eric, these individuals quickly formed a committee to inform the Caribbean communities in Britain and abroad about Rodney's case and the repressive developments in Jamaica. Initially, the idea was to duplicate, using a Gestetner machine, some of these lectures and, following what was happening in Black communities in the US, entitle them *Walter Rodney Speaks*. As various possibilities about effective dissemination occurred to the group, the idea came from either Jessica Huntley or Ewart Thomas that the whole series of lectures could be published under the title *The Groundings With My Brothers*; Thomas offered to edit them while Small offered to contribute an introduction to the collection and they agreed to go for immediate publication. But the group faced the problem of how to finance the venture. As Jessica explained:

> of course, the whole question is where are we going to get the money from? That was everybody's response. And I said, 'I will ask my friend, what about you asking your friend?' ... and right there I picked up the phone and I start ringing people and people promise a, b, c, d pounds. And Barbara Joseph who was at the meeting said she will give £50, in those days that was a lot money. [Interview with Eric and Jessica Huntley, 22 October 1992]

After much discussion it was decided not to approach white people or their agencies for financial support, but to depend on the group's own resources. Barbara Joseph, a Trinidadian student of architecture, and other individuals played a part in the publication by holding fund-raising parties. Apart from editing Rodney's notes and providing an Introduction to the text, Ewart Thomas went with Jessica Huntley to discuss the matter with John LaRose who already had more experience of publishing in Britain. John was supportive and introduced them to his printer, John Sankey of Villiers Press who was 'very concerned as to where we are going to get the money from, but I was so convinced we would get the money' (Interview with Eric and Jessica Huntley, 22 October 1992). Over two decades later, by which time both she and Eric had naturally become less than certain about the exact cost of printing, Jessica recollected that it would have been between £300 and £500. The publication was a campaigning document which highlighted the situation in Jamaica, and while the first edition was sold for six shillings and six pence, most copies were given away in the cause of raising consciousness of the post-colonial order that was emerging in the region.

But if the group's financial resource was meagre, they certainly possessed considerable social capital. For example, Richard Small[19] was from a prominent Jamaican family of lawyers, and while a law student in London had also been one of the leading figures in the Campaign Against Racial Discrimination (CARD) (see Heineman, 1972); in the late 1970s and the early 1980s Small was a member of the legal team representing Rodney and his comrades in the Working People's Alliance (WPA) in Guyana when President Forbes Burnham accused Rodney and his associates of anti-government activities. Ewart Thomas,[20] who had been at school in Georgetown with Rodney had, like him, come to England (Cambridge in Thomas' case) after University of West Indies (UWI) to do his doctorate in mathematics; he went on to a successful career at Stanford University. In other words while material resources were limited, the group had considerable human capital at its disposal, and individuals undertook different tasks. Eric had been editor of his post office trade union newsletter and contributor to Thunder, the organ of the People Progressive Party (PPP) in Georgetown, and therefore contributed his skills and experience.

The Groundings With My Brothers (1969) quickly became a best-seller amongst Caribbean groups in Britain and overseas, particularly in the US. It achieved its aim of disseminating information about the immediate post-colonial society in Jamaica, and extended Rodney's international reputation as a serious, well-informed and educated radical, unlike most of the African Americans who had emerged as major spokespersons in the late 1960s. He was not just seeking to acquire knowledge about Africa: he had direct experience of the most exciting and radical state on the continent – Julius Nverere's post-Arusha Tanzania; he spoke and wrote about West Africa at a crucial point in that region's links with Europe which resulted in part in the African diaspora. *The Groundings* had a strong urgency and relevance for young Caribbeans in England eager to know something about the African past and to have that past linked to the Caribbean of which they knew comparatively little. It was not surprising therefore that *The Groundings* was reprinted in 1970, 1971, 1975 1983 and 1990; the publisher's notes, introductions and editor's preface have become important additions to a valuable original document of protest in the struggles of Caribbean people both in the region and outside.

The text itself is a mere 56 pages. But within this space the reader hears the voice not merely of an angry young man, but a scholar who is master of a subject that had been conspicuous by its absence in Caribbean education circles - Africa as reality as distinct from Africa only as myth. Rodney linked African and the contemporary differential situations of Africans in the Americas, Europe and Jamaican society. He modified the radical language of Black Power leaders in the US to show how all shades of Black people occupied subordinate positions in a world dominated by imperialism. Where many radical Black Americans drew a simple line between Black and white Rodney's work hinted at a more complex situation in which racial and ethnic identities were wrapped up with the interlacing histories of a wide Atlantic world. In Jamaica and elsewhere imperialism had its supporters and such class interests cut against racial lines. This explained the Jamaican government's banning of the late Kwame Toure (then Stokeley Carmichael), H. Rap Brown, and James Forman, as well as books by Malcolm X, Elijah Mohammed and Hamilton and Carmichael's powerful and highly influential *Black Power: the Politics of Liberation*. Just as Rodney's lectures had had a marked impact on his audiences in Kingston, so in London *The Groundings* became an immediate success. It not only established Rodney as a leading Third World radical with an international status, it also launched the Bogle L'Ouverture Publications as a major independent publishing house operating within the Black communities in Britain and through its subsequent publications served as a link with a wider diasporic world.

This point could be illustrated with reference to BLP's other publications, but it may be more relevant to do so through their continued links with Rodney, particularly given a growing interest in his work and his all too short career. For example, although BLP was not the first to publish Linton Kwesi Johnson's poetry, it was their publication of his *Dread Beat and Blood* (1976) which substantially introduced him to the British reading public and gave voice to a new generation of Black British literature as distinct from Caribbean writers living in England. The Huntleys see Johnson's poetry as the voice of alienated Black youths in the late 1970s and early 1980s which resulted in the explosions on the streets of British cities in 1979 and 1981. The simplified biographies of Marcus Garvey and of Cheddi Jagan by Eric Huntley for children, the poetry collections of Valerie Bloom, and the posters and cards produced over the years have been important. In 1990 BLP was declared bankrupt as a consequence of the combination of a number of factors: increased rent for premises, cutbacks in educational and library expenditures, pressing demands from the banks, the Huntleys not receiving payments for books ordered and sent to Nigeria as well as a bitter and unfortunate case with Patricia Rodney (Walter's widow) over royalties of her late husband's works. The last of these tribulations has left a deep and ugly scar in the legacy of Walter Rodney and has cast a shadow over the remarkable partnership the Huntleys and Rodney established to give voice to Caribbeans in the wider African diaspora.

The emerging historiography (see Lewis, 1998) around Rodney threatens to continue this unfortunate rift, but the hope must be that with time the scar will heal, and indeed there are signs that some of the protagonists are reaching out to each other across the barriers. More immediately, having survived the tribulations of bankruptcy, by the mid-1990s Jessica and

Eric were able to recommence publishing, but in a significantly changed publishing world. It would now appear that there are several mainstream publishers who are willing to publish young or relatively unknown Caribbean writers, or at any rate, there is now a recognisable British Caribbean writing tradition and young writers appear not to have insoluble problems with commercial publishers. Indeed, community-based publishers such as the Huntleys and LaRose forged a path and created a market, but it is the mainstream commercial publishers who are in a position to take financial advantage of that market.

In these new circumstances, BLP may need to discover a new niche in a crowded publishing world, but there can be no denial that they have made a considerable contribution in the shaping of a wider Caribbean diasporic order. In recent years, however, BLP has shown a willingness to publish writers such as Hylton (1997b) and Walker (2000) who show keen interest in what they call an Africentric approach to scholarship, no doubt drawing on Asante (1998). This notion of Afro-centric scholarship is unlikely to provide the kind of niche in the market they could develop to make the contribution they made earlier. Indeed, much of the work produced in this genre is often poor derivative scholarship at the opposite end of the academic scale from the work the late Walter Rodney produced and encouraged as a scholar of Africa. The risk BLP takes with such work, however, may be just the kind of risk that is necessary for small niche publishers to take, because to paraphrase Durkheim's aphorism, today's oddity may be tomorrow's orthodoxy.

But to continue the story of BLP and Walter Rodney, it is important to narrate how the Huntleys played a central role in the production of Rodney's most well-known work, his polemic *How Europe Underdeveloped Africa*. This was simultaneously published by BLP in London and in Dar es Salaam in Tanzania by Tanzania Publishing House (TPH), under the leadership of Walter Bygoya, in 1972; it was a joint effort, with TPH having the rights for Africa and BLP the rights for the rest of the world. Far more than *The Groundings*, *How Europe Underdeveloped Africa* has come to occupy a central position in radical popular literature in the African diaspora and will probably be remembered as the central text produced by the first generation of post-colonial Caribbean scholars who benefited from higher education within the region but who more than any other generation before or since earnestly sought to link the various parts of the Caribbean Atlantic heritage. For Rodney, the aim of this work was 'to try and reach Africans who wish to explore further the nature of their exploitation, rather than to satisfy the 'standards' set by our oppressors and their spokesmen in the academic world' (Rodney, 1972, p. 8). (Editor's Note: See Goulbourne [2002, p. 150] for the overview on the content of the book). The important point here is that the book caught the imagination of Caribbean and African intellectuals in the Atlantic world. The book's influence was felt even farther afield, however, as it was translated into Japanese, French, Spanish and German (the Huntleys insist that they never received any payment for the French publication).

The different parts of the Atlantic-African diaspora are connected by complex relationships, and within this world two major Caribbean figures stand out above others during the second half of the twentieth century - Bob Marley, singer, poet, visionary, and Walter Rodney, scholar and political activist. Marley achieved linking popular myths of Africa with the lived experiences of people across the wide Atlantic divide, and the invitation to be the guest performer at Zimbabwe's independence celebrations in 1980 was in many ways a telling and fitting recognition of that fact. One of Rodney's great achievements was to have produced a work that spoke not only to Africans on the continent, but to the whole African diaspora. His work has been variously celebrated throughout the diaspora. One instance of this was the Zimbabwean parliament's recognition of the Huntleys when, in late 1998, they attended the legislative body, immediately after morning prayer, the speaker said: 'I announce the presence in the Speaker's Gallery of Mrs Jessica Huntley and Mr Eric Huntley, the publishers of that truly ground breaking publication on [sic] *How Europe Underdeveloped Africa*' (Zimbabwe Parliamentary Proceedings, 1998). This statement was received by shouts of 'hear, hear' from members, reflecting the high regard with which Rodney and his publishers are held in Africa, particularly in those parts such as Zimbabwe which gained independence as a result of ardent and sometimes violent struggles against European encroachment and settlement.

John Larose and New Beacon Books

Like BLP, New Beacon Books (NBB) had its inspiration in developments which occurred in the Caribbean. John LaRose had been an activist from his late teens in Trinidad, worked in Venezuela and had been in close contact with radical movements and individuals in the French, Spanish and English-speaking Caribbean and South and Central America. With this background, John was poised to become the quintessential Caribbean person who was best placed to perform the role he was to create for himself and members of his family in the heart of the Caribbean communities in England: a knowledgeable and well-connected, considerate and always helpful person through whom the interwoven experiences of Caribbean transnationality is individually and collectively lived.

While maintaining his close links with the Caribbean and developing new ones with Africa, LaRose entered a new phase of his rich transnational life around 1965, when he shifted from 'concentrating upon building up the relations with West Indians here [UK], especially those who had been involved in the revolution in the Caribbean, for further development of the struggle for revolutionary social and economic changes in the Caribbean itself (interview with J. LaRose, 3 October 1991) to concentrating on Britain. But the new phase was also itself born of Caribbean concerns, namely, to 'go into publishing as a serious aspect of the thing' (interview with J. LaRose, 3 October 1991). This 'thing' for him was earlier made clear in our conversations when he stated:

> I never thought that, considering what I had in mind for New Beacon ... it was never our intention to become beyond anything but a small to medium publisher and bookseller, and publishing institution. We knew the other political and cultural commitments that we had, and we continued to want to make, and that therefore we couldn't really think of ourselves as being a full-time, actually full-time publishers and booksellers, in the way that if you were going into this business as a commercial operation. [Interview with J. LaRose, 3 June 1991]

NBB was therefore born of Caribbean dreams. It took on tangible form when in August 1966 NBB published LaRose's own collection of poetry entitled *Foundations* under the name of Anthony LaRose. This was quickly followed by the re-publication of a major book in Caribbean and British historiography, John Jacob Thomas' *Froudacity* (1888). This had been first published as a well-argued and spirited reply to the English imperialist and racist historian Anthony Froude's negrophobic account of the post-emancipation West Indies. Eric Williams noted, in his survey of how English historians perceived the post-Emancipation West Indies, that Froude was the only professional English historian of the Victorian age who took the region seriously, and after his visit in 1887 recorded his support for the past slavery society in the region, his belief in Black inferiority and English superiority (consistent with his disdain for the Irish and for Catholics) in his *The English in the West Indies, or the Bow of Ulysses* (see Williams, 1964, ch. 10). Thomas, who was born before Emancipation in 1838, was one of the first major Caribbean intellectuals and in 1869 had published *The Theory and Practice of Creole Grammar* (reprinted 1969). Thomas's two books had long been out of print, but they were known to LaRose and many of his contemporaries in Port-of-Spain in the 1940s and had inspired them in their intellectual struggles against imperialism. Thomas' riposte of Froude had been important in establishing what became a strong Caribbean pride in intellectual prowess that would match that of anything that the imperial intellectuals could marshal. An essential aspect of this tradition was that competition should be fair and the rules of competition should be transparent. In this way fair-minded people would be able to assess and judge fairly.

In re-publishing the text, LaRose first sought to get the distinguished Guyanese historian, the late Elsa Goveia, to write an introduction, and held discussions with Eddie Brathwaite (historian and poet) from Barbados as well as Wilson Harris (novelist and essayist) from Guyana about the text. Goveia was engrossed in research at the time and eventually Ken Ramchand wrote the Introduction, and Thomas's work became available again, particularly to a new generation seeking to repair the breach in an intellectual tradition the contours of which were little known. In the same year LaRose's premises became the meeting place for the newly formed Caribbean Artists Movement (CAM), to which we return below.

In a broader sense, it was the intellectual fervour of the late 1920s and early 1930s in Trinidad which had a lasting impression on LaRose and led to the founding of New Beacon Books in London over thirty years later. Born in 1927, LaRose was not himself part of the generation of national awakening which boasted C.L.R. James, Albert Gomes and Alfred Mendes. But LaRose had been deeply influenced by James and profoundly impressed by the efforts to found an authentic, indigenous but critical literary movement in Trinidad, at the centre of which had been Mendes and James. Gomes, who was to become one of Trinidad's first nationalist leaders, founded and ran the Beacon for two years (1931-33). Both Gomes and Mendes were of Portuguese backgrounds, their forebears having migrated to Trinidad after 1838 when the planters' response to Emancipation led eventually to the importation of cheap labour from as far afield as China and India, but initially from Madeira, where the failure of grape production encouraged a short period of indenture labour to the region (see Tinker, 1974; Wood, 1968). This new age of indenture labour was particularly important for Guyana and Trinidad, which had come into British possession relatively late in the eighteenth and early nineteenth centuries, respectively, and in which there was plenty of land to be settled by the new British masters.

The *Beacon* was a general magazine which published pieces on general culture and politics; it also carried short stories and reviews. It attracted contributors and readers from the different racial and cultural communities who made up Trinidadian society, and who were concerned about the life of the colony. With people from Britain, France, Spain, China, India, Africa and elsewhere, Trinidad for LaRose was a cosmopolitan society existing within a colonial order. But it was not until he came to live in England that he fully realised that he was the inheritor of this sophisticated, complex world in which the individual is invited to negotiate a way through and amongst people of initially different cultures, religions, customs and so on. Out of this cultural kaleidoscopic world came a cultural explosion evidenced by a number of publications by the Beacon members. Chief amongst these were C. L. R. James's novel *Minty Alley* published in 1936, the same year as the appearance of his seminal work on Toussaint L'Ouverture and the Haitian Revolution, *The Black Jacobins* (see also James, 1938).[21] Earlier in 1934 Mendes' first novel, *Pitch Lake* was published. As Kenneth Ramchand reminds us in his Introduction to New Beacon's re-publication of *Minty Alley* (1971), the literary explosion which was taking place in Trinidad was part of a wider experience throughout the English-speaking Caribbean. It was a literary revolution which was to have its impact on new

Caribbean communities in London several decades later, Just as Rodney's lectures in Kingston were to have their impact in the 1970s.

LaRose's New Beacon Books was the realisation of a vision to revive and keep alive the work of the Port-of-Spain's Beacon group. Like its predecessor, New Beacon intended to spread its net wide, and publish books on every aspect of Caribbean life, including politics and the arts. This was because for LaRose and the Trinidad Beacon group, these aspects of human life are to be seen as closely interconnected and cannot be neatly separated or compartmentalised. Decades later and in what had been the centre of the imperial order LaRose was to stress that 'everything begins and ends with culture' (interview with LaRose, 25 September 1991). The work of publishing and the meetings organised by CAM taught him that 'although we were talking about cultural things, we were talking about its history ... all kinds of relations: historical relations, political relations, economic relations, both inside the Caribbean and the rest of the world, and what it meant' (interview with LaRose, 25 September 1991).

As noted the new venture was concerned to provide a vehicle for poetry and re-publications of long neglected works such as those of J.J. Thomas. As noted, New Beacon went on to re-publish James's *Minty Alley*, Mendes' *Pitch Lake*, and Sir Arthur Lewis's *Labour in the West Indies*, which was first published in London in 1939 by the Fabian Society in an effort to bring to the attention of the British left the conditions and demands of West Indian labour during the period of sustained revolt in the region in the second half of the 1930s, culminating in the dramatic events in Jamaica in 1938 and the subsequent Moyne Commission (see, for example, Post, 1978; Munroe, 1972; Goulbourne, 1988a).

But New Beacon Books also sought, from its early days, to publish contemporary writers. Apart from LaRose's own *Foundations* (under the name of Anthony LaRose), NBB also soon published Adolphe Edwards' *Marcus Garvey* (1967), some critical essays by Ivan Van Sertima entitled *Caribbean Writers* (1968), and Wilson Harris's now famous critical essays *Tradition, the Writer & Society* (1967), which is a significant precursor of many postmodern literary debates about narrative, character and historical events. Like BLP, New Beacon Books' list has extended over time to include not only the Caribbean, but importantly the Caribbean in Britain, developments in Africa, the US, Central and South America, and elsewhere.

The New Beacon bookshop on Stroud Green Road in North London is an important aspect of this enterprise. Here LaRose's group has been able to offer what is widely regarded to be the best stock of books in Britain on the worlds straddled by Caribbeans in Britain - the Caribbean, Africa and parts of Latin America. Their stock include the full range of academic and more polemic texts, and the group's George Padmore Institute provides an added feature for researchers into the making of Caribbean communities in Britain.

Self-help and community action

It is obvious that New Beacon and Bogle L'Ouverture have had a number of things in common in terms of the personalities involved, their beginnings, aims, size, scale of community commitments and activities engaged in as well as global outreach beyond race and ethnic boundaries. It is worth briefly commenting on aspects of these in order to convey similarities as well as a deep-rooted commitment to the larger African diaspora, and more specifically their commitment to the emergent Caribbean diaspora.

First, both publishing concerns have been comparatively small affairs, depending on family and friends for support rather than on banks and/or local public assistance, and refusing to be taken over by bigger companies in the marketplace. To a degree, many of the various radical publishing concerns that emerged during the same years in the 1970s have faced this kind of problem and have acted in ways that they thought best suited to their circumstances, such as being absorbed by larger groups. Whilst taken together the impact of NBB and BLP has been immense, it must be borne in mind that both publishers have been run more on the basis of domestic labour than on the basis of large-scale business enterprises. BLP, as noted, operated from the home of its owners; so too did NBB, until more generous space was found not far away on Stroud Green Road, where the bookshop as well as the group's Padmore Institute[22] are located. In the case of the Huntleys, some neighbours complained about the numbers and frequency of visitors. Premises were later rented at 5a Chigwell Place in Ealing where a bookshop was opened. After the murder of Walter Rodney in Georgetown, Guyana in 1980, the bookshop was renamed in his honour, but became the object of attacks by right-wing groups, which were particularly active in British cities in the wake of Margaret Thatcher's victory at the polls in 1979. One response by radical bookshops which were under such attacks was to form the Bookshops Joint Action group to campaign against right-wing activities. Taken together, the Huntleys' home and bookshop in Ealing became for well over two decades a central location in West London for visitors from abroad, for book launches, workshops for schools, and for the dissemination of news of developments in various parts of the African diaspora. For example, during those years such well-known figures as Selvon, Louise Bennett, Salkey, Johnson and Faustin Charles gave poetry and prose readings, and campaigns such as the anti-SUS laws in the 1980s were launched by BLP.

Second, whilst both publishing concerns were closely linked with international networks of writers and intellectuals, they also served as independent community advice and organising centres. As noted above, they doubled as bookshops - with NBB's presence as a bookshop being more pronounced than its publishing activities. In a sense, they became rather like the Caribbean barbershops of earlier decades, that is, sites for dropping in for news, discussions and renewal or maintenance of friendships and acquaintance. Although LaRose's home in Stroud Green was always open to anyone who cared to stop by for a discussion, his bookshop situated on Stroud Green Road availed the public of a place stocked with books, leaflets, pamphlets, information about groups in London, the Caribbean, Africa, the US and so on, as well as LaRose, Sarah White or one of their sons or helpers to discuss current or historical matters. Stroud Green Road is the main thoroughfare between Finsbury Park tube station and Crouch End, and the bookshop forms part of what has become a lively shopping area. This has been the result of settlement in the vicinity by groups of post-colonial immigrants from the Caribbean, East Africa, Southern Europe and the Indian subcontinent. The groups have given new life to the area, and the New Beacon bookshop enhances the locality's cosmopolitan flavour. Thus, to be with LaRose for a morning or an afternoon, any day of the week, is to experience a gentle but vigorous ebb and flow of intellectuals from Africa, the US, the Caribbean and elsewhere passing through and 'touching base'. Sometimes people drop in from the fringes of Britain or are visiting from continental Europe. There is always a steady flow of individuals off the street and from the immediate vicinity.

At Chigwell Place where the BLP bookshop was located the situation appeared less busy but was nearly always much the same as at Stroud Green Road. But, being farther from the dynamic main thoroughfare of cosmopolitan London, it is perhaps true to say that BLP was not as central as Stroud Green Road, situated close to Finsbury Park underground and frequent bus services to central London. While participation in conferences at universities may have been more actively pursued by BLP, the closer links between the New Beacon group and the wider British academic, social and left-wing communities meant that they tended over the years to enjoy the greater exposure. This has left the impression that New Beacon was the more varied in the coverage of cultural and political activities, as well as interviews with relevant topical publications and other media. In particular, LaRose was close to figures such as A. Sivanandan and his Institute of Race Relations, which publishes the journal *Race and*

Class (with their headquarters on Pentonville Road in King's Cross) and the Brixton-based Race Today Collective, which published the now-defunct *Race Today*, and was led by Darcus Howe (a nephew of C.L.R. James and, later, a television personality, particularly as the notorious 'Devil's Advocate'). New Beacon was also more accessible to the national media than Bogle L'Ouverture as well as being closer to the English radical intelligentsia through Sarah White. Sarah's relationship to the local Caribbean and the wider communities is instructive with regard to what Americans in the late 1990s and at the beginning of the present century clumsily call 'cross-over' between different racial and ethnic groups: a scientist with an interest in Soviet science, Sarah came from the centre of the British intellectual establishment, her father having been a founding figure of the Arts Council with progressive views about cultures and peoples. Sarah's technical and intellectual contribution to the success of New Beacon has been immense, and all the more so in that she has set about her work almost silently and in an unassuming manner. Her contribution to this shared enterprise is therefore sometimes shielded or muted by the dynamics of the politics of racial or ethnic curtailment, that is, where it is perceived to be important to conceal the role played by individuals of different communities. This may be particularly strong in the Caribbean community in Britain, where there is a significant degree of collaboration at the public level as well as within families.

Conclusion

Although groups such as the BUFP would see themselves as being primarily political, in essence their work was one of community building, but their community work was guided by well-thought-out and deeply committed political perspectives. While not strictly of a political nature, that is, competing for public office on a general platform, such work none the less prepared the community for the more radical direct political participation of Britain's Black population in the late 1970s and throughout the 1980s to the turn of the century. Of equal significance, however, was the use made of Africa and the Caribbean as sources of strength for the emerging communities in Britain. The issues raised and the sources of inspiration were to become central pillars in the consciousness of these communities.

Two general conclusions must be drawn about the NBB and the BLP from the accounts of their activities sketched here. First, they have been closely associated and collaborated over major projects. One of these has been the Third World and Radical Book Fair which was initiated in the early 1980s by both groups and lasted for teen years, with support from Howe's group in Brixton. The groups, particularly LaRose's, were at the centre of the call for public investigations into the deaths of 13 young Black people at a birthday party in New Cross in the 1970s. Earlier, both groups were involved with campaigns in London over education, busing, and related issues. Second, it must be clear that both groups were distinguished from several other similar enterprises by being deeply grounded within specific communities in different parts of the city. As noted, they have grown up with the Caribbean communities that have sprung up in the last decades of the twentieth century. They continue to be central to radical Caribbean diasporic consciousness, linking England with the wider African diaspora. Both John LaRose and the Huntleys have been honoured for their contribution: John and Jessica have been awarded honorary doctorates by Sheffield Hallam University and South Bank University, London, respectively and there have been a number of specific events held by members of their communities to recognise their contributions and to register appreciation. These are individuals whose modesty can easily mislead so that the casual observer would miss their seminal importance to Britain's Caribbean communities and the wider African diaspora. Both LaRose and the Huntleys would be first to say that their contributions to the definition and tone of Caribbean communities in Britain and its links with the wider African diaspora form part of a more general articulation of Caribbeanness and that other contemporary contributors also call for recognition.

Notes

1. The case of Rolan Adams is returned to later in this discussion. Aseta Simms died in Stoke Newington police station during the night of 13 May 1971. It appears that she was taken in off the street at about 11.30 p.m. and died sometime between 12.00 and 12.30 a.m. A doctor, apparently representing the police commission, who examined the body was reported to say that he could not 'say what was the cause of her death' (BUFP pamphlet, 1972, p. 3). The verdict was death by misadventure. The North London branch of the party led a campaign involving publications, demonstrations, meetings, etc., to demand a public enquiry into the circumstances of Mrs Simms' death (see *Black Voice*, 1972 *passim*).
2. Ron Phillips was the eldest of three well-known brothers, the others being the crime writer Mike Phillips and Trevor Phillips, chair of the London Assembly; Ron later re-migrated to the US, and died in the mid-1990s in Philadelphia.
3. The names Kwame Toure were taken from Carmichael's two heroes Kwame Nkrumah and Sekou Toure of Ghana and Guinea respectively. Kwame Toure died of cancer in the late 1990s, after living for decades in Guinea, West Africa, and gaining recognition throughout the African diaspora, including his native Trinidad.
4. The JCWI itself suffered a similar fate in the early 1990s, when its Birmingham branch separated to form an independent body from its London headquarters.
5. There were, of course, other groups, such as the Black Liberation Front headed by Tony Soares, and various collectives in different parts of London.
6. In John LaRose's view, Althea Jones (as she then was) personified Black British youth protest in the 1970s. Born and brought up in a Trinidadian middle-class family, she came to England to study, and at the time of the Mangrove Nine trial Althea Jones was conducting research for a doctorate in chemistry at London University. She later became a lecturer at the University of the West Indies, where she also studied medicine, before returning to the UK, apparently as a general practitioner.
7. The term came from Harriet Beecher Stowe's novel *Uncle Tom's Cabin* published at the height of the anti-slavery movement in the Northern states of the US in the 1850s.
8. Internally, the BUFP sought to establish a women's group and a youth group. Discussions around the kinds of problems youth and women faced were promoted, but in practice the membership tended to act in unison over the general problems the organisation addressed. The group arranged discussion groups around Marxist philosophy, Black history, developments in Africa, Asia, the Americas and so on. It arranged for visitors to the country to address groups in specific communities, and members met on a regular basis to monitor events in their neighbourhoods.
9. Philip Murphy, who read philosophy at the University of Southampton, went on to become a prominent Labour councillor on Birmingham City Council, and an officer at the Commission for Racial Equality in the city.
10. Roger Lofters, who had returned to Jamaica in the late 1970s and became the electrics manager at the University of the West Indies' Hospital in Kingston came to an untimely death in an accident in the summer of 1997. A gathering in his honour was later held in

11. Brixton, organised by members of the then BUFP and a number of old members from different parts of the country attended.
11. Nearly all these individuals (for example, Edward Kamau Brathwaite, Orlando Patterson) were to go on to distinguished careers in the Caribbean and North America, and relatively few (such as John LaRose) remaining in England to make a lasting mark in Caribbean communities.
12. These were George Jackson, Fleeta Drumgo and John Clutchette, whose experience in prison politicised them, and made them heroes of radical Black America and Britain.
13. This date was deliberately chosen to reflect the importance of the Cuban Revolution for Caribbean people living in Britain and elsewhere.
14. This was so no doubt because the death of Mao in September 1976 and the subsequent struggle in China for control of state power revealed some of the injustices of the Cultural Revolution and subsequent abominations in the name of socialist justice in the 1980s and 1990s.
15. This concern in the Black communities in Britain was to continue and was forcefully restated in the Stephen Lawrence case, as set out in the Macpherson Report of February 1999.
16. Lenin argued, following Frederick Engels, that an aristocracy of labour had emerged in West Europe. This meant that with the emergence of reformist social-democratic parties and trades unions, capitalists were able to gain the support of the working classes by offering non-essential reforms of capitalism. Union leaders played a crucial part in this process, because it is through them that the 'deal', or class collaboration, has been effected.
17. Of course, the early beginnings of the Black churches in the 1950s and 1960s in the rooms of devout families and individuals, involved holding Sunday schools in much the same way as these alternative classes were organised.
18. This was later published as *A History of the Upper Guinea Coast 1545-1800* (London: The Clarendon Press, 1971).
19. Small later returned to Jamaica and established himself as a prominent lawyer, and a major figure in the Jamaica Council for Human Rights.
20. He was later to became a prominent Stanford University academic.
21. It is worth noting that it was the year before that the Soviet writer, Anatoli Vinogradov's novel The Black Consul (London: Gollancz, 1935, translated by Emile Burns) about L'Ouverture's struggle against Napoleonic France and the British, became available to the English reading world.
22. Named in honour of Guyanese/Trinidadian pan-Africanist, George Padmore, who was a moving spirit at the 1945 Manchester Pan African Congress, attended by several giants of the movement, such as Kwame Nkrumah of Ghana, Jomo Kenyatta of Kenya, and W.E.B. DuBois of the US.

References

Asante, M. K. (1998) *The Afrocentric Idea*. Philadelphia: Temple University Press

Boyce Davis, C. (2001) Imperialism and the Super-Exploitation of the Black Woman: Claudia Jones Transnational Black Feminism, ESRC *International Conference on the Caribbean Diaspora,* 30 August—1 September 2001, London: South Bank University.

Carter, T. (1986) *Shattering Illusions: West Indians in British Politics.* London: Lawrence & Wishart

Coard, B. (1971) *How the West Indian Child is Made Educationally Sub-Normal in the British School System.* London: New Beacon Books

Edwards, A. (1967) *Marcus Garvey: 1887—1940,* London: New Beacon Books
Goulbourne, H. (1988) *Teachers, Education and Politics in Jamaica, 1882—1972.* London: Macmillan
Goulbourne, H. (ed.) (1990) *Black Politics in Britain.* Aldershot: Avebury
Goulbourne, H. (1991a) *Ethnicity and Nationalism in Post-Imperial Britain.* Cambridge: Cambridge University Press
Goulbourne, H. (1991b) The Offence of the West Indian: Political Leadership and the Communal Option, in: M. Anwar & P. Werbner (eds.) *Black and Ethnic Leaderships: the Cultural Dimensions of Political Action.* London: Routledge
Goulbourne, H. (1998) *Race Relations in Britain Since 1945.* London: Macmillan
Goulbourne, H. (2002) *Caribbean Transnational Experience.* London: Pluto Press
Hall, S. et al (1978) *Policing the Crisis: Mugging, the State and Law and Order.* London: Macmillan Press
Harris, W. (1967) *Tradition, the Writer and Society.* London: New Beacon Books
Heineman, B. (1972) *The Politics of the Powerless.* Oxford: Oxford University Press
Hiro, D. (1971) *Black British White British.* London: Eyre & Spottiswoode
Hylton, C. (ed) (1997) *Black Men in Britain: Marching into the Millennium.* Leeds: Bogle-L'Ouverture & Black Men's Forum
James, C. L. R. (1982) Walter Rodney and the Question of Power, in E. Alpers & P-M. Fontaine (eds.) *Walter Rodney — Revolutionary and Scholar: a Tribute.* Los Angeles: Centre for Afro-American Studies & African Studies Center, University of California
Lewis, R. (1998) *Walter Rodney's Intellectual and Political Thought.* Mona & Detroit: University of the West Indies Press & Wayne State University Press
Lewis, R. and Bryan, P. (eds.) (1986) *Garvey: His Work and Impact.* Mona: Institute of Social & Economic Research, University of the West Indies
Lewis, R. and Warner, M. (eds.) (1988) *Garvey: Africa, Europe, The Americas.* Mona: Institute of Social & Economic Research, University of the West Indies
Modood, T. (1988) 'Black', Racial Equality and Asian Identity', *New Community,* 14: 3
Munroe, T. (1972) *The Politics of Constitutional Decolonization: Jamaica 1944—62.* Kingston: Institute of Social & Economic Research, University of the West Indies
Post, K. (1978) *Arise Ye Starvellings: The Jamaican Labour Rebellion of 1938 and its Aftermaths.* The Hague: Martinus Nijhoff
Sivanandan, A. (1986) *From Resistance to Rebellion: Asian and Afro-Caribbean Struggles in Britain.* London: Institute of Race Relations
Sherwood, M. (ed) (1999) *Claudia Jones: A Life in Exile.* London: Lawrence and Wishart
Thomas, J. J. (1969) *The Theory and Practice of Creole Grammar.* London: New Beacon Books
Van Sertima, I. (1968) *Caribbean Writers.* London: New Beacon Books
Walker, R. (2000) *The Classical Roots of Black Culture.* London: Bogle L'Ouverture
Walmsley, A. (1992) *The Caribbean Artist Movement 1966—1972: a Literary & Cultural History.* London: New Beacon Books
Weber, M. (1930) *The Protestant Ethic and the Spirit of Capitalism.* London: Allen & Unwin
Williams, E. (1964) *Capitalism and Slavery.* London: Andre Deutsch

Chapter 2

Media Representations: Continuity, Contradiction and Change

Simon Cottle

How have British media representations of 'race', racism and minority cultures changed across recent years? Or, to turn the question around, how have ideas of what it is to be 'British' been reconfigured through time and what part has the media played in this? Can we discern measurable and meaningful movement away from earlier media landscapes disfigured by negative stereotypes, conflict-driven news agendas, and paternalistic discourses? Are our TV screens, radios and newspapers, libraries, art galleries and museums, cinemas and video stores, and now home-based computers and other technologies of interactivity, conveying images and ideas that help constitute an inclusive definition of what it is to be British, or do they continue to reinscribe and police the boundaries of otherness through the monochrome assumptions and dominant outlooks of the past? These fundamental questions are in part empirical ones that have begun to be answered by systematic, comparative and analytical research. But they are also political questions since much depends on the choice of categories and benchmarks used and the values guiding the focus of analysis. Before directly addressing the question of representational continuity or change in Britain's media, therefore, we need first to consider the analytical frameworks, or the 'problematics', guiding research into questions of 'race', racism and minority ethnicity more generally. This chapter, drawing on two of the author's recent publications (*Ethnic Minorities and the Media: Changing Cultural Boundaries*, pp. 1-15, 218-219; Open University Press 2000; and 'Representation' in E. Cashmore (ed.) *Encyclopedia of Race and Ethnic Studies*, Routledge, 2003), first outlines the changing problematics of 'race', racism and minority ethnicity before summarising research into media representations which can help to determine the continuities and changes found in British mainstream media across the years.

Changing Research Problematics

As I have outlined in *Ethnic Minorities and the Media* (2000), <u>three</u> 'problematics' of 'race-relations', 'racism/racialisation' and 'new ethnicities' have tended to guide the questions asked by researchers as well as the conceptualisation of differing objects of inquiry. The notion of a 'problematic' in this context refers, then, to the wider theoretical and political frameworks that conceptualise and prioritise different research 'problems' or questions and which structure our thinking and debates about the social and discursive realities of 'race', racism and ethnicity. Today three general 'problematics', described below, contend for wider theoretical recognition and help to structure the research field (see: Miles, 1993; Miles and Torres, 1999; Solomos and Back, 1996; 1999 and Hall, 1988; 1999).

The 'race relations' problematic

The 'race relations' problematic is deeply embedded within common-sense views in both the UK and many other countries and continues to inform academic discussion and study to this day (Mason, 1999). Early sociological approaches to the study of *'race'* had sought to theorise *'race relations'* in terms of *inter-group processes* of adjustment, assimilation and in relation to conflicts over status claims and resources (Park, Burgess and Mackenzie, 1923; Rex and Moore, 1967). This way of conceptualising 'race relations' has subsequently been criticised for failing to adequately theorise the systemic processes and persistent structures of inequality, the exclusions of power and the prevalent culture and experience of racisms that condition such 'inter-group' encounters. Moreover, the very terms deployed, 'race relations', appear to presume *'race'* not only as a self-evident category but also as the key explanatory factor thought to explain *racial conflict situations*. This appears, then, to endorse erroneous common sense ideas of 'race' as biologically real (Miles, 1982; Miles and Torres, 1999) even though most sociologists would today argue that 'race' can only be taken as 'real' in terms of its *material consequences* and *discursive effects* (Mason, 1995; Omi and Winant, 1995). Under this problematic the concept of 'race' often remained unquestioned and was assumed to be at the root of 'racial conflict situations'. Media representations were also often implicitly treated as seemingly irrelevant or as straightforward accounts of reality.

The 'racism/racialisation' problematic

Based on the critique of the 'race relations' problematic Robert Miles, amongst others, has consistently argued that what we should actually be studying is how material inequalities and signifying processes combine to 'racialise' groups as 'races' and thereby help sustain, for example, the structures and processes of class inequality and the exploitation of migrant workers. *Racialisation* 'refers to a process of categorisation, a representational process of defining an Other (usually, but not exclusively) somatically' (Miles, 1989, p. 75; cf. Small, 1999). In the context of the US, Michael Omi and Howard Winant have proposed a similar view of *racial formations*, which is defined as 'the sociohistorical process by which racial categories are created, inhabited, transformed and destroyed' (1995, p. 55), and they analyse the role played by 'race' in political projects and in relation to hegemonic structures of power. In the UK influential analyses of the so-called *'new racism'* have been theorised not as 'the result of autonomous racial conflicts' or as 'the outcome of abstract laws of capitalist development' (Solomos et al, 1982, p. 27) but in relation to an 'organic' crisis of capitalism in which 'race' becomes discursively mobilised, and articulated, in relation to the state's attempts to 'police the crisis' and maintain hegemonic dominance (Hall et al, 1978; Hall, 1980). Today however, the term 'new racism' is often used to refer to public statements and cultural forms of representation which racially essentialise others but which do not necessarily involve a conjunctural analysis of state and politics (see, for example, van Dijk, 2000).

Together these positions and debates, then, help to define the *'racism/racialisation'* problematic in opposition to common sense views of 'race relations' and the focus shifts to the historical and contemporary processes by which social groups become 'racialised' or *'raced'* and how ideologies and discourses of 'race' are both constituted by, and constitutive of, racist exclusions and practices – whether in relation to the state, institutions, or every day practices (see Fiske, 2000). *Multi-racial feminists* have here played a leading role in opening up the discursive complexities of *sexuality, gender* and class and how these are variously refracted within and through discourses and representations of 'race'. Together, these theoretical co-ordinates point to the relevance of attending to (and challenging) media representations of 'race' (see McLintock, 1995), as well as minority under-representation within media institutions and associated processes of institutionalised racism (Cohen and Gardner,

1982; Wadsworth, 1986). Clearly, this second problematic helps draw attention to the roles of media in circulating racist ideas and images in society, including cultural ideas of 'new racism', and its specific involvement in processes of racialisation.

The 'new ethnicities' problematic

Finally, a third, 'new ethnicities' (Hall, 1988) problematic has emerged which seeks to engage with the cultural complexities of ethnic identities, processes of identity formation and change and with the *'new cultural politics of difference'* (West, 1993). These writers theorise the discursive complexities and 'positionalities' involved in *ethnic identity* – approached not as essentially fixed or *primordial* – but as culturally fluid, internally contested, and politically engaged (Brah, 1996; Hall, 1999; Yuval-Davis, 1999). The earlier and strategic political mobilisation of *'the essential black subject'* (Hall, 1988) here gives way to an acknowledgement of important ethnic minority differences and the multiple *'subject positions'* found within and between these.

These changes are often contextualised in relation to the contradictory processes and flows of *globalisation* and how these can lead both to the defensive reassertion of *'ethnic absolutisms'* organised around *Tradition* as well as to 'new ethnicities' organised around processes of cultural *Translation* comprising cultural crossover and syncretism, and *post-colonial hybridity* (Gilroy, 1987; Bhabha, 1990; Robins, 1991; Hall, 1992a, 1992b) – processes, furthermore, that are increasingly media dependent (Morley and Robins, 1995) and actively negotiated within local settings and cultural milieux (Back, 1996). Many of today's diasporic communities, with their simultaneous identifications with place(s), within myths and memories, and between different cultures and homes, thus problematise essentialising ideas of cultural *'roots'*, and point rather to the influence of the disparate *'routes'* travelled and how these inform biographies, the complex layering of ethnic identities and outlooks, and the formation of collective projects (Clifford, 1997; Gilroy, 1993; Hall, 1999).

This emergent problematic thus encourages us to take seriously – for the first time perhaps - issues of ethnic minority differences and the complexities of media use, appropriation and sense-making within processes of identity formation, contestation and change. How *diasporic communities* and those positioned at the margins of society creatively utilise media technologies and integrate mainstream media within their daily lives and local cultural practices are theoretically prefigured in this problematic. Interestingly, the focus on processes of identity formation and change at the margins is also thought to help illuminate processes of *hegemonic 'ethnicity'* and the construction of *'whiteness'* at the centre (Hall, 1988; Julian and Mercer, 1988).

The influence of these three overarching 'problematics' can be detected in the research approaches to media representations of race, racism and ethnicity now briefly reviewed below.

Researching Representation

Media representations comprise the images and ideas, signs and symbols, discourses and debates that feature within, and are circulated by, the different mediums and genres of the mass media. Essentially media representations are about 'meanings' and how these enter into the life of society. In societies marked by racism, segregated by 'race' or characterised by multi-ethnic identities, the meanings circulated by the media and consumed by audiences in particular historical times and social contexts are not without consequence. This is because media representations do not simply 'reflect' society, but can play an active part in constituting what the nature of that society is, of how its social relations are conducted, and in defining what its future can be. We should not be surprised; therefore, that academics working in the field of race and ethnic studies have often turned their attention to media representations.

Base-line research findings

Considerable research now exists that has examined the British media's representations of 'race', racism and ethnic minorities over a considerable period of time. The collective findings of this research effort can generally be summarised as follows: the British media have often perpetuated under-representation and stereotypical characterisation within entertainment genres and negative problem-oriented portrayal within factuality and news forms, and exhibit a tendency to ignore structural inequalities and lived racism experienced by ethnic minorities in both. In Britain from the late 1950s through to the 1970s, for example, studies observed how immigrants were reported in relation to the so-called 'race riots' of 1958 (Miles, 1984), public health scares (Butterworth, 1967), problems of 'numbers' and tensions of 'race relations' and how this effectively concealed problems of British racism (Hartmann and Husband, 1974; Hartmann, Husband and Clark, 1974; Critcher, Parker and Sondhi, 1977; Troyna, 1981). In the 1970s and across the 1980s, studies of news, and other factuality genres, identified the ways in which a 'moral panic' orchestrated around 'mugging' (Hall et al., 1978), the portrayal of street violence (Holland, 1981), and inner city disorders served to criminalise Britain's black population and ignored continuing social inequalities and growing anger at policing practices and harassment (Sumner, 1982; Tumber, 1982; Joshua, Wallace and Booth, 1983; Murdock, 1984; Burgess, 1985; Downing, 1985; Hansen and Murdock, 1985; Solomos, 1986, 1989; Cottle, 1993a). From the late 1980s continuing to the present, studies have charted virulent press attacks on anti-racism campaigns, the vilification of black representatives and the support given to statements of 'new racism' by prominent politicians, as well as xenophobic reportage of refugees and migrants – actively disparaging attempts to further multi-cultural and anti-racist agendas (Murray, 1986; Gordon and Rosenberg 1989; Van Dijk, 1991; McLaughlin, 1999; Philo and Beattie, 1999). Across the years, numerous studies have also observed the media's use of stock stereotypes of black people as 'trouble-maker', 'entertainer' and 'dependent' (Hartmann and Husband, 1974; Barry, 1988; Twitchin, 1988; Hall 1990).

These and many other studies, then, provide us with evidence of the general patterns, impoverished representations and sometimes starkly racist portrayal found in mainstream media. As *general* findings, however, they can perhaps inadvertently create a sense of media representations as historically static and ideologically uniform and, in consequence, cover over important processes of historical change, media differentiation and representational complexity. The remainder of this essay begins to unpack some of these complexities.

Media representations: Dynamic and differentiated

Studies are now beginning to historically recover how changing ideas and political agendas, whether those of 'assimilation', 'anti-racism' or multi-culturalism', have informed the development of media representations across the year including those of television, the press and cinema (Daniels and Gerson, 1989; Pines, 1992; Daniels, 1994; Ross, 1996; Bourne, 1998; Law, 2002; Malik, 2002). The influence of 'liberal' TV producers (Seymour-Ure, 1974; Braham, 1982) as well as 'responsible' newspaper journalists and newspapers have also been observed to contribute to, respectively, the downplaying of White racist fears and the selective curbing of sensational press treatments of civil disorder in earlier periods of conflict reporting. Studies such as these demonstrate something of the less than uniform representational portrayal of past media output. And we can also note the limited but real advances in ethnic minority media presence in recent years, whether in respect of TV genres of light entertainment, comedy and advertising in the UK (Givanni, 1995; Hall, 1995; Beattie, Khan and Philo, 1999), or the importation of successful 'soaps' based on Black characters from the U.S (Downing, 1988; Jhally and Lewis, 1994; Gray, 1995), as well as in the commercial crossover and commodification of black music, dance and fashion (Cashmore, 1997). These too are important features of contemporary ethnic minority media representation. British society increasingly accommodates ideas of 'multi-culturalism', a growing sensibility that can also, however, provoke forms of white backlash culture (Gabriel, 2000) as well as more subtle forms of racism. In my study of UK regional television news, for example, I observed how ethnic minorities are now often portrayed in deliberate 'multi-culturalist' ways through a (superficial) focus on cultural festivals, individual success stories and the cultural exotica of ethnic minority cultures (Cottle, 1993a, 1993b). Such representations can be explained in terms of the populist pursuit of positive stories and celebratory features as well as a growing multi-cultural sensibility within the newsroom. Nonetheless, despite the best intentions of the news producers such multi-culturalist representations may serve to reinforce culturally sedimented views of ethnic minorities as 'Other' and simultaneously appear to give the lie to arguments about structural disadvantage and inequality.

These and other studies, then, increasingly point to the dynamic nature and subtleties of media discourse and representation, features that cannot always be captured through simplistic and static applications of the concept of 'stereotype' (Mercer, 1988 1989, 1994; Daniels, 1990; Cottle, 1992). Ideas concerning new ethnicities and the cultural politics of difference, with their fluid understanding of contested subject-positions are today prompting a more diversified stance towards the politics of representation – one that increasingly questions essentialist stereotypes whether 'negative' or 'positive'. Ella Shohat and Robert Stam (1997) in *Unthinking Eurocentrism: Multiculturalism and the Media*, for example, document representational complexities in the historical developments of film and uncover the continuing tensions within multi-cultural representations.

Recovering the play of difference

In order to address such representational complexities studies today increasingly deploy an array of sophisticated textual methods when analysing the myths, narratives, discourses and language embedded within media representations of 'race'. The work of Kobena Mercer (1994) and his discussion of the erotic photographs of Robert Mapplethorpe, and Stuart Hall's (1997) discussion of racialised advertising and other images, both, for example, demonstrate how recent images of black bodies often 'embody' ambivalent meanings that deliberately play on ideas of cultural difference, stereotypes and inter-textuality and thereby prompt readings that go 'against the grain'. Other studies also generally detect at least some discursive contestation and/or challenge to dominant viewpoints across mainstream genres and within minority media outlets. Sarita Malik, for example, in her recent study *Representing Black Britain* concludes:

> As we have seen, these meanings around 'race' are never fixed and always changing, but then 'culture' itself is always in motion and is always a potential site of struggle. This makes it difficult to identify a simple progress model in representations of 'Blackness' on British television. We are not talking about a television society that is more or less racist now compared to then; we are experiencing different approaches, languages and ideologies around race … (Malik, 2002, pp. 173-174).

To be clear, most researchers today do not want to suggest that dominant views of 'race' no longer inform media representations or that these do not often serve to 'racialise' media events, but rather that there is a complexity and movement here which is itself a product of social and discursive processes mediated through cultural forms. The latter are not historically fixed or a foregone conclusion and they most certainly are not beyond challenge or change.

Sensitised to the textual forms and discursive nature of media representations, recent studies have tended to reflect the growing influence of cultural studies and the wider linguistic (and cultural) turn in contemporary social theory. British cultural studies had earlier theorised popular culture as the terrain on which, and through which, hegemonic struggles for consent are ideologically conditioned and discursively played out and thus seek to keep both the interactions (and 'articulations') of the 'cultural' and the 'social' in view. *Policing the Crisis* by Stuart Hall and his colleagues (1978), for example, had sought to analyse how Black youth had become criminalised and symbolised as a new 'folk devil' by the media in the 'mugging' scare of the early 1970s. This 'moral panic', it was argued, helped pave the ideological way for a new form of state 'authoritarian populism' (neo-conservative politics) that itself was a response to processes of national economic decline and growing political dissensus. This analysis relating representations of 'race' to wider state interests and processes of manufacturing consent proved highly influential, though its explanation of the exact mechanisms linking media institutions, professional practices and cultural representations to political forces of change may now appear under- (or over-) theorised and in need of empirical support.

Media events and media performance

Published studies in the US may also have relevance for how we can better understand certain forms of media representation in the UK. These have sought to demonstrate how high profile media events such as the O. J. Simpson trial and the riots following the publicly aired video film of LA police beating Rodney King serve to galvanise deep cultural anxieties around issues of 'race'. These studies generally also observe that though 'raced' media events can often serve conservative political projects they can also sustain counter-hegemonic discourses (Fiske, 1996; Hunt, 1997). In the context of the UK, mainstream media exceptionally served to propel issues of race and social injustice to the top of the political agenda when, as in the case of the reporting of the racist murder of Stephen Lawrence across the period 1993-2003, they appeared to adopt a championing role in support of Stephen Lawrence's parents and their calls for justice.

Research currently underway (Cottle, forthcoming) details how the media contributed invaluable resources and sustained pressure across the period 1993 to 2003 keeping the Stephen Lawrence affair alive and propelling it to the top of the political agenda. The public inquiry eventually enacted and mediated on the public stage called prominent centres of political and social power as well as individuals to account, and demonstrated how the media can enact a 'public crisis' and perform a potentially transformative role in shifting the contours of racist Britain. Going against the grain of earlier 'base-line' research expectations, then, prominent sections of the media, both press and TV, performed a complex of roles in which elite authorities and institutional power (notably, the Crown Prosecution Service, the Metropolitan Police and its Chief Constable Sir Paul Condon, Sir William Macpherson the Public Inquiry Chair, the Home Secretary Jack Straw, and the Home Office) all became embroiled in intense public criticism. Symbolic power here played a part in sustaining critique and challenge from below. Two 'ordinary' people, Doreen and Neville Lawrence the parents of Stephen Lawrence, effectively took possession of the moral high-ground via the media in their quest for justice for Stephen, and by extension all those subject to racist violence and discrimination. In such ways the racist murder of their son turned into a 'mediatised public crisis' and, as such, conditioned elite discourse and served to move public awareness from the indicative mode – of 'what is' – to a subjunctive mode - of 'what should be'. Media performance, in this instance, served to galvanise public opinion and unleashed widespread processes of institutional and social reflexivity.

Studies such as these, then, remind us of how media representations can both register and contribute to the shifting terrain of 'race', racism and ethnicity, a contested landscape that by definition is constantly on the move. They also serve to underline the central nature of media representations that are best approached not as 'reflections' of society but rather as active agents that exert influence and have consequences within the life of society.

Conclusion

Historically, as we have heard, Britain's media representations can reveal the dominant thinking about 'race' at a particular moment in time and how the prevailing culture legitimises racist practices and the perpetuation of racial inequalities. Expressive of both history and culture the meanings of media representations need not only serve to legitimise dominant ideas of race and symbolically naturalise racial inequalities however. They can also become the site of contestation and exhibit their own internal complexities. This too is evident from our review of research into Britain's changing media landscape and its representations. Today we are better able to understand that the meanings of media representations are neither fixed for all time nor necessarily always accepted, and we can also acknowledge that, on occasion, they can and do actively perform a more benevolent (sometimes patronising) role in the changing cultural politics of 'race' and ethnic identity in multi-cultural Britain. Today's media, it seems, remain capable of polluting the cultural pool of images and ideas about minority groups thereby reinforcing or re-inscribing prejudicial views and racist practices, but they can sometimes also challenge past stereotypes and serve to promote multi-cultural understanding and inter-cultural dialogue. Today's media often continue to legitimise inequalities of race and ethnicity through 'naturalising' discourses and structured silences, but so too can they culturally legislate against the racisms of segregated societies and condemn their essential inhumanity. Representational boundaries erected by today's media extend to the outer geo-political frontiers of nation states designed to keep migrants and asylum seekers out as well as inwards to the core of one's intimate sense of self and personal identity. But so too do the media have the capacity to promote increased recognition and understanding of ethnic differences, the histories and struggles that inform these, as well as the richness and gains that identities of difference can bring to culturally diverse societies. In such continuing, changing and contradictory ways, then, media representations variously, and sometimes powerfully, enter into the life of society.

References

Back, L. (1996) *New Ethnicities and Urban Culture: Racisms and Multiculture in Young Lives*. London: University College London Press.
Barry, A. (1988) Black Mythologies: Representation of Black People on British Television, in J. Twitchin (ed.) *The Black and White Media Show Book*, pp. 83-102. Stoke on Trent: Trentham Books.
Beattie, L., Khan, F. and Philo, G. (1999) Race, Advertising and the Public Face of Television, pp. 149-170 in G. Philo (ed.) Message Received. Harlow: Longman.
Bhabha, H. K. (ed.) (1990) *Nation and Narration*. London: Routledge.
Bourne, S. (1998) *Blacks in the British Frame*. London: Cassell.
Brah, A. (1996) *Cartographies of Diaspora: Contesting Identities*. London: Routledge.
Braham, P. (1982) How the Media Report Race, in M. Gurevitch, T. Bennett, J. Curran and J. Woollacott (eds.) *Culture, Society and the Media*. London: Methuen.

Burgess, J. A. (1985) News From Nowhere: The Press, the Riots and the Myth of the Inner City, in J. A. Burgess and R.A. Gold (eds.), Geography, the Media and Popular Culture, pp. 192-228. London: Croom Helm.

Butterworth, E. (1967) The 1962 Smallpox Outbreak and the British Press, *Race* 7:4, pp. 347-364.

Cashmore, E. (1997) *The Black Culture Industry*. London: Routledge

Clifford, J. (1997) *Routes: Travel and Translation in the late Twentieth Century*. Boston, Massachusetts: Harvard University Press.

Cohen, C. and Gardner, P. (eds.) (1982) *It Ain't Half Racist Mum*. London: Comedia.

Cottle, S. (1992) 'Race', Racialization and the Media: A Review and Update of Research, *Sage Race Relations Abstracts* 17: 2, pp. 3-57.

Cottle, S. (1993a) *TV News, Urban Conflict and the Inner City*. Leicester: Leicester University Press.

Cottle, S. (1993b) 'Race' and Regional Television News: Multi-culturalism and the Production of Popular TV, *New Community* 19: 4, pp. 581-592.

Cottle, S. (ed.) (2000) *Ethnic Minorities and the Media: Changing Cultural Boundaries*. Buckingham and Philadelphia: Open University Press.

Cottle, S. (2003) 'Representation' in E. Cashmore (ed.), *Encyclopaedia of Race and Ethnic Studies*. London: Routledge.

Cottle, S. (forthcoming) *Media Performance and Public Transformation: The Racist Murder of Stephen Lawrence and its Aftermath*. Westport CT: Praeger.

Critcher, C., Parker, M. and Sondhi, R. (1977) *Race in the Provincial Press*. Paris: UNESCO.

Daniels, T. (1990) 'Beyond Negative or Positive Images, in J. Willis and T. Wollen (eds.) *The Neglected Audience*, pp.66-71. London: British Film Institute.

Daniels, T. (1994) Programmes For Black Audiences, in S. Hood (ed.) *Behind The Screens: The Structure of British Television in the Nineties*. London: Lawrence and Wishart.

Daniels, T. and Gerson, J. (eds.)(1989) *The Colour Black: Black Images in British Television*. London: British Film Institute.

Downing, J. (1985) 'Coillons' ... Shryned in an Hoggs Toord: British News Media Discourse on Race', in T. van Dijk (ed.) Discourse and Communication. pp. 295-323. Berlin: Walter de Gruyter.

Downing, J. (1988) 'The Cosby Show' and American Racial Discourse', in G. Smitherman-Donaldson and T. van Dijk (eds.) *Discourse and Discrimination*. Detroit, MI: Wayne State University Press.

Fiske, J. (1996) *Media Matters: Race and Gender in U.S. Politics* (revised edition) Minneapolis, MI: University of Minnesota Press.

Fiske, J. (2000) White Watch, in S. Cottle (ed.) *Ethnic Minorities and the Media: Changing Cultural Boundaries*. Buckingham: Open University Press.

Gabriel (2000) Dreaming of a White..., in S. Cottle (ed.) *Ethnic Minorities and the Media: Changing Cultural Boundaries*. Buckingham: Open University Press.

Gilroy, P. (1987) *There Ain't No Black in the Union Jack*. London: Hutchinson.

Gilroy, P. (1993) *The Black Atlantic: Modernity and Double Consciousness*, London and New York: Verso.

Givanni, J. (ed.) (1995) *Remote Control*. London: British Film Institute.

Gordon, P. and Rosenberg, D. (1989) *Daily Racism -The Press and Black People in Britain*. London: Runnymede Trust.

Gray, H. (1995) *Watching Race: Television and the Struggle for 'Blackness'*, Minneapolis, MI/London: University of Minnesota Press.

Hall, S. (1980) Race, Articulation and Societies Structured in Dominance, in UNESCO *Sociological Theories: Race and Colonialism.* Paris: UNESCO.

Hall, S. (1988) New Ethnicities, in K. Mercer (ed.) *Black Film, British Cinema*, pp. 27-31. ICA Documents 7. London: British Film Institute.

Hall, S. (1990) The Whites of their Eyes: Racist Ideologies and the Media, in M. Alvarado and J. O. Thompson (eds.) *The Media Reader*, pp.8-23. London: British Film Institute.

Hall, S. (1992a) The Question of Cultural Identity, in S. Hall, D. Held and T. McGrew (eds.) *Modernity and its Futures* p. 273-325. Cambridge: Polity Press.

Hall, S. (1992b), What is this 'Black' in Black Popular Culture?, in G. Dent (ed.) *Black Popular Culture* pp.21-36. Seattle: Bay Press.

Hall, S. (1995) Black and White in Television, in J. Givanni (ed.) *Remote Control.* London: British Film Institute.

Hall, S. (1997) The Spectacle of the 'Other', in S. Hall (ed.) *Representation: Cultural Representations and Signifying Practices*, pp.223-279. London: Sage Publications.

Hall, S. (1999) Interview with Stuart Hall: Culture and Power, in R. Torres, L.F. Miron and J. X India (eds.) *Race, Identity and Citizenship - A Reader*, pp. 389-412. Oxford: Blackwell Publishers.

Hall, S., Chritcher, C., Jefferson, T., Clarke, J. and Roberts, B. (1978) *Policing the Crisis: Mugging, the State, and Law and Order*. Basingstoke: Macmillan.

Hansen, A. and Murdock, G. (1985) Constructing the Crowd: Populist Discourse and Press Presentation, in V. Mosco and M. Wasco (eds.) *Popular Culture and Media Events*, Vol. III, pp.227-57. The Critical Communication Review. New Jersey: Ablex.

Hartmann, P. and Husband C. (1974) *Racism and the Mass Media.* London: Davis Poynter.

Hartmann, P., Husband. C. and Clark, J. (1974) Race as News: A Study in the Handling of Race in the British Press from 1963 to 1970, in UNESCO (ed.) *Race as News.* Paris: UNESCO.

Holland, P. (1981) The New Cross Fire and the Popular Press, *Multi-Racial Education* 9: 3, pp. 61-80.

Hunt, D. (1997) *Screening the Los Angeles 'Riots': Race, Seeing and Resistance.* Cambridge: Cambridge University Press.

Jhally, S. and Lewis, J. (1994) *Enlightened Racism: The Cosby Show, Audiences and the Myth of the American Dream.* Boulder, Colorado: Westview Press.

Joshua, H., Wallace, T. and Booth, H. (1983) *To Ride the Storm: The 1980 Bristol 'Riots' and the State.* London: Heinemann.

Julian, I. and Mercer, K. (1988) Introduction: De Margin and De Centre, *Screen*, 29: 4, pp. 2-10.

Law, I. (2002) *Race in the News.* Basingstoke: Palgrave.

Malik, S. (2002) *Representing Black Britain: Black and Asian Images on Television.* London: Sage.

Mason, D. (1995) *Race and Ethnicity in Modern Britain.* Oxford: Oxford University Press.

Mason, D. (1999) The Continuing Significance of Race? Teaching Ethnic and Racial Studies in Sociology, in M. Bulmer and J. Solomos (eds.) *Ethnic and Racial Studies Today*, pp. 13-28. London: Routledge.

McLaughlin, G. (1999) Refugees, Migrants and the Fall of the Berlin Wall, in G. Philo (ed.) *Message Received*, pp.197-209. Harlow: Longman.

McLintock, A. (1995) *Imperial Leather: Race, Gender and Sexuality in the Colonial Context.* London: Routledge.

Mercer, K. (ed.) (1988) *Black Film, Black Cinema.* ICA Documents 7: British Film Institute.

Mercer, K. (1989) General Introduction, in T. Daniels and J. Gerson (eds.) *The Colour Black – Black Images in British Television*, pp. 1-11. London: British Film Institute.

Mercer, K. (1994) *Welcome to the Jungle*. London: Routledge.

Miles, R. (1982) *Racism and Migrant Labour*. London: Routledge and Kegan Paul.

Miles, R. (1984) The Riots of 1958: Notes on the Ideological Construction of 'Race Relations' as a Political Issue in Britain, *Immigrants and Minorities*, 3: 3, pp. 252-75.

Miles, R. (1989) *Racism*. London: Routledge.

Miles, R. (1993) *Racism After 'Race Relations'*. London: Routledge.

Miles, R. and Torres, R. D. (1999) Does 'Race' Matter? Transatlantic Perspectives on Racism after 'Race Relations' in R. Torres, L. F. Miron and J. X. India (eds.) *Race, Identity and Citizenship - A Reader*, pp. 19-38. Oxford: Blackwell Publishers.

Morley, D. and Robins, K. (1995) *Spaces of Identity*. London: Routledge.

Murdock, G. (1984) Reporting the Riots: Images and Impacts, in J. Benyon (ed.) *Scarman and After*. Oxford: Pergamon.

Murray, N. (1986) Anti-Racists and Other Demons: The Press and Ideology in Thatcher's Britain, *Race and Class*, 27, pp. 1-20.

Omi, M. and Winant, H. (1995) *Racial Formations in the United States*, (2nd ed.). London: Routledge.

Park, R.E., Burgess, E., and Mackenzie, R. (1923) *The City* Chicago: University of Chicago Press.

Philo, G. and Beattie, L. (1999) Race, Migration and Media, in G. Philo (ed.) *Message Received*. Harlow: Longman.

Pines, J. (ed.) (1992) *Black and White in Colour: Black People in British Television since 1936*. London: British Film Institute.

Rex, J. and Moore, R. (1967) *Race, Community and Conflict*. London: Oxford University Press.

Robins, K. (1991) Tradition and Translation: National Culture in Global Context, in J. Corner and S. Harvey (eds.), *Enterprise and Heritage: Crosscurrents of National Culture*. London: Routledge.

Ross, K. (1996) *Black And White Media: Black Images in Popular Film And Television*. Cambridge: Polity Press.

Seymour-Ure, C. (1974) Enoch Powell's 'Earthquake', in C. Seymour-Ure, *The Political Impact of the Mass Media*. London: Constable.

Shohat, E. and Stam, R. (1997) *Unthinking Eurocentrism: Multiculturalism and the Media*. London: Routledge.

Small, (1999) The Contours of Racialization: Structures, Representations and Resistance in the United States, in R. Torres, L.F. Miron and J. X. India (eds.) *Race, Identity and Citizenship - A Reader*, pp. 47-64. Oxford: Blackwell.

Solomos, J. (1986) Political Language and Violent Protest: Ideological and Policy Responses to the 1981 and 1985 Riots, *Youth and Policy* 18, pp. 12-24.

Solomos, J. (1989) *Race and Racism in Contemporary Britain*. London: Macmillan.

Solomos, J., Findley, B., Jones, S. and Gilroy, P. (1982) The Organic Crisis of British Capitalism and Race: The Experience of the Seventies, in Centre for Contemporary Cultural Studies (eds.) *The Empire Strikes Back*. London: Hutchinson.

Solomos, J. and Back, L. (1996) *Racism and Society*. London: Macmillan.

Solomos, J. and Back, L. (1999) Marxism, Racism and Ethnicity, in R. Torres, L.F. Miron and J. X. India (eds.) *Race, Identity and Citizenship - A Reader*, pp.65-78. Oxford: Blackwell Publishers.

Sumner, C. (1982) 'Political Hooliganism' and 'Rampaging Mobs': The National Press Coverage of the Toxteth Riots, in C. Sumner (ed.) *Crime, Justice and the Mass Media*, pp. 22-35. Cambridge Institute of Criminology: Cambridge University Press.

Troyna, B. (1981) *Public Awareness and the Media: A Study of Reporting on Race*. London: Commission for Racial Equality.

Tumber, H. (1982) *Television and the Riots*. Broadcasting Research Unit, London: British Film Institute.

Twitchin, J. (1988) Stereotypical Thinking in TV News and Current Affairs, in J. Twitchin (ed.) *The Black and White Media Show Book,* pp.214-35. Stoke on Trent: Trentham Books.

Van Dijk, T. A. (1991). *Racism and the Press*. London New York: Routledge.

Van Dijk, T.A. (2000) New(s) Racism: A Discourse Analytical Approach, in S.Cottle (ed.) *Ethnic Minorities and the Media: Changing Cultural Boundaries.* Buckingham: Open University Press.

Wadsworth, M. (1986) Racism in Broadcasting, in J. Curran (ed.) *Bending Reality– The State of the Media*, pp. 38-46. London: Pluto Press.

West, C. (1993) The New Cultural Politics of Difference, in S. During (ed.) *The Cultural Studies Reader*, pp.203-217. London: Routledge.

Yuval-Davis, N. (1999) Ethnicity, Gender Relations and Multiculturalism, in R. Torres, L.F. Miron and J. X. India (eds.) *Race, Identity and Citizenship - A Reader*, pp. 112-125. Oxford: Blackwell Publishers.

Chapter 3

'We don't just make tea': redefining political activism[1]

Julia Sudbury

Many scholars have taken a gender blind approach, concentrating solely on Black/White divisions and ignoring gender inequalities (Goulbourne, 1990; Anwar, 1986). A handful of researchers have made concessions towards gender transparency, acknowledging the small numbers of Black women who have an active role in the processes they describe (Carter, 1986; Geddes, 1993). However, they have relied uncritically on conventional wisdom that Black women, doubly burdened by the practices and ideologies of racism and sexism, have simply failed to access the political arena. This essay will illustrate the shortcomings of both approaches and will utilise Black women's own definitions in order to arrive at an alternative framework for the analysis of Black political participation. I shall then examine political activism which has been developed by Black women's organisations. Finally, I shall look at the role of key groups of Black women as catalysts for political change.

Contemporary studies of Black political participation can be broadly categorised around four themes. First, there are quantitative studies of electoral behaviour (Saggar, 1992; Anwar, 1986, 1991; Layton-Henry, 1992). An early example of this approach is offered by the Community Relations Commission, whose 1974 study first posited the significance of the 'Black vote' and thus put Black voters on the mainstream political agenda (Fitzgerald 1984, pp. 7). This analysis contains two elements: comparisons between rates of registration for White, and Asian potential voters and actual or estimated voting patterns. Analysts utilising such data tend to look at the real or imagined 'Black vote' and at which party stands to gain from it. They aim to discover to what extent commonsense ideas about Black political loyalty to the Labour Party are valid. Recent studies have challenged the notion of a homogenous Black vote and suggested that the diversity of Black communities prohibits such a phenomenon from developing in Britain (Miles, 1988; Solomos and Back, 1995).

Second, scholars have analysed the numbers, locations and impact of Black parliamentary candidates, MPs, Lords and councillors (Geddes, 1993; Wadsworth, 1992), and more recently, the racialised politics of selection and deselection processes (Solomos and Back, 1995). This work aims to illustrate the contributions of Black people to British politics and to facilitate a greater understanding of the barriers to their participation. The third theme is the examination of Black caucuses within White political structures. Notable among these studies are Shukra (1990) and Jeffers' (1991) studies of Black sections within the Labour Party.

Finally, there has been an increasing awareness by researchers of the existence and importance of autonomous Black political organisations and institutions. A number of studies have analysed the political impact and agendas of local community organisations (Werbner, 1991; Anthias, Yuval-Davies, Cain, 1992; Carter, 1986). Anwar (1991, p. 56) states that there are over two thousand 'ethnic minority' organisations in Britain. However, listings in *Hansib Directory* 1994 indicate that there are more than 9,000. Of these, the Notting Hill Carnival and associated local campaigns have been a particularly rich source of data (Carter, 1986; Gilroy, 1987). In addition, there has been some discussion of Black organisations with a national brief (Josephides, 1991; Heineman, 1972).

These recent contributions have challenged the notion that Black people are passive victims of exclusionary political practices. In examining Black people's actions and decisions as voters, as politicians and as participants of grassroots organisations, they have shown that Black people are active agents for change. Goulbourne (1990) has characterised this new approach as encompassing a 'view from below' which includes Black people's own interpretations of their actions, focusing not just on institutional change, but also on individuals who bring it about (1990, p. 3). Historically informed accounts are particularly important in that they illustrate that Black people have been active in British politics for as long as they have been in this country, although most studies only record the actions of visible public figures from William Cuffay, son of Kittian slaves and a leader of the Chartists, to Shapurji Saklatvala, MP for Battersea in the 1920s (Wadsworth, 1992; Anwar, 1991).

The Textual Replication Of Gender Inequality

How do these studies attempt to engage with gender differentiation within the political sphere? The answer is that with few exceptions, gender inequities are unquestioningly replicated in the texts themselves. In many of the texts, 'Black' could simply be substituted with 'Black male' without changing any of the data. In most cases there is simply no reference to the gender of the Black participants. When names are mentioned, however, it becomes clear that the politicians are men (Rex, 1991). Activist intellectuals are no less phallocentric. For example, Wadsworth's (1992) illuminating description of Black politicians in pre-Second World War Britain makes no reference to any Black woman in her own right, but also fails to acknowledge this omission. Carter (1986) is an exception in that he acknowledges that his narrative is primarily male (and London-based), and attempts to redress the balance by including eulogies to Claudia Jones and Pansy Jeffries (1986, p. 17). However, this last minute inclusion merely serves to underline the stark absence of women in the remainder of the text.

A revealing twist on gender blindness is Solomos and Back's analysis of the Labour Party in Birmingham (Solomos and Back, 1995). This work is notable for its erasure of Black women while simultaneously foregrounding White women. This occurs, for example, when the authors describe the divergent political priorities of White and Black [male] councillors. A male Asian politician discusses the imposition of women shortlists in the following terms:

> Why should we say that we have to support women, we have to support lesbians, we have to support homosexuals. . . If you're a Black woman fair enough. But they know we haven't got many Black women who are politically active, they're trying to exclude us.
> (Solomos and Back 1995, p. 152)

This conflict between Black and women's politics necessarily involves a reconfiguration of the term 'woman' to include a silent 'White'. Women, it is proposed, can only advance in opposition to Black politicians and asking Black politicians to support women is equivalent to asking them to support gays and lesbians, who are also conceptualised as White.

What is disappointing about this quotation is not the councillor's position - in a local political context in which powerful women's or gay and lesbian groups tend to be White, this construction is in part a response to a material reality - but the authors' failure to criticise the implicit racialisation of the term 'woman' and its implications for Black women's participation. This failure in turn reinforces commonsense notions about Black women's exclusion from political processes, to the extent that the authors do not find it necessary to explore the statement `we haven't got many Black women who are politically active'. Black women's passivity is simply a given and does not warrant further investigation. Solomos and Back's analysis of `the uneasy relationship between Black politics and sexual politics' is actually an exploration of the uneasy relationship between Black men and White women politicians. Despite being a recent work, it ignores the simultaneity of Black and `sexual' politics, and thus erases the presence of Black women (Solomos and Back 1995, p. 101).

Black women are visible in the few accounts which make use of gender transparent statistics. Layton-Henry (1992) acknowledges that Black women in the 1987 general election were slightly less likely to vote Conservative than were Black men and also 'less certain about going to vote' (1992, p. 57). However, this difference is not analysed and we are left unsure of its implications. Geddes (1993) undertakes a more in depth exploration of gender differences in his analysis of Black representation at local level. Yet the major disparity he finds in participation by men and women is hardly reflected in the amount of time he puts into analysing his data:

> Of the 342 Asian and Afro-Caribbean councillors picked up by the survey around 6 per cent are women. This may be indicative of cultural constraints within, for example, the Asian community on female political activity. It may also suggest a 'hierarchy of oppression'. (Geddes, 1993 p. 55)

This minimal analysis deploys stereotypes of women of Asian and African descent and certainly does nothing to unravel the complexities of racialised sexism. In describing the barriers facing Asian women as cultural, the author ignores the role of sexism in structuring dynamics within Black communities. The implication is that such inequalities are inevitable and therefore not worthy of discussion.

Where Black women do play a key role in accounts of Black political mobilisation, that role is not of activists, but of symbols of Black oppression. The deaths of Cynthia Jarret in Tottenham and of Cherry Groce in Brixton led to the uprisings in those areas in 1985. The parallels with the alleged murder by immigration officers of Joy Gardner in August 1993 are obvious. Joy Gardner's death sharpened Black community awareness of the new immigration controls suggested in the Asylum Bill. Descriptions of her death, in front of her five-year-old son Graeme in Haringey, caused outrage in the Black community. While recognising the very real pain that the loss of these women caused to family and friends, it is also possible to identify how these deaths are utilised to foreground a suffering and martyred Black womanhood (Werbner, 1991, p. 20). Images of Black women as victims become alternatives to the possibility of Black women's political agency. Black women are at once invisible, and highly visible in the public political sphere.

En-Gendering A New Racialised Politics

An alternative paradigm is needed. This paradigm should embrace what Black communities and individuals are doing, rather than comparing them to White communities and finding them lacking. It should account for Black agency, while retaining gender transparency and incorporating the active roles of women. It should seek to examine all aspects of Black political participation, that which explicitly engages with mainstream [White] political processes and that which speaks primarily or entirely to a Black audience.

We need to re-examine our conceptualisation of political activism. The aforementioned texts use a narrow definition of legitimate political expression. Political activism is expected to be collective, expressed via recognised bodies such as parties or unions, and addressed to the power-brokers or the White public. Many of the Black women's organisations which I studied during the course of this research questioned such hegemonic notions of political participation. A common theme of the interviews was the failure of the parliamentary process to address the concerns of Black women in any meaningful way. Many interviewees felt that their aspirations were not represented by any party. The traditional view that Black voters' concerns are represented by the Labour Party is challenged by one respondent:

> I think Black women wouldn't find an automatic easy alliance with political groups, the Labour Party, although a lot of Black women might have socialist perspectives in an informal sense. I think there are some issues which they might be seen as right-wing on, in terms of education and a clear traditional view of education, not what has been called '80s liberal education. But on other things they are very clearly, very strongly anti-Tory. (Brenda, Caribbean woman, organisation)

Interviewees also felt that traditional forms of political participation were alienating and exclusionary. The Black women interviewed tended to view the mechanisms of formal participation, both political parties and trade unions, as 'White politics'. This view may be shared by the high numbers of young Black people in particular who are not on the electoral register (*Voice* 12 December 1995[2]; Fitzgerald, 1984). One interviewee who had been actively involved in the Labour movement at local and national levels explained that Black women were regularly 'ignored and marginalised' (Faith, African, Black organisation). This situation was exacerbated by a lack of support for women activists juggling housekeeping, childcare and paid employment. The concentration of Black women in low paid employment and the tendency for many women to work long hours to support their families also contributed to their exclusion:

> A lot of us African women have been involved in bringing up our children, running homes, doing two or three jobs because our men are unemployed, dealing with day to day reality. And in those circumstances, it's not always possible for women to join political parties and go to ward meetings and go to constituency meetings (Faith).

Only one of the interviewees had expressed her political convictions through a mainstream political party. Most of the interviewees contrasted their perception of traditional political participation with their own, much more encompassing view:

> I think that politics for Black women is an everyday event, because we're always out there struggling and to actually struggle with your children and to get through the system is a political kind of thing (Alekiri, African, organisation).

Black women consistently asserted the immediacy of their politics compared to what they viewed as a much more theoretical and abstract approach by political parties. For them, political interventions are shaped by their personal experiences, which in turn provide a sense of urgency and importance in their campaigns:

> If you've been affected by domestic violence and you have experienced problems with services, because you've had first hand experiences, then you're going to be more involved in the political arena and saying what the issues are. I think you have a lot more to give (Anita, Asian, Asian organisation).

Feminist scholars and activists, in their rejection of the division between public and private spheres, have also asserted the importance of personal experience in their assertion 'the personal is political'. By bringing aspects of what had previously been considered private life into the public arena - housework, abortion, sexual violence, domestic violence, incest and sexuality - they created a much broader notion of what is political. This is explained by Lorde (1988, p.14):

> If what we are talking about is feminism, then the personal is political and we can subject everything in our lives to scrutiny ... The subject of revolution is ourselves, is our lives.

And elaborated by Essed (1996, p. 97):

> For women, everyday life can be a site of political struggle. The kitchen, living room, or doorway of a school becomes a political space where women cooking, drinking coffee, or waiting for children to get out of school exchange family stories, as well as consult with each other about the future of the children in school.

This conceptualisation of the political sphere enables us to challenge the stereotypical notion of Black women's non-engagement, by asserting that they are involved in a range of political struggles in their everyday lives:

> A lot of the time women are making sure their kids are not being expelled from school, making sure that they're doing their home≤work, very practical things which is political, which is involved in the community, involved in churches. So I don't put a superior value to the way in which we manifest our political activity (Faith, African, Black organisation).

In an educational system in which children are disproportionately excluded and in which Asian children are seen as linguistically deficient, the task of ensuring that Black children receive an adequate education becomes a profoundly political act which challenges their social classification as uneducable or educationally sub-normal (*Voice* 9 April 1996, p. 19; OWAAD, 1979). For Black women, the family becomes a site of political resistance, not just to patriarchy[3] but to institutionalised racism.

The centrality of children to Black women's politics was a feature of many of the interviews. In addition to expressing the need to fight for their children's right to receive an adequate academic education, many of the women felt that one of the most important gains from their involvement in a Black women's organisation had been their children's politicisation. This had contributed towards the children's identity formation as well as helping them to challenge manifestations of racism. An African mother of three children of mixed heritage described the process thus:

> Whereas before I became a member of the Black women's group, my concern about my children's identity was very much more towards where my children don't look as Black as me and there≤fore they're not going to experience prejudice. Which left them in a kind of limbo about 'who am I?'. But I think that giving them a Black identity despite their light skin has actually given them a sense of who they are (Hilda, African, organisation).

Interviewees stated that their involvement in building alliances with Black women of different ethnicities had influenced their children's perception of other Black communities. In one instance, a Caribbean interviewee noted that her child had stopped using derogatory but commonplace language such as 'the Paki shop'. Another interviewee saw her children learning to have greater tolerance and understanding for the emotional and behavioural difficulties experienced by some Somali refugee schoolmates. One woman commented on her children's political education:

> At school one of the things that's always said about my children is that they have a really strong sense of justice, and also the fact that our children have been equipped to challenge the racism that they experience at school constructively and they can tell the difference. They know about racism, they know about sexism (Sonia, Caribbean, organisation).

For many of the interviewees, children represented the intersection of the individual and the community. As one respondent emphasised: 'Many Black women see children as communal' (Brenda, Caribbean, organisation). This view of children as a shared responsibility gives rise to a desire to create collective solutions to problems experienced initially at an individual and family level. Establishing daycare where children could be left in a safe, anti-racist environment was one common response. Children's programmes, such as that developed by one refuge worker, were often designed to counter the negative effects of racism and abuse on children's self esteem:

> I believe in having a mirror and I think that's important therapeutically. So they can see that they are beautiful. To make comparisons that there are different shades in all of us. That can strengthen them to go into that world out there (Sophia, Asian, Black organisation).

Another interviewee described how their group had undertaken trail-blazing work around the needs of Black children with a violent parent: 'We were the first refuge in the city to have a children's worker and out of her action research type of work [what's happened] is that other hostels and refuges have followed suit' (Balwant, Asian, Asian organisation). Yet another group had been involved in raising awareness about the impact of the Child Support Act. The group had organised workshops on women's right to non≤cooperation in naming violent fathers and had appeared on regional television to highlight the act's role in exacerbating the impoverishment of children with one resident parent. Black women's political activism around their children therefore encompasses education for political consciousness of their own children, dealing with a lack of adequate childcare, challenging racist abuse of children in institutional settings, recognising and challenging the impact of violence within the family on children and opposing changes in welfare benefits which disadvantage Black single mothers. These struggles take place at the level of the family, within the community and with the local and national state.

Invisible Activism: Empowering Self, Family And Community

The above analysis illuminates the specific interpretation of the personal as political utilised by Black women's organisations. This interpretation does not diminish the importance of collective action. It takes as the starting-point of that action the personal experiences of women and recognises the importance of political education as a basis of collective resistance.

Sivanandan (1990) alerts us to the dangers inherent in embracing the personal as political without a commitment to collective action. We run the risk, he claims, of losing sight of the communal and organisational element crucial to the creation of social change:

The 'personal is the political' has also had the effect of shifting the gravitational pull of Black struggle from the community to the individual at a time when Black was already breaking into ethnics. It gave the individual an out not to take part in issues that affected the community: immigration raids, deportations, deaths in custody, racial violence, the rise of fascism ... There was now another venue for politics: oneself, and another politics: of one's sexuality, ethnicity, gender ... I am, therefore I resist (1990, p. 39).

Sivanandan's critique is pertinent to the feminist conceptualisation of political action. He warns us against seeing sustained political group action as inherently 'masculinist', and the only authentic women's politics as individual acts of self affirmation. These acts, while individually empowering, may do little to challenge oppressive structures and institutions. However, Sivanandan does nothing to resolve the apparent dichotomy of self actualisation versus collective action. He simply rejects the former in favour of the latter without acknowledging the necessary role of personal empowerment in the creation of alternative political discourses. Sivanandan's political actor is ready made and requires no personal growth in order to engage in Black working class struggle. In reality, this Black political actor does not simply exist, but is created and recreates herself constantly through resistance and struggle.

Writing in the North American context, Patricia Hill Collins (1990), rejects this either/or dichotomy of the individual versus the collective. In its place, she suggests a holistic approach which incorporates both the struggle to change structures of oppression and the creation of individual and familial sites of resistance:

> The Black women's activist tradition of individual and group action designed to bring about social change has occurred along two primary dimensions. The struggle for group survival is the first dimension. Consisting in actions taken to create Black female spheres of influence ... The second dimension of Black women's activism consists of the struggle for institutional transformation (1990, p. 141).

The experience of Black women's organisations and the politics of child-rearing is an empirical example of the strengths of Collins's theoretical approach. In examining and Asian organisations it becomes clear that Collins's analysis is not unique to African diasporic women. Her theoretical approach speaks not only to the experiences of women of African descent in Britain, but also to the struggles of Asian women.

Crucial to this approach is an understanding that Black political activism speaks to different audiences at different times. Therefore, both political discourses which engage with mainstream political processes and ideologies, and those which address dynamics internal to Black communities are worthy of examination. Hence, the struggles of Black women for recognition and respect from Black men, and their opposition to Black male violence, while often hidden from view to White communities and academics, are recognised as authentic expressions of political mobilisation. Similarly, the activism of Black lesbians and gays, within organisations such as the Black Gay and Lesbian Centre, Zami and the Anti-Racist Alliance, can accurately be described as articulating not only a politics of difference, but also a politics of change.

An expanded and centralisation of political action of the kind that is being proposed here enables us to acknowledge a wide range of political activity within Black women's organisations. Drawing on Collins's (1990, pp. 141-142) analysis of Black women's activism, we can identify six arenas of political activism. These arenas can be divided into those that are internal to the Black communities: the individual, the family, the community and those which engage with mainstream power structures: the local, the national and the international. In the following pages I expand and develop this categorisation.

The concept of individual empowerment is an important one within social movements which aim to counter the internalisation of the dominant mode of social interaction (Lorde, 1984; Freire, 1972). For the organisations studied, the idea of the personal empowerment of Black women featured as a common theme. Empowerment was seen as encompassing a broad range of practical and emotional issues which I have grouped around three themes: self-confidence, education and economic development. The first area was the most commonly mentioned. One interviewee described women escaping violent partners in the following terms:

> They were at the lowest of the low and now they've rebuilt their lives and they've achieved so much. Those women had been so empowered, given so much confidence to go on and live their independent life (Anita, Asian, Asian organisation).

There is an implicit danger however in focusing attention on Black women's lack of confidence, rather than on discriminatory structures and practices. This approach can lead to Black women being designated a 'problem' requiring remedial action. The latter conceptualisation is an all too familiar tenet of governmental programmes established to tackle 'disadvantaged' Black communities such as Section 11 of the Local Government Act 1966 (Anthias, Yuval-Davies and Cain, 1992, pp. 164-166). An alternative understanding of the need for personal growth and confidence building is that many Black women need a space in which they can distance themselves from the daily onslaught of derogatory and hostile representations and experiences which are commonplace within British society:

> In terms of my political development, it's around having somewhere to take all that crap you experience in the outside world ... All Black women in this country need a really good sisterhood network to survive. Because otherwise it's so easy to start internalising the crap and to start to think that you've got a problem which clearly isn't the case (Sonia, Caribbean, organisation).

The second aspect of empowerment emphasises the need for an alternative to the mainstream education system. Most of the interviewees questioned felt that they had been bombarded with inaccurate representations of Black womanhood which erased Black women's historical contributions and current achievements. They therefore felt that they needed a re-education process in order to identify the gendered racialised barriers facing them, learn about the role of Black women achievers both historically and in the present day and create alternative visions of social relations. An interviewee described her group's focus on personal empowerment as follows:

> I think to be able to take a political stance on something you have to know who you are, what you value and how you'd like to see that reflected in the way the society works. And we were many of us just getting to the stage where we were trying to work out our own norms, our own mores, so we weren't just accepting the stuff that we'd been fed (Abiola, African, Black organisation).

This re-education process takes place through informal 'reasoning' sessions, in assertiveness classes and in Black history courses.[4] It is the 'education for critical consciousness' described by bell hooks (1994) in her development of a progressive politics of pedagogy and is resonant of Paolo Freire's (1972) notion of 'conscientazion', a concept which has had a significant influence on Black feminism in Britain and the United States.

Many Black women educated in the British school system have also been denied opportunities to gain mainstream academic qualifications and therefore need education, normally in the form of access courses which provide the opportunity to gain basic skills as the basis for further education. While education for political consciousness and access to basic education appear quite distinct, both suggest that the road to empowerment is via the acquisition of knowledge:

> Those women at our organisation who over a period of two years, sitting talking, reasoning, going out, getting on courses. Some of them are at university, others have got qualifications. All of that happened [in assertiveness courses] in three days where Black women came to a consciousness of themselves as Black women where they gained support and they share that indefinable something that just happens when Black women get together (Brenda, Caribbean, organisation).

This educational process was also seen as equipping Black women to deal with the personal impact of racialised discrimination and hostility. In this sense it was seen as creating an essential pragmatic underpinning to the hard-won self confidence:

> 'You've got be confident, yes you've got all of these rights, but you've also got to have strategies for dealing with failure which is not personal failure, but is societal and institutional' (Jennifer, Caribbean, Black organisation).

The third realm of empowerment was that of economic development. Poverty is a critical issue facing many Black women. Escaping poverty through employment or entrepreneurship was therefore an important goal. In addition, many women viewed dependence either on a male partner or on state benefits as preventing women from becoming fully self actualised and from pursuing their individual goals. Economic independence is also a key to creating options for women escaping violence. Women at the two women's refuges in this study actively assisted women to access employment in order to facilitate the choice to leave an abusive partner.

Empowerment has been conceptualised as a process whereby the boundary between the personal and the communal is transcended, enabling the individual to connect fundamentally with collective movements for social change (Collins, 1990; Yuval-Davis, 1994). Subjective feelings of empowerment should not be accepted at face value without interrogating the material basis for any claim that an individual or group's situation has improved. It is essential therefore that personal voyages of self discovery and assertion are accompanied by organised collective efforts for social change. As Collins accurately asserts: 'while individual empowerment is the key, only collective action can effectively generate lasting social transformation of political and economic institutions' (Collins 1990, p. 237). Most organisations studied emphasised that empowerment connected the individual to the collective sphere. One interviewee described the relation between confidence building and the willingness to challenge discriminatory institutional practices:

> How do you separate out empowerment of the self to empowerment and impact on your environment? I think that our organisation changed many women's lives and I think that one change would have had a knock on effect on other changes. ... Inevitably I think,

> one of the outcomes was that some of those women were feeling confident to challenge the housing people, to say, 'look, I'm a confident person, you can't write me off". So for me the notion of empowerment is taking or recognising what's ours by right (Brenda, Caribbean, organisation).

However, the idea that personal empowerment has political ramifications was not uncontested. One interviewee insisted that empowerment and political activism were quite separate activities. Her organisation provides counselling for Muslim women and the coordinator was quite adamant in her claim that the group was apolitical:

> During the Gulf crisis, we used to get a lot of calls from Muslims trying to really get us to do something, to get involved. We could not. ... Because our aim is really to concentrate on giving counselling to Muslim women and helping them (Zaheda, Middle Eastern, Muslim organisation).

The interviewee suggested that if I wanted to know about Muslim women involved in politics, I should attempt to meet with the Muslim Parliament.[5] Nevertheless, enabling women to claim their rights was central to the organisation's counselling. Users were informed about their rights under Islamic law to education, divorce, a spouse of their choice and to property and money. The organisation's work was seen as equipping women with the emotional strength and self confidence to lead their lives more fully: 'How can you get involved in society fully if you have a lot of problems? ... you have to be happier, you have to be inwardly and outwardly feeling very beautiful and once you have reached that stage, then you are able to contribute more' (Zaheda).

However, it also had a subtext of challenging cultural norms which are oppressive to women. The presentation of the organisation as simply 'helping women' was therefore a powerful tool in winning the support of Muslim communities and in particular religious leaders while actively challenging some of the very practices institutionalised by the more traditional mosques.

Recent feminist analysis has suggested that empowerment is a more problematic goal than has previously been envisaged. While proponents assert that the power gained in the process of empowerment is a benign power over one's own destiny, rather than an oppressive power over others, Yuval-Davis (1994) suggests that such an assertion is naive. It is unlikely that the empowerment of one oppressed group will in every instant be compatible with that of another. Indeed, empowering some members of a given group may involve the silencing of others within the group. The ostracism of Black lesbians from some Black women's organisations is a pertinent example of this problem. In practice grassroots activism has always engaged in a process of shifting the boundaries of who is included and who is excluded. The politics of empowerment is not inevitably exclusionary or oppressive to subordinate and marginal groupings, nor is it always progressive. Rather, it contains the possibility of building a diverse social movement which emerges vibrantly from the personal struggles of its members.

A second arena in which Black women's activism is often invisible to 'outsiders' is the family. Since mordant critiques by Carby (1982) and Amos and Parmar (1984) revealed that White feminists had imposed their experience of the family as universal, it has become commonplace in the work of more progressive critical thinkers to indicate that for Black women, the family is less a site of oppression than one of affirmation and resistance to racism (see also Whelehan, 1995). A striking feature of many of the interviews was the support offered by many Black male partners to women wishing to become involved in Black women's organisations:

> So, the people that had men in the lives at the times, [the men] were cooking the rice and peas, were coming to pick up the kids, maybe were looking after the children. And I would say that my husband played a role in that he would be supervising the children whilst I was going out on a Sunday afternoon to work with a group of women. And then they would come along at the end and maybe sit down for half an hour and get involved in the debates that women had (Alekiri, African, organisation).

As a result of this support, many Black women's organisations welcomed men onto their premises, with the obvious exception of those that were involved in refuge provision. The exclusion of men was seen as an aspect of White women's organisations from which Black women wished to distance themselves:

> There was a White women's organisation in the High Street and the comments I had from Black women I started talking to about setting up an organisation were 'we don't want to be like that'. ... And one of the things we discussed was that a Black women's centre can be whatever we want it to be. If we think that men should be a part of the centre, that doesn't mean that it's not a women's centre (Pat, Caribbean, organisation).

In many cases, women were influenced by common experiences of racism to turn a blind eye to oppressive gender roles. This apparent willingness to 'forgive' sexism from Black men, and in particular family members, was rarely a result of a lack of awareness about the existence of sexism, rather it was a choice expressed by women facing multiple sites of oppression:

> I think we're quite forgiving really in terms of our menfolk. We forgive them loads in terms of sexism, because we have a much more pressing issue, the issue of racism and discrimination ... we tend to be having more solidarity for our brother or our father or our husband, because he's suffering the same experiences as we do. Therefore we are more forgiving I think. That doesn't make the Black man or the Arab man or the Asian man less sexist, but us much more tolerant. (Mona, Middle Eastern, Black organisation)

Several of the interviewees associated sexism with White men and institutions such as the police, and employers generally. There was less willingness to address issues of Black male sexism. Rather than consciously challenging the sexism of their partners, many women found their relationships gradually drifting apart. These changes were linked to men's failure to deal with their partners' newly found confidence and were often regretted:

> It was almost like I had been looking out of one window and all of a sudden there was another window there that I didn't know existed. And when that other window opened I couldn't get enough of it. And I just soaked myself in it twenty-four [hours] seven [days a week] and for me I suppose there were no boundaries around that and the impact and the toll it had was on my relationship with my ex-husband who unfortunately wasn't in there and moving at the same pace with me (Alekiri, African, organisation).

The prioritisation of racism over sexism as separate systems of oppression was not uncontested. Women working within refuges on the issue of male violence against women were more likely to take a strong position against all forms of misogyny and to maintain an integrative analysis of racism-sexism. This was frequently in the face of accusations from male partners of women as users and of being 'marriage breakers' or of 'splitting families' (Southall Black Sisters, 1989; Roy, 1995). While many workers in such environments espoused a rigorous Black feminist analysis of male violence, they were equally aware that not all women using the organisation shared such a perspective, but did not view this as problematic. Indeed, they felt that the feminist principles underpinning their work were often unstated. The practical implementation of these principles did not necessarily involve encouraging women to see themselves as Black feminists, nor did it involve attempting to evangelise:

> We've got women coming to us who are in crisis. The last thing you do is shove in their face, 'look we're feminists and you've got to do this'. … But what you do see is that over the years, women empower themselves, knowingly, unknowingly they do it and it's really good to see that. They may not call it feminism, they may call it feminism, they may call it self-esteem (Misa, Asian, Black organisation).

While police and housing officials appeared to expect White women's refuge workers to work to feminist principles, Asian women were pressured to handle cases of domestic violence in a more reconciliatory way. The idea that women's independence was alien to Asian communities in particular was reinforced by male community leaders' who were most often involved in consultative mechanisms on work with Asian communities:

> There is that pressure and that stereotype that Asian women's organisations have got to offer reconciliation work from the community. In those days, it was very difficult because one, where do you go, and two, it was unheard of that a woman would live on her own with her children, it just didn't happen (Manjit, Asian, Asian organisation).

The interviewees' feminism was therefore as much an expression of their opposition to the racialised gender stereotypes fostered by these agencies as a response to Black male violence (Mama, 1989). Where feminism was embraced as a method of understanding and challenging gender relations, it was explicitly defined as 'Black feminism', In this way, Black refuge workers distanced themselves from White feminism(s) by invoking the struggle against racism as well as that against patriarchal violence.

Engaging politically with the notion of the family also involved support for alternative family structures. Central to most of the Black women's organisations studied was their support for Black single mothers. While women were able to choose single parenthood for economic reasons without fear of community sanctions, South Asian and Chinese women raising children alone after leaving a violent relationship were often ostracised. In addition, all single mothers were felt by the respondents to be under attack by the state and stigmatised by the media and politicians. This view is well supported by academic studies (Omolade, 1995; Solinger, 1994). Organisations were active in creating alternative visions of single parenthood which recognised the strength and loving within many families with one resident parent, and opposed this to the often dysfunctional nature of some two parent families. Women also found important support in creating networks of adults with whom their children could interact.

However, one parent families were not the only alternative families under construction and contestation. Black lesbian women were involved in creating healthy family structures despite opposition from many heterosexual women and a paucity of models on which to base Black lesbian relationships. The lesbian women interviewed described their experiences of 'coming out' as an experience which frequently led to alienation from mixed sexuality women's groups. One of the women involved in the establishment of a London-based Black lesbian group described a traumatic experience at the 1981 OWAAD conference where women demanded a lesbian-only space:

> The room erupted, it really did. Women started shouting mash 'em, I'm telling you. And I'm thinking 'Oh my God, this is terrible, I'll just sneak out'. I don't know where these women found their courage from, but individual women from isolated parts of the country, can you imagine what it feels like to stand among two-hundred Black women and know that what they're shouting against is you (Adiola, African, Black organisation).

By the 1990s the overt hostility of the early 1980s had in some cases given way to a more complex reaction from heterosexual women. Christian and Muslim women shared religious convictions against homosexuality, however, this was expressed within the context of a contradictory desire to respect and support all Black women:

> Because many of us go to church, many of us are Christian and we don't really say much around lesbians. . . . There are a couple of lesbians in the group and some of us know about it. It's not known publicly. But we don't go into details or treat them with disrespect, or so on (Natalie, Caribbean, organisation).

This desire 'not to judge' lesbian women has led many women's organisations to have a 'don't ask, don't tell'[6] policy whereby lesbian women are known to some members as lesbians, but do not openly discuss their sexuality at a group level. This stance while ideologically contradictory, is nevertheless an indication of the political gains made by lesbian women in making overt expressions of hostility less acceptable within the context of mixed sexuality Black women's organisations. This muted tolerance was echoed by one interviewee: 'On a personal level, as long as they don't promote it in the centre, it's OK. We do a lot of casework with clients and that would be confidential between the member of staff and the client' (Mai, Chinese, Chinese organisation). Two of the women's organisations had taken a more proactive stance against homophobia and in recognition of the specific experiences of Black lesbian women. One women's refuge worker described the organisation's struggle to get lesbian women's experiences recognised by other domestic violence organisations:

> [Sexuality is] not talked about in the women's movement, here actually it has been. We've been one of the very few who have campaigned about the whole issue of abuse not being just about male perpetrators, but also women against women violence. We looked at mother in law abuse, daughters in law. Mothers who have abused their daughters. We weren't popular but the Scottish Women's Aid had to change the whole definition of violence (Balwant, Asian, Black organisation).

This work is also revealing because it illustrates a willingness to look at an issue which has frequently been seen as taboo within the [White] women's movement - women as perpetrators of violence. This insight is quite probably linked to an experience of White women as perpetrators of racist abuse. Having recognised the possibility of women as abusers in one context, it becomes credible that Black women could abuse one another (see K. Bhavnani 1988).

What is notable in the discussions of the family as a site both of affirmation and of resistance is the relative absence of discussions about relationships between Black women and White partners. It is clear that many of the women interviewed had a dichotomous view of Black and White community interactions which precluded the inclusion of 'mixed' relationships as a valid family structure. This meant that when relationships were discussed, most of the women presumed that the question concerned Black on Black relationships. Even those interviewees who I knew to be in relationships with White partners tended to make this assumption. However, some of the women were willing to transgress boundaries. One interviewee challenged the assumption that she had more in common with a Black woman with whom she had split up than with a White partner:

> It was like, 'look what you've done to this woman, she's a righteous Black woman' and whatever. And actually, the reality is that I am middle class. I know that Britain doesn't see that and it's hard to be middle class as a Black person, but I am. Me and this woman had a lot more in common than the woman I'd left, even though ostensibly she was Black and I was Black. (Adiola, African, Black organisation)

Another woman who had been in a relationship with a White man when she first became involved in Black women's organisations, but subsequently had relationships with Black men only, claimed that 'mixed' relationships were a topic of great contention in the groups she had been involved with:

> In some Black women's organisations... There's always been issues like if the women are involved in mixed race relationships, what that means for them, and how easy it is for them to talk about it or to join in with Black women, because in a sense they feel a contradiction and a split (Brenda, Caribbean, organisation).

This debate indicates that far-reaching use of the personal as political by Black women's organisations. Many of the women interviewed were determined that all women should be accountable for their personal allowances. In an environment in which Black men and women are under threat, Black thumb is undermined and belittled and healthy Black on Black relationships rarely represented in the media, these relationships, whether same sex or heterosexual can actually be seen as a political, affirming choice. This affirmation becomes problematic when it translates into hostility towards and ostracism of women choosing White partners.

The third area that Black women were highly active was that of awareness raising within local communities. This was seen by many of the organisations studied as a logical next step in creating a Black woman-centred politics. The emphasis of the consciousness raising varied over time and in different organisations, as did the conception of 'community'. One interviewee summarised her multiple experiences of community:

> Sometimes I perceive myself as part of a community of Black women, sometimes as part of a community of single parents. Sometimes I'm part of the community people of African heritage. They're all important to me, I have many different experiences of community (Sonia, Caribbean, organisation).

For the organisations which catered for more than one ethnic or racialised group, there were also multiple communities with which to communicate. The Sheffield Black Women's

Group was an example where women related to a number of discrete communities - Somali, Pakistani and so on. In this instance, there appeared to be very little interaction between the different communities in the city and the group focused on educating the different communities to recognise the similarities of their struggles and to resist 'divide and rule tactics by the local authority (see Mukherjee, 1988, p. 222):

> Responding to the divide and rule is my little bit. ... It is not to play the system. Sheffield is a tiny place with a tiny grant aid budget. If you divide it between the different Black communities, what you do is make us keep busy fighting each other about the crumbs. The little there is. Instead of looking at the real issue which is lack of funding and resources for Black community groups (Mona, Middle Eastern, Black organisation).

Operating with a more unitary sense of community, the African Caribbean women's groups focused their educational campaigns around a limited concept of community. One such group utilised the relative homogeneity of the community to their advantage in performing theatre which spoke to the community's experiences of gendered racism. The group, based in south London, utilised very specific stereotypes about single mothers and well known localities such as Brixton, to create an insider critique of community dynamics. Another group resisted the expansion of their community when White mothers of Black children of mixed origins attempted to join the group. They were allowed to attend for the sake of the children, but were not welcomed into the Black women's 'reasoning' sessions. The group's wish to educate the 'community' did not in this instance encompass White women, who, it was suspected, would 'take over' the organisation. Given the limited and hard-won resources available to Black women, this policy of partial exclusion was necessary in order to protect the group's focus on Black women's concerns.

Relationships with local communities, whether utilising a broad or narrow definition, were not always easy. Many of the groups had been accused of attempting to 'split the community'. This accusation was usually made by Black men involved in community organisations which had failed to address Black women's needs. It was a corollary in many ways of the accusation of 'splitting families' and was intended to discourage women from organising autonomously. Ironically, many women described defending their right to organise as a highly politicising experience. It was an experience which coalesced their politics and forced them to take a stand on sexism within Black communities. An interviewee involved in setting up a Black women's group in a small town in the mid-1980s described her experience thus:

> They didn't like the implication that Black women needed space from Black men, they really refused to accept that Black men also can abuse women or abuse children. It was a time of political idealism where Black people could do no wrong, you know, the real enemy out there was the White state and White people: that's who we must focus on. Even if things were happening within Black families you shouldn't speak about it, you shouldn't make it public and by making this public, by breaking away and forming our own group, it was making a public declaration. (Hilda, African, organisation)

However, it was not only Black men that questioned women's right to organise autonomously, Black women too were wary of the implications of such action. Discussing the rationale behind autonomous organisations therefore created the space to break the silence about racialised gendered oppression:

> A lot of women actually saw it as separatism and didn't think one should organise separately from Black men and indeed one shouldn't; it was wrong to set up something separate from White women. A lot of people believed that and were ambivalent about joining and when they heard racism discussed as well, they left. There were a lot of unpleasant realities in their own lives that they couldn't face (Hilda).

Encounters with hostile communities led some women's organisations to turn inwards. This was often a feature of those organisations most under attack because they dealt with a contentious issue such as male violence or anti-lesbian homophobia. The need in these cases to create a safe space for women was seen by one interviewee as preventing these organisations from community education which might bring about long term changes in attitudes:

> In our type of work you can become insulated, that's my experience of the refuge movement, you become really introspective, things happening around you in your little area. ... Community development, at the end of the day you're not just there to provide a service, you want them to change. . . . I hate to use the word 'attitude', but that's the only one I can think of (Balwant, Asian, Black organisation).

However, this position was countered by other women who felt that educating men about sexism or heterosexual women about homophobia was not their responsibility. The 'community' is therefore a contested political arena where Black women assert their right to self-determination in the face of considerable hostility.

From Local To Global: Making The Connections

I have looked at forms of political activism directed internally to the Black community. In the final three arenas of this six point schema, Black women's organisations seek to influence the power-brokers: in particular, the multiple manifestations of the state in women's lives. The fourth arena is local government. Black women's organisations play an important role in equipping women with the tools, knowledge and confidence to challenge their treatment by officials. For many women the experience of making group representations on issues affecting their lives was an important part of their political growth:

> One of the things a lot of us are scared of is talking to local authority, whether it's housing or whatever, because it reminds us of school days. ... So, when you get women at the place where they have the confidence to go off and talk to any White person in authority that's brilliant and lots of women, they do it (Natalie, Caribbean, organisation).

Groups were actively involved in campaigns in their local community, such as those against racist assaults, deportations and police violence. In challenging local agencies, Black women often gained skills and knowledge which were valued in the community at large. One interviewee described how they had become organic advocates in relation to the local authority after their success in a number of cases became known:

> It just grew from people saying, 'can you do this and that?', and

> what happens now is that we operate a vigilante group. So, someone
> will ring up and say: 'I'm having a serious problem with my child
> in school around racism and can you support us?'. And two of us
> would go and sit with them and work out a strategy and support
> them at school or in court (Sonia, Caribbean, organisation).

At other times, Black women's organisations were incorporated into less challenging consultation processes. Incorporation also brought with it validation: 'We will say things and people will listen, people will take notice and we are valued for our opinions and our expertise, even though people wouldn't overtly always say, we are' (Manjit, Asian, Asian organisation).

It is clear that the niche of 'expert' is one which offers both recognition and the promise of a more secure funding base. However reframing Black women's protest as a consultative interaction between two groups with different sets of expertise, can also gloss over differences in power and access to resources between the two sets of actors. The consultation mechanism can then become an alternative to changing the way in which mainstream services are delivered. One interviewee pointed out how the designation of 'expert' was abused, so that staff of Black women's organisations were expected to be experts on all Black community needs. Having been designated as the sole experts, Black women's organisations would also be expected to be the main service providers for Black women, thus providing an escape route for local authority workers wishing to pass complex cases to an outside agency:

> That's something we're looking at now in terms of the housing, the
> social workers and stuff like that, perhaps it's worked to our
> disadvantage because we've actually done too much for people . . .
> service providers, they've looked on us as being 'experts' and they
> wanted us to become experts in one particular area to absolve them
> of responsibility (Balwant, Asian, Black organisation).

However, the organisations involved in consultation mechanisms actively resisted this marginalisation of their concerns on two levels. They did this by criticising the practices and policies of service delivery agencies:

> We actually advocate on behalf of women all the time, and we're
> constantly challenging these people. … And not just at a grass≤roots
> service delivery level, it's on a campaigning policy level, in terms of
> challenging institutions and organisations about their understanding
> of Asian women and domestic violence. (Manjit, Asian, Asian
> organisation)

They also engaged in more direct and less easily contained forms of protest. When consultation and dialogue were seen to have failed, organisations would frequently utilise direct action such as sit-ins, marches and demonstrations. For many women, their counter with grant aid mechanisms introduced them to direct political engagement with the local authority through pickets of council meetings where grant allocations would be decided.

Accessing funding became a highly political statement of Black women's right to self-determination which in turn spoke to the inadequacy of mainstream services. Most organisations had to counter arguments about separatism in order to become part of the grant aid programme. This opposition often took the form of an alliance between Black men who had been given the status of 'community leaders' and the local authority. One organisation was threatened with closure by an Asian male councillor if they continued encouraging women to leave violent homes; another group were undermined by letters written by male members of the local Community Relations Council to the local authority, claiming that they were splitting the community. This dual jeopardy was described by an interviewee:

> When it was first being set up, one there was all this internal stuff in the community, seeing it as a direct threat to family life, and then of course this whole thing from the White community about why is there a need for a special, as they called it, a special Asian women's service, why can't it be done from an existing White organisation? (Manjit, Asian, Asian Organisation)

Despite this opposition, local authority funding was often the only option for organisations wishing to acquire premises and the increased visibility offered by a centre or office was also seen as a highly political symbol. This sort of symbolism is an essential part of changing ideological constructions of Black women in specific localities. For Black women in Cambridge, a small town, where Black people were usually assumed to be transient foreign students, it was a matter of stating 'we are here to stay'. For women in an inner city area of Coventry where Black women were highly visible in local media portrayals and folklore as prostitutes and inadequate single parents, the women's centre created a powerful counter-image of Black women reviving the local community.

The fifth arena is national government. While most of the women's organisations studied engaged extensively with the local state, most of them reported only occasional attempts to create a voice at a national level. This was explained by one interviewee who described the difficulty for many women involved in daily struggles for survival, to appreciate the relevance of national issues: 'It's no point jumping to national or party politics when you actually haven't handled your local politics. … It's important to start where people feel confident and at the moment local politics is quite tangible' (Mona, Middle Eastern, Black organisation).

Nevertheless, where national issues had an evident impact on Black women's lives, the organisations studied had made interventions. Overt attacks on Black communities would often elicit a public statement in response. One organisation responded to Norman Tebbit's 'cricket test' in a radio interview.[7] Other women described campaigns against racist immigration rules which particularly affected Black women and mobilised in protest over the Child Support Act which was seen to attack poor single mothers.

In contrast to the highly localised concerns of the majority of the organisations, three organisations had a national brief. The Organisation of Women of African and Asian Descent (OWAAD), was highly effective in bringing together local Black women and Black women's organisations to create a national agenda in the early 1980s. However, OWAAD's unfunded status meant that the women involved were drained emotionally and financially to maintain its momentum. This lack of resources was one important factor in the organisation's failure to survive after the founder members moved on.

The National Association of Women of Afrikan Descent (NAWAD) was established in 1989 as a result of the lack of national coordination of issues which affect 'Afrikan/Caribbean women' (NAWAD leaflet, undated). The organisation received some local authority funding and was able to establish offices in East London. NAWAD held a number of national events and made public statements about issues affecting the Caribbean community in particular. However, it was unable to expand far beyond the initial membership of Caribbean women based in the southeast. When a founder member passed away in November 1995, the organisation lost momentum and at the time of writing was no longer active. Finally, Black Women for Wages for Housework (BWfWfH) have a national campaign brief pressing for recognition of Black women's unwaged work and improved rights to benefits. BWfWfH are unfunded and yet produce copious campaign literature and educational packs and are frequently cited in the press. However, despite their national networks and clear political perspective, the organisation is not well known with the other Black women's organisations and therefore does not enjoy broad national affiliation.

The importance of effective national structures was emphasised by an interviewee who had become involved in national issues via her involvement with the committee of Sia: the National Development Agency for the Black Voluntary Sector, a relatively well resourced Black umbrella organisation which has established a National Network of Black Women's Organisations (Sia, 1996a, 1996b). This involvement had enabled the interviewee to envision the establishment of an independent Black women's aid network which would be able to coordinate and mobilise around Black women and violence at a national level:

> There were Black women's networks, but there was never the funding of the people to facilitate that; it was always voluntary, on top of everything else they had to do. But I think there's a real opportunity now, real potential for that to get underway. I would like to see a Black WAFE, the Women's Aid Federation of England, who absolutely deny the issues to do with Black women.

However, the difficulties of maintaining a broad based national body representative of the geographical, racialised and ethnic diversity of Black women in Britain and which is well resourced, but independent, have yet to be overcome.

Moving beyond national boundaries, many Black women's organisations express a desire to make contact with women's struggles in other parts of the world and to create an agenda which puts the experiences of Black women in Britain within the context of global trends and movements. This constitutes the sixth arena of Black women's activism. While life experiences, from employment to the environment, are shaped at a global level, local organisation seldom have access to influence policy at that level. One interviewee expressed the contradiction at the centre of many organisations that while they recognise the importance of international struggles and networks, they are nevertheless hard pressed to look farther than the local level:

> In a way we don't have the luxury to put our heads above waterline, but we can't keep our heads buried and just survive. We have to network; we have to link; we have to have world solidarity, but it's very hard to have world solidarity when you're scared, you're vulnerable, when you've been abused and I think that dilemma is one that Black women have always faced and one that Black women are facing more acutely now (Brenda, Caribbean, organisation).

Nevertheless, most of the interviewees expressed interest in the situation of Black women outside of Britain. All of the organisations had members born outside Britain, which led to a continuing interest in their countries of origin. Many of the women emphasised that they were 'international people' in contrast to White people who were seen as parochial and insular. In several organisations, this awareness had been heightened by the participation of members in an international exchange with Black women from other European countries, or at an international conference. Three of the organisations studied had sent a delegation to the United Nations World Conferences on Women in 1985 in Nairobi, or in 1995 in Beijing. One organisation had been active in preparing the agenda for the Beijing conference leading to the incorporation of some of their concerns in the resulting 'platform for action'. The platform was later signed by 189 countries committing them to a programme of action to reduce illiteracy, sexual exploitation and other forms of abuse (Ms magazine January/February 1996). The Beijing conference was seen as a victory for women's ability to work together to create an international agenda for change and the women who attended expressed their excitement and renewed commitment:

> One of the things we decided was looking at the world through women's eyes and that women are good decision makers. ... We don't just make tea or coffee or make the beds or do the work in the house. We can make decisions, we can do policy, we can make recommendations, the sky's the limit. Cut poverty, education, stop using young girls as prostitute trafficking, stop treating women as if they haven't any commonsense. (Natalie, Caribbean, organisation)

The conference also served as a catalyst in bringing together a number of Black women's organisations in preparation, under the umbrella of the International Network of Women of Colour (INWOC). INWOC received no funding for its work and most of the women had to pay their own fares and accommodation at the conference. Organising at an international level was therefore poorly resourced and yet benefited from the international contacts and experiences of the women involved.

Barriers To Political Activism

The preceding sections have given a fresh interpretation of the breath of political activities undertaken by Black women's organisations, ranging from individual consciousness-raising to influencing international forums. Despite ample evidence of a commitment to activism among the women interviewed, there were also indications that this role was internally contested and externally opposed. In order to maintain political awareness and translate that consciousness into action, women had to negotiate a number of barriers. At any one moment in the history of an organisation, one or other of these might take precedence, and the balance of politicising and depoliticising forces could swing in either direction.

One of the key barriers to maintaining a critical stance to gendered racism was the attitudes of some of the members themselves. Many of the women preferred to talk about painful or frustrating experiences at work, school or the benefits office, rather than looking at how these experiences might be challenged. Other women experienced the groups as a form of escape from the harsh realities of their lives. Black women's organisations were seen as offering a space where gendered racialised oppression did not exist and where life affirming cultural practices such as cooking, hair-plaiting and discussions in Urdu, Bengali or Black vernacular could take place:

> Having a refuge just for Asian women meant they could relax and not have to live up to expectations. Because when you're with other communities, you can't always be yourself and say, speak in your own language. You always have to put up a front (Anita, Asian, Asian organisation).

Members often did not wish to be reminded of the daily challenges to their humanity:

> A lot of the women, they can't be bothered with politics. They just want to get out and come and hear what's going on where they can feel good. Sometimes, they say it's too political for them, it's too much of issues. It's like the education don't get them to that standard and they're tired and knackered to come in from work and to come out and listen to politics and they want something that make them laugh (Natalie, Caribbean, organisation).

This escapism would sometimes take the form of denial of the existence of gendered racialised inequalities. Black women who established organisations in the early to mid-eighties described this attitude as particularly prevalent:

> If you talked about somebody being racist towards you, it was like you were being political, and they didn't want to join a political group. What they really wanted was to get together and cook and knit. They really were very much into separate gender roles and how women can learn to be better wives and mothers. They really thought that was what the organisation ought to be about, not facing issues like sexism, when you talk about the city council, and kind of racism or anything like that, they defined that as political and they weren't comfortable (Hilda, African, organisation).

This attitude was more prevalent in smaller towns such as Coventry or Cambridge, where the Black population had developed less organisational infrastructure and where access to Black media such as *Asian Times*, *Voice* and *Caribbean Times* newspapers, which were likely to highlight evidence of racism, was restricted:

> The mentality in Coventry was much more of a challenge so that if you were able to put up an argument in any way referring to the system as racist, you were seen as almost on the level of revolutionaries (Pat, Caribbean, organisation)

It is commonplace that White people are less likely to believe discrimination affects the life chances of Black people than Black people are themselves. It is also a common stereotype that Black people 'have a chip on their shoulder' which leads them to cry 'racism' where it does not exist. What has received less attention is evidence that Black people in Britain are unlikely to identify the presence of racial discrimination even where they have been the victims of it (Fryer, 1988; C. Brown, 1984, p. 265).

bell hooks in her recent examination of 'Black race' argues that there is a form of denial which enables Black people to avoid the pain of facing their experiences of oppression. Part of this avoidance strategy ≤is that of ridiculing the oppressors, masking painful experiences with laughter. In this way, separate spaces, far from nurturing critical thinking, can become spaces for unhealthy laughter and escapism:

> In the past, separate space meant down time, time for recovery and renewal. It was the time to dream resistance, time to theorise, plan, create strategies and go forward. The time to go forward is still upon us and we have long since surrendered segregated spaces of radical opposition. Our separation now is usually mere escape - a sanctuary for hiding and forgetting (bell hooks, 1995, p. 6).

bell hooks' insightful analysis goes to the core of the dual role of autonomous organisations as a site both of resistance and escape. However, in positing a chronological regression whereby the separate space has changed from a nurturing ground of radical resistance to a haven of escapism, bell hooks fails to capture the contested nature of these spaces. Black women's organisations allow respite and relaxation, the moment of forgetting that gives one the strength to carry on in a soul-destroying job, or in the face of stereotypes. They are also sites for the creation of resistance strategies. Women who attend them have varying needs and this will influence how the organisation responds at any given time.

The second potential barrier to activism was the manipulation of funding. Many scholars have identified a close relationship between state funding of Black community organisations and the inability or unwillingness of these organisations to take on a political role (Ben Tovim et al., 1986; Solomos and Back, 1995). Funding has been seen as a strategy to co-opt grassroots struggle into more manageable forms of activity, by turning activists into service deliverers, Black working class struggle into ethnic enclaves and creating a tier of 'race relations professionals' to control Black youth energies. (Anthias, Yuval-Davies and Cain, 1992; Gilroy, 1987). There is evidence that censorship and an overload in paperwork has the potential to restrict the activities of funded Black women's organisations. One interview identified potential sanctions by funders as a barrier to criticising statutory agencies: 'People get caught up in the safety of what they're doing and they don't want to challenge. Because if they challenge, it might affect their funding' (Balwant, Asian, Black organisation). An interviewee with previous experience of allocating Greater London Council (GLC) funds to community organisations characterised the situation as follows:

> If you want to do political work, if you want to work around consciousness-raising ... around resistance to the state, don't ask the state for money. For one thing, in order to get it you'll have to tone down what you do. You also spend such a lot of time in meetings and monitoring that there actually isn't time to do the business that you set out to do (Faith, African, Black organisation).

The potential loss of independence was a factor in the decision of one case study organisation in not seeking funding from the local authority, even though they had been invited to apply:

> I think that's why we were so successful was that we said what we liked. And I don't thing you can do that once you've got the master who's playing the tune above your head all the time and is calling the tune in terms of what you call yourself, what you can say and that it's not OK to say that. (Alekiri, African, organisation)

This organisation felt that officials were responding to their popularity by attempting to bring them under their control. The organisation, which performed consciousness-raising drama, was very wary of the possibility that their highly critical material would be compromised if they accepted funding. Such examples seem to support the case against funding.

However, the idea of a simple causal relationship between funding and political censorship fails to explain the existence of the funded organisations studied which were highly politicised. Such organisations stated that claiming their right to local authority grant aid and central government funding under programmes such as Section 11, Urban Programme and subsequently the Single Regeneration Budget, was in itself a political act. It also fails to explain the track record of many local authorities in refusing to support Black organisations which are challenging their hegemony at a local level. In other words, if funding did indeed follow political activism, the pattern in most local authorities of substantial allocations of funds to highly professionalised White voluntary organisations and limited funding for Black organisations would be reversed (Wenham, 1993). Finally, the argument fails to take into account the differentiation of the state. Receiving funding from central government often puts Black organisations in a strong position to be able to challenge the local authority. In this study, several organisations which had obtained central government funds in the form of Urban Programme funds were able to mount significant criticisms of the local authority. Their strong resource base made them both less likely to be the object of local authority reprisals for such criticism and more able to survive cuts in funding.

The relationship between funding and political censorship is not static and changes over time. One organisation was quite adamant about their refusal to allow local government to influence the way their organisation operated when they first started receiving funding in 1985 and would not allow the authority to place a representative on the management committee:

> One of the things that we made very clear to the local authority was that we did not want them to dictate how we were going to organise and how we were going to do what we were going to do ... if we break the law in so doing, yes you can do something about it, other than that we don't want any conditions (Hilda, African, Organisation).

Ten years later, the same organisation had a White council officer on the committee and appeared to be more closely controlled stating 'the city doesn't want us to be political' (Ngozi, organisation). The change in relationship was also linked to a period during which the chair of the organisation was also a council officer and was under pressure from her line manager to take a less oppositional stance. Nevertheless the organisation, which had initially focused almost entirely on local politics, had recently become very involved in international politics and had sent a representative to the United Nations fourth World Conference on Women in Beijing. Furthermore, the organisation had begun to channel their local concerns through an umbrella group called the Ethnic Community Forum. The shift in relationship with the local authority had therefore led to greater networking and coalition building with other racialised groups as well as making other political horizons more attractive.

Attempts by local authorities to use funding as a form of control were actively opposed. The organisations which did receive funding invented strategies to avoid this control. In some cases, this took the form of overt non-cooperation as in the case of one organisation which refused to complete new monitoring forms which reduced women's experiences of violence to misleading statistics. In other cases, women created imaginative strategies which avoided overt confrontation:

> We're thinking maybe we have to work a certain way internally and project a certain image. So we will project the image they want to see, but internally we will carry on working the way we always have. ... And that's how it's going to have to be, for survival's sake. And the groups which are folding and are disappearing are groups that haven't been able to adapt in that way as much (Manjit, Asian, Asian organisation).

These organisations were creating parallel worlds which offered the local authority what they wished to see, but enabled the organisation to continue behind closed doors with activities which might be opposed by officials. This dissimulation was mentioned by many organisations in relation to the local authority and is an approach which may not be evident to the researcher who is not seen as 'one of us.' It takes varied forms: editing minutes sent to council officers, using other organisational names or umbrella groups to send critical letters and organise campaigns and encouraging women with young children to picket the town hall on an 'individual' basis. This research indicates that funded Black women's organisations, far often act as subversive political agents.

Closely linked to the ability to access funding is the decision of whether or not to apply for charitable status. Charitable status enables organisations to avoid property taxes and to apply for some restricted funds. While charity legislation ensures that registered charities do not utilise their funds to support activities which could be viewed as partly political or to present 'biased' information, many Black organisations interpret this to mean that they cannot be involved in political activities or campaigns. This has been exacerbated by the Charity Commission's refusal for some years to recognise the terms `racism' or `Black' in charitable objects (Sia, December 1995). One organisation which had considered the option stated: 'That's part of why for ages we hadn't become a charity as really you can't be too political' (Ngozi).

Few of the organisations studied had become registered charities due to their fear of control and censorship. However, those which had, while experiencing frustrating delays and difficulties in achieving their registration, once registered had little interaction with the Charity Commission. There is no evidence therefore that the organisations suffered from any external restrictions because of charity legislation. Fear of such action is far more likely than actual intervention by the commission to have a censorial impact.

The containment of fear is a little studied factor in Black political mobilisation, yet it constitutes a third barrier to organising politically: 'I think Chinese women are afraid of stirring things up. They are frightened and don't know what is likely to happen' (Mai, Chinese, Chinese organisation). This perspective was not unfounded or based on unjustified anxiety. Black women were frequently the victims of hostility, from both Black and White people. One interviewee described the trauma of being verbally attacked by Black men involved in the local Community Relations Council when she attempted to set up a Black women's group: 'We were made to feel like traitors, that we were undermining the Black community with our actions, that we were rampant feminists' (Hilda, organisation).

Fear is therefore a critical weapon in controlling Black women and preventing them from organising. In this case, it was fear of rejection from a community which provides protection from racial discrimination and violence. Protection by Black males from racism and protection from male violence are often incompatible. Black women working in refuges experienced rejection and occasionally physical threats when male partners discovered that they were offering shelter to their spouses, as was the experience of a refuge worker:

> In one sense we are ostracised and we are treated with suspicion but it's the same for us because we don't want to become too easily identifiable. … We've had people calling up and saying 'we want to know where such and such is' and we say: 'sorry who?' (Balwant, Asian, Black organisation).

The threat of violence, however, comes most frequently from the White community. One organisation found that opening a centre attracted the attention of a skinhead who repeatedly physically threatened the volunteers on reception. This sort of event was so recurrent that the organisation was forced to put on a course on 'dealing with aggression' for the staff and volunteers. On occasions women received anonymous phone calls, or premises were exposed to racist graffiti or were damaged. The police response to these incidents was minimal.

A study of abortion clinics in the United States suggests that the experience of overt hostility from the outside community, while contributing to emotional exhaustion, also fuels a sense of resistance (Simonds, 1995). In the organisations studied, it appeared to create a form of close bonding against common opponents and a renewed resolve. However, Simonds does not analyse the affect on women not involved in organisations for whom the threat of ostracism and possible violence may be a significant deterrent. The ability of organisations to present themselves as apolitical may be a significant factor in avoiding such hostility and may in turn enable the involvement of greater numbers of women. Once again dissimulation emerges as an important factor in the survival of Black women's organisations.

Creating Alternative Visions: Black Women Catalysts

These barriers to political expression mean that 'coming to voice' is not simply an organic process which occurs whenever Black women are gathered together. The translation of common experience into collective action requires some additional impetus. That impetus frequently comes from one or more pioneer women (Essed, 1996, p. 96). These women have a catalytic impact on the women in a given community or locality and begin the process of awareness raising and mobilisation. Omolade (1995) likens this role to that taken by Ella Baker in the Student Non-Violent Coordinating Committee in the United States, the 'woman in front', the visionary and initiator: 'The woman in front "puts her body into the movement". She, like Ella, is found working long hours, squeezing in family obligations and sacrificing personal pleasures. Policy, programs and work evolves from and is most often initiated by her' (Omolade, 1995, p. 175).

Like Jayaben Desai, inspirational leader of the 1976 Grunwich strike, these 'women in front' are non-hierarchical and are therefore able to exchange their role at any time for that of 'sister in the circle', utilising a more collective form of decision making (A. Wilson, 1978). However, it is these women who initiate organisations, ≤intervene when organisations are at a standpoint, and reactive to those that have become de-politicised. The organisations studied revealed various types of 'woman in front'. Women shaped and educated by their access to international political struggles played a key role. Women in this category were involved in anti≤colonial and independence struggles in Africa, Asia and the Caribbean and came as adults to Britain. These women have developed oppositional ideologies and are able to draw on skills and experience not readily available to Black women in Britain. These skills include experience of non-hierarchical ways of working and women's involvement in decision making. One interviewee pointed out that women's active roles in the governance of her home village in India were a formative influence: 'I was brought up with my father and my grandmother [in India]... and that's why I remember women working together and coming into the house with discussion and decision making' (Sophia, Asian, Black organisation).

Women involved in movements against White rule in the former Rhodesia and South Africa played a key role in the establishment of the Organisation of Women of Africa and African Descent (OWAAD), the first national Black women's political body. The tactic of non-violent protest utilised by the Indian Home Rule movement was also a source of inspiration for women involved in picketing and demonstrations.

Another group of women in front with origins in anti-colonial struggle are Rasta women.[8] A focus by academics and media of the supposed rebelliousness and criminality of Rastafari has masked the way in which it synthesises lived experiences of racialised and class oppression with religious and spiritual symbolism to create a radical alternative vision of social organisation (Cashmore, 1979; Campbell, 1985). Rastafari advocates living in harmony with nature, it refutes hierarchical and bureaucratic forms of organisation, materialism and artificial drugs and foods and aspires to an equal and just society, 'Shashamane'. In this sense Rastafari is both the successor of Garveyist Pan-Africanism and a pre-cursor of popular protest movements such as the Green Movement, Band Aid and the Anti-Nuclear Movement. This alternative vision placed many Rasta women at the forefront in the late 1970s and early 1980s when Black women's organisations were emerging.

Rasta women have largely been absent from sociological studies which have replicated the media construction of Rastafari as male. For example, Cashmore's influential study of Rastafari in Birmingham was simply entitled *Rastaman: The Rastafarian Movement in England* (1979) and Small's report on Rastafari in London subtitled 'A group of young Black people' (1983) focused entirely on men. Where there has been some interest in women, they have been accorded an exalted but socially circumscribed role as 'queen' and mother (Churches Commission for Racial Justice, in Greater London Council, 1984, p. 14; see also Yawney, 1994). This view of women's role in Rastafari communities has been reinforced by dominant views of traditional head coverings and dress and the acceptance by some of biblically defined gender roles (Greater London Council 1984, p. 14). It is important, however, to appreciate the gendered components of Rastafari in the context of the rise in African nationalist sentiment in Britain in the 1970s. Covering the head and body was seen by many women as a form of opposition to the sexual commodification of women's bodies characterising capitalist society and to the degradation of African women's bodies in particular. Furthermore, the nationalist belief that men received the brunt of state brutality led some women to declare their deference in the hope that this would restore 'Black manhood'.

Despite this public face, Rasta women were involved in community organising in the form of the 'Twelve Tribes' events which occurred throughout the 1970s bringing together Rastafari followers nationwide. This experience would be critical in developing the skills and commitment necessary to build early Black women's organisations:

> In a lot of cases, it tended to be Rasta women that were involved as well in the early stages as well . . . if you think about the time, it would have been the seventies when they were starting which was obviously when Rasta was at its highest - and those women would have been more ideologically placed and structurally placed to create those sorts of networks. ... You can compare it to the Church in that you have that structure there provided by Rasta ideology and physical networks that Rasta women had (Lynette, Caribbean, organisation).

Rastafari was and continues to be a important resource for community struggles. In addition to providing practical resources, networks and skills, it functions 'as a catalyst for a new conscious and of reordering the world in the minds of the people' (Garrison, 1979, p. 27). The creation of non-hierarchical, 'ital'[9] Black women only space is one way in which Rasta women could express their visions of utopia. These spaces subsequently became the basis for the creation of a new politics which integrated a Rasta analysis of a 'Babylon' system with Black women's experiences of gendered opposition to create a new and unique oppositional vision. This new vision has been called 'the new Rastafari'.

> The new Rastafari has emerged through a process whereby Black feminisms have garnered the weight and media access necessary to enable them to appropriate Rastafari and redefine its content. This has also been a process of rediscovery of the history of women in struggle and an excavation of global gender, class and race relations (Turner, 1994, p. 55).

While scholars have noted a decline in the influence of traditional male dominated Rastafari from the mid-1980s, the new Rastafari, embodied in musicians such as Tracy Chapman, is a powerful radicalising force which lives on in the cultural and political practices of Black women's organisations in Britain a resistance movements worldwide (Gilroy, 1987; Turner 1994, p. 15).

A further group of 'women in front' are those who are in some way 'displaced' from their communities of origin. This displacement has a liberating impact in that it frees women from the fear of ostracism experienced by many Black women who take a pioneering role. One interviewee describes a group of women who came together to establish the first Black lesbian group:

> We were mainly displaced women, so you would get [African] American women, women from Scotland, who it wouldn't matter what [group] they were from. ... I tell you what else, a lot of people who have been fostered, in care and were a long way away . . . my theory is actually if you've fought that hard, I mean I was in care for a long time, if you're fostered or adopted, it's hard. You get used to being different and you learn to deal with it. (Adiola, African, Black organisations)

The women's experiences of displacement were more fundamental than the shared experience of 'being Black in a White society', they spoke to more profound experiences of isolation. Similarly, a Sikh woman whose partner was Muslim provided the strength and radical vision necessary to establish an Asian women's refuge in the late 1970s without bowing to community pressures to prioritise marital integrity over women's safety:

> The staff make the organisation because they're there at the cut and thrust of it day in day out and if your staff are vocal and political and radical then the organisation will be automatically. ... The [first] worker was extremely radical. Here was a Sikh woman living with a Muslim man. So it was really progressive and serious. (Manjit, Asian, Asian organisation)

The worker's rejection from both communities had prepared her for the hostility that the refuge would face.[10] Women who were brought up outside of established Black communities and were the only Black child in their school, women who were taken into the care system or brought up by White foster or adoptive parents, women who had come out as lesbians women who had defied cultural expectations by dating 'out', all had experienced social ostracism and had become emotionally strong in the face of rejection.

The important role of these women has frequently been erased in the oral history of Black women's organisations. In one case, a Black organisation which had been founded primarily by lesbian women was trying to disown that history in order to attract a wider membership.

> One of the co-founders was a lesbian woman and the organisation had a reputation for being predominantly lesbian women by the time I was there. I use the word reputation, but it was a reputation in the sense that proved to be problematic because a lot of women who had heard of it didn't want to get involved because they thought it was a lesbian organisation. (Lynette, Caribbean, organisation)

In other cases, women who have been in institutional care as children are unwilling to share their experiences and are assumed to have been brought up in Black families. This erasure of the role of 'displaced' women prevents us from recognising the fundamentally diverse nature of Black women's organising in Britain. Nevertheless, these often hidden histories are a testimony to the contributions of women who have been considered 'not quite Black enough'.[11]

Conclusions

This chapter has illustrated the wealth of political activism which becomes evident when the blinkers of commonsense notions about the political realm are removed. Drawing on Black women's perspectives I have redefined political activism to acknowledge its personal experience, while retaining a focus on the communal action which grows out of such experience. I have also emphasised the multiple sites of political action and highlighted some arenas which have previously been ignored. In so doing, I have shown that Black women's organisations are at the forefront of empowering Black women, challenging inequalities and abuse within Black families and communities, as well as creating broad based demands for change at local, national and international levels. While acknowledging the many obstacles to Black women's involvement, I have also challenged assumptions which have been about Black women's inability to overcome the barriers which would seek to keep them from political activism. Finally, this chapter has located some agents of change who have been central to the development of Black women's organisational agendas but who are hidden from view when scholars focus attention only on those political actors who have received status and recognition from mainstream political system. These Black women catalysts have mobilised alternative visions of socio-economic relations which are essential in the creation of any radical agenda for change.

NOTES

1 Editor's note: This chapter is a modified reprint of Sudbury, J. (1998) *Other kinds of Dreams: Black Women's Organisations and the Politics of Transformation*, ch. 3. London: Routledge.

2 'Political activists are urging Black people not to opt out of the mainstream political system. The call comes after figures showing that as many as one in four young Black people are not on the electoral roll.' ('Would-be Voters Urged to Register', *Voice* 12 December 1995: 2)

3 Since Black women also experience the family as a site of male violence, Black women's refuges must balance the oppositional and oppressive aspects of family life. This tension is reflected in Chapter 5.

4 'Reasoning' is a term which originates in the Rastafari practice of attending lengthy discussion sessions often based on bible study which aim to educate and uplift. In common Black usage the term normally refers to a non-religious discussion in which serious issues are addressed (S. Small 1983).

5 The Muslim Parliament was established in 1995 as an alternative to mainstream party politics for Muslims of all nationalities in Britain. Its legitimacy has however been contested.

6 A policy introduced by Clinton as a compromise position on anti-gay discrimination in the US army.

7 Norman Tebbit, the former Conservative cabinet minister, argued for a particularly limited vision of Britishness when he claimed that Asians did not feel allegiance to Britain if they supported a cricket team from Pakistan or India (Brah 1996: 194).

8 Although most sociological works use the term 'Rastafarianism' and 'Rastafarian', I prefer using the terms which are used by followers of Rastafari (Ras - King; Tafari - name of Haile Selassie).

9 'Ital' is a Rasta word which translates roughly as pure or 'kosher'. It originated in reference to food, but is used more broadly to signify any attribute which adheres to the principles of simplicity, naturalness and consciousness.

10 Desai (1963) gives a vivid description of the process of 'outcasting' which accompanied marrying out of traditional communities.

11 A concept taken from Marlon Riggs' groundbreaking documentary *Black is, Black Ain't* (1995).

References

Amos, V. and Parmar, P. (1984) Challenging Imperial Feminism, *Feminist Review*, 17, pp. 3-20

Anthias, F. Yuval-Davies, N. and Cain, H. (1992) *Racialised Boundaries.* London: Routledge

Anwar, M. (1986) *Race and Politics: Ethnic Minorities and the British Political System.* London: Taviston Publication

Anwar, M. (1991) The Content of Leadership: Migration, Settlement and Racial discrimination, P. Werbner and M. Anwar (Eds.) *Black Ethnic Leadership in Britain: The Cultural Dimensions of Political Action.* London: Routledge

Ben-Tovim, G., Gabriel, J., Law, 1. and Stredder, K. (1986) A Political Analysis of Local Struggles for Racial Equality, in J. Rex and D: Mason, *Theories of Race and Ethnic Relation.* Cambridge: Cambridge University Press

Bhavnani, K. (1988) Is Violence Masculine?: a Black Feminist Perspective, in S. Grewal, J. Kay, L. Landor, G. Lewis and P. Parmar, *Charting the Journey: Writings by Black and Third World Women.* London: Sheba Feminist Press

Brown, C. (1984) *Black and White Britain: The Third PSI Survey.* London: Heinemann

Campbell, H. (1985) *Rasta and Resistance: From Marcus Garvey to Walter Rodney.* London: Hansib Publications

Carby, H. (1982) White Woman Listen!: Black Feminism and the Boundaries of Sisterhood, in Centre for Contemporary Cultural Studies, *The Empire Strikes Back: Race and Racism in 70s Britain.* London: Hutchinson

Carter, T. (1986) *Shattered Illusions: West Indians in British Politics.* London: Lawrence & Wishart

Cashmore, E. (1979) *Rastaman: The Rastafarian Movement in England.* London: Allen & Unwin

Collins, P. H. (1990) *Black Feminist Thought: Knowledge, Consciousness and the Politics of Empowerment.* Boston, MA and.London: Unwin Hyman.

Essed, P. (1996) Diversity: *Gender; Color and Culture.* Amherst, MA: University of Massachusetts Press

Fitzgerald, M. (1984) *Political Parties and Black People.* London: Runnymede Trust

Freire, R (1972) *Pedagogy of the Oppressed.* London and New York: Penguin.

Fryer, P. (1988) *Staying Power: The History of Black People in Britain,* London: Pluto Press.

Garrison, L. (1979) *Black Youth, Rastafarianism and the Identity Crisis in Britain.* London: Educational Resource

Geddes, A. (1993) Asians and Afro-Caribbean Representation in Elected Local Government in England and Wales, *New Community 20, 1:* 43-58

Gilroy, P (1987) *Ain't no Black in the Union Jack: the Cultural Politics* of *Race and Nation.* London: Hutchinson

Goulbourne, H. (1990) *Black Politics in Britain.* Aldershot: Avebury

Greater London Council (1984) *Rastafarianism in Greater London* London: Greater London Council

Hansib Directory (1994) *Third Sector.* London: Hansib Publishing

Heineman, B. W (1972) *The Politics* of *the Powerless: A Study* of *CARD.* London: Institute of Race Relations and Oxford University Press

hook, b. (1994) *Teaching to Transgress: Education as the Practice of Freedom.* London and New York: Routledge

hook, b. (1995) *Killing Race, Ending Racism.* New York: Henry Holt

Jeffers, S. (1991) Black Sections in the Labour Party: the End of Ethnicity and 'Godfather' Politics?, in R Werbner and M. Anwar (Eds.) *Black and Ethnic Leaderships in Britain: The Cultural Dimensions of Political Action*. London: Routledge.

Josephides, S. (1991) Organisational Splits and Political Ideology in the Indian Workers Association, in P. Werbner and A. Muhammad (Eds.) *Black and Ethnic Leaderships in Britain: The Cultural Dimensions of Political Action*. London and New York: Routledge

Layton-Henry, Z. (1992) *The Politics of Immigration: Immigration, 'Race' and 'Race' Relations in Post-War Britain*. Oxford and Cambridge, MA: Blackwell Publishers

Lorde, A. (1984) *Sister Outsider*. New York: The Crossing Press

Lorde, A. (1988) *A Burst of Light*. New York: Firebrand Books

Mama, A. (1989) Violence Against Black Women: Gender, Race and State Responses, *Feminist Review* 32: pp. 30-48

Miles, R. (1988) Racism, Marxism and British Politics, *Economy and Society*, 17,3: pp. 428-460 Ms (1996) January/February issue

Mukherjee, T (1988) The Journey Back, in P. Cohen and H. Bains (Eds.) *Multi-Racist Britain*. Basingstoke and London: Macmillan Press

Omolade, B. (1995) *The Rising Song of African American Women*. New York and London: Routledge

Organisation of Women of African and Asian Descent (OWAAD) (1979) FOWAAD! London: Organisation of Women of African and Asian Descent

Rex, J. (1991) *Ethnic Identity and Ethnic Mobilisation in Britain*. Coventry: Centre for Research in Ethnic Relations

Roy, A. (1995) Asian Women's Activism in Northamptonshire, in G. Griffin (ed) *Feminist Activism in the 1990s*. London and Bristol, WA: Taylor & Francis

Saggar, S. (1992) *Race and Politics in Britain*. New York and London: Harvester Wheatsheaf

Shukra, K. (1990) Black Sections in the Labour Party, in H. Goulbourne (Ed.) *Black Politics in Britain*. Aldershot: Avebury

Sia, (December 1995) *Information Bulletin*. London: Sia.

Sia, (1996a) *Developing Black Women's Organisations*. London: Sia.

Sia, (1996b) *National Directory of Black Women's Organisations*. London: Sia

Sivanandan, A. (1990) *Communities of Resistance*. London and New York: Verso

Solinger, R. (1994) *Wake up Little Susie: Single Pregnancy and Race before Roe v. Made*, London and New York: Routledge

Solomos, J. and Back, L. (1995) *Race, Politics and Social Change*. London and New York: Routledge

Southall Black Sisters (1989) *Against the Grain: A Celebration of Survival and Struggle, Southall Black Sisters. 1979-1989*. London: Southall Black Sisters

Turner, T. E. (1994) Rastafari and the New Society: Caribbean and East African Feminist Roots of a Popular Movement to Reclaim the Earthly Commons, in T E. Turner (Ed.) *Arise Ye Mighty People!: Gender, Class and Race in Popular Struggles*. New Jersey: Africa World Press

Voice (12 December 1995) *Would-be Voters Urged to Register*. London: Vee Tee Ay Publishing, 2.

Voice (9 April 1996) *Lessons in Education*. London: Vee Tee Ay Publishing, 19.

Wadsworth, M. (1992) Black Politics: a Historical Perspective, *Race and Class*. 34, 2: pp. 63-74

Wenham, M. (1993) *Funded to Fail: Nuff Pain, No Gain: the Under-resourcing of the Voluntary Sector in London*. London: London Voluntary Service Council

Werbner, P. (1991) Black and Ethnic Leadership in Britain: a Theoretical Overview, in P. Werbner and M. Muhammad (Eds.) *Black and Ethnic Leadership in Britain: The Cultural Dimensions of Political Action.* London: Routledge

Whelehan, I. (1995) *Modern Feminist Thought: From the Second Wave to Post-Feminism.* New York: New York University Press

Wilson, A. (1978) *Finding a voice: Asia Women in Britain.* London: Virago

Yawney, C. (1994) Moving with the Dawtas of Rastafari, in T. E. Turner (Ed.) *Arise Ye Mighty People: Gender, Class and Race in Popular Struggles.* New Jersey: Africa World Press

Yuval-Davies, N. (1994) Women, Ethnicity and Empowerment, in K. Bhavnani and A. Phoenix (Eds.) *Shifting Identities, Shifting Racisms.* London: Sage.

Appendix

Summary of case study organisations

Akina Mama Wa Afrika (London)

AMwA is a national non-governmental organisation of African women. The organisation's name signifies 'African sisterhood' in Swahili and reflects the membership of women from different parts of Africa, including migrants, refugees, students, professionals and women of dual heritage. AMwA grew out of an International Women's Day event in London in 1985. The organisation has a two-prong approach to their work. First, they provide support, education and networking for African women in Britain. Second, they support leadership, education and community development and are involved in the women's movement in Africa. AMwA coordinates the African Women Prisoners Project at Holloway Prison (est. 1991) and is involved in educational campaigns against skin bleaching and female genital mutilation. They have a quarterly publication called African Woman and undertake research and policy development. AMwA has funding from a variety of sources including trusts, the regional health authority and local authorities.

Black Lesbian Group (London)

The BLG was established in 1982 following a painful experience of hostility and exclusion at the 1981 OWAAD conference. The group utilised an inclusive definition of Blackness and included women from across Britain of Asian, African and Caribbean origins. The group struggled to find premises and after being ejected by Brixton Black Women's Group, eventually found space at A Woman's Space, a White feminist centre. Although meetings were held in London, a fare pool policy enabled women from the north to attend. The group focused on personal development, exploration and support as well as tackling isolation and providing opportunities for socialising. Members used their experiences to build careers in media, film and equal opportunities, however, the group, which was never funded, folded in the late 1980s.

Black Women for Wages for Housework (London)

recognition for unwaged women's work. BWfWfH was established in the early 1970s by members of the Wages For Housework Campaign and (until spring 1996) shared premises in King's Cross, London. The group has a policy of not seeking funding and campaigns on racism, immigration controls, economic restructuring, Third World 'debt', environmental racism and rights of sex workers, gays and lesbians. BWfWfH coordinates the International Network of Women of Colour and the Black Women's Rape Action Project which works to ensure both that the rape of Black women is not hidden and that Black men are not stereotyped as rapists. The group operates a political definition of Blackness in the British context, although the term 'women of colour' is utilised in mobilising international campaigns.

Black Women's Resource Centre (Sheffield)

The resource centre was established in an unlet council house in the multi-racial and impoverished area of Burngreave in March 1994, following eighteen months of prepatory work by a city council community worker in partnership with a group of local volunteers. The centre is funded 'in kind' by the city council and has a grant from the Church Urban Fund. The centre actively works to overcome ethnic barriers and operates a political definition of Blackness. Members consist of West African, Pakistani, Bangladeshi, Somali and Yemeni women. The centre provides training courses including English language, computers and sewing, advice and welfare rights work and informal drop-in social events with a cross-cultural emphasis.

Cambridge Black Women's Support Group (CBWSG)

CBWSG was established as a house group in 1980 by African and women. Initial seed funding from Kings College, Cambridge University enabled the group to apply successfully for funds from the city council and Commission for Racial Equality in 1986. The group provides social and educational opportunities for Black women and operates the Mary Seacole day nursery (est. 1990) and holiday playschemes for children. The group also participates in local authority consultations, particularly on educational issues. Their location in a relatively prosperous small town has excluded the group from most funding schemes targeting Black communities. They share a building with other women's groups in a commercial area near the station. The majority of members are of African descent, although Asian women have also been involved in smaller numbers and the definition of Blackness has oscillated between narrow and more inclusive usage.

Liverpool Black Sisters (Liverpool)

Liverpool Black Sisters was established in the early 1970s. 'Black' is promoted by the group as an umbrella term to describe all those who experience racism. The group's initial concerns were lack of childcare provision, inadequate mental health support mechanisms and inadequate recruitment of Black foster carers. The Sisters were also involved in campaigning against immigration legislation and deportations. In the late 1980s the group secured trust funding for a coordinator and in the early 1990s, funding for training, childcare and administration was obtained from Urban Aid, Granby Toxteth Task≤force, Children in Need and a number of other agencies. The group currently operates from a shared building in Liverpool where it provides summer playschemes, after school care and training courses including Black studies, computers and personal development.

Muslim Women's Helpline (London)

Motivation for the establishment of the helpline came from a conference at the Islamic Cultural Centre in West London in 1987, when women shared experiences of divorce, domestic violence, sexual abuse and concerns about arranged marriage. After two years of preparation, a national helpline was launched in autumn 1989 with a paid coordinator and a rota of volunteers. The helpline provides spiritual counselling and guidance from a Muslim perspective and reached 1,145 women by telephone and face to face in 1994. The helpline receives no grant aid and relies on donations from the Muslim community for its running costs. The organisation views Islam as transcending barriers of 'race' and ethnicity and has Arab, Asian and some White users.

Onyx (New Addington)

Onyx was initiated in 1986 by an African woman social work trainee undertaking a community work placement. The group was formed primarily of single mothers who were isolated in large industrial council estate. Meeting initially in the city council community development office, the group decided to use creativity and the arts to challenge racism. They therefore organised an open day where racism and discrimination were humorously tackled through poetry, drama and music. Subsequently, the group began to act as advocates for local Black families in their dealings with the local authority. Onyx decided not to apply for funding in order to retain their critical independence. However, by the early 1990s, the group lost its momentum as members moved away or started jobs. Currently, Onyx exists as a loose network of women which occasionally does performances at community events, but no longer has formal meetings.

Osaba Women's Centre (Coventry)

Osaba Women's Centre was established in 1984 by members of an African dance group with sponsorship by the Coventry West Indian Youth Council. The group aimed to provide opportunities for women and children in the fields of social welfare, health, education, employment, training and culture. Premises were obtained in the inner city deprived area of Hillfields, initially in social services premises and then in a former shop. Early members tended to be single mothers and Rasta women had a key role in the centre's development. In 1993 the group moved to spacious newly renovated premises purchased with an Urban Aid grant. The centre provides training including Black history, personal development and job search; childcare including summer playschemes, playgroup and day care; a newsletter; cultural events and a drop-in facility. The centre has also been involved in establishing a centre for women experiencing domestic violence.

Panahghar (Coventry)

Panahghar was established in 1979 when an Asian male councillor, working in partnership with Asian women council employees, obtained Section 11 funding for a service for Asian women escaping violence in the home. Initially the project was located within the Haven, a White women's refuge, however, in 1986 Panahghar obtained a house and became independent. The organisation provides services in four areas: the refuge, including counselling, legal advice and advocacy; aftercare for women resettling in the community; outreach work to support women unable to leave their homes; support groups and surgeries. The organisation also participates in policy debates and is a constant critic of the local authority. Funding by the social services department and Children in Need, Safer Cities and Orbit Housing was supplemented in 1996 with a large grant from the National Lottery Charities Board to purchase a community centre and to pay for additional staff posts. Although Panahghar provides a refuge for Asian women only, they operate a political definition of 'Black' and were involved in establishing a similar service for African Caribbean women in Coventry.

Shakti Women's Aid (Edinburgh)

Shakti was established in 1986 by a group of Black and White women. Initially, the organisation was a part of Edinburgh Women's Aid, but subsequently it became independent and obtained separate premises. Shakti provides support and safe temporary accommodation to Asian, African Caribbean and Chinese women and children escaping domestic violence throughout Scotland. The organisation provides advice on welfare benefits, legal rights, immigration/nationality, racial harassment, education and employment and has an interpreting service. Shakti also challenges institutional discriminatory practices in housing, social services, health, education and immigration and is actively involved in campaigns such as 'Zero Tolerance'. Shakti works to operationalise and defend a political definition of Blackness.

Wai Yin Chinese Women's Society (Manchester)

The society was established in 1988 and in 1995 obtained European Community funding to purchase and renovate a building in central Manchester. Funding from a range of sources including central and local government, the Consortium on Opportunities for Volunteers government quango and the National Lottery Charities Board facilitates a range of cultural and educational opportunities including Mandarin, calligraphy, Cantonese opera singing, as well as training courses such as English language, interview techniques and computer training. In addition, the society provides a drop-in centre, information, emotional support and vocational guidance. The centre also coordinates involvement in celebrations such as Chinese New Year, Dragon Boat Festival and International Women's Week. The centre focuses on empowering Chinese women to overcome marginalisation, isolation and cultural/linguistic barriers and enabling children to participate in cultural activities.

Chapter 4

The success of our mothers: Caribbean mothering, childrearing and strategies in resisting racism

Tracey Reynolds

Introduction

Childrearing involves the physical, material, emotional and psychological care and well-being of children. For Caribbean mothers, and mothers belonging to other minority ethnic groups, a key aspect of successful mothering work involves teaching their children to deal with the fact that as Black children living in Britain it is likely that they will encounter some form of racism or racial discrimination in their everyday lives. The success of Caribbean mothers is achieved through their childrearing practices. This is because they have successfully utilised their childrearing practices and skills to develop four key strategies that enable their children to challenge racism in their lives and not view it as an obstacle for individual success and advancement. These four encompass firstly, mentally and emotionally preparing their children to challenge racist practices in their everyday lives; secondly, the monitoring of their children's education; thirdly, the celebration of Black Diasporic and Caribbean culture and traditions to promote a collective identity and a sense of 'cultural belongingness, and finally, the close monitoring and policing of children's activities in public spaces. The article explores the childrearing strategies utilised by Caribbean mothers in order to respond to racist practices in their children's lives.

The discussion opens by setting out the research context and providing a brief summation of how racism is conceptualised by policymakers and race relation theorists. It then explores the specific strategies that the mothers utilise in their childrearing to challenge racism by drawing on views expressed by thirty Caribbean mothers living in London, UK. The extent to which the mothers draw upon and utilise their own experiences of being parented in the Caribbean or Britain in their childrearing will also be critically explored as well as generation and social class differences that influence the mothers' perceptions and response to racism in their children's lives.

Mothering, childrearing and conceptualising racism

The study is based on qualitative in-depth interviews with thirty mothers of Caribbean heritage, who live in London, England. The study investigates the mothering and family experiences of Caribbean women in Britain from the post war period (late 1940s onwards) through to the present day. In particular, it addresses the way in which race, notions of cultural identity and racism create collective mothering experiences despite generation and social class differences between the mothers (Reynolds, 1999a). The sample size of mothers interviewed is relatively small. However, the main advantage of the small sample was that it allowed me to focus in-depth on the lives and experiences of each individual mother concerned. This was particularly important because there is limited research data available in Britain that focuses exclusively on the experiences of Caribbean mothers. The mothers who participated in the study were aged between nineteen and eighty-one. This wide age range encouraged an analysis of inter-generational similarities and differences. In the context of the study generation difference is loosely defined. The first generation mothers are those who arrived in Britain from the post-war period. The second generation mothers are those mothers born in Britain and the third generation mothers have mothers who are themselves born in this country. Similarly, class difference is defined in relation to the mothers' own understanding of their social status and a combination of objective and subjective definitions of social class were used. Objective definitions are based on conventional systems of classification such as, the Registrar General and income levels. Subjective definitions look to family background to identify a class status and also the mothers' social and cultural capital (Reynolds, 1999b).

Racism is a concept that is multi-faceted, constantly shifting and re-negotiating itself according to its social, economic, cultural and political environments (Brah, 1996). The focus of policy debates and the race relations field had been towards examining this process of change and renegotiation as we move towards a multi-ethnic society within a globalised world. Racism is defined as 'those ideologies and social processes which discriminate against others on the basis of their putatively different membership' (Solomos, 1993, p. 9). This membership, which Solomos refers to, is racially and culturally distinctive. In contemporary Britain, people that belong to Caribbean, and other minority ethnic groups, have their cultural and racial membership to the nation state questioned. As a consequence they assume a tenuous position in British society (Brah, 1992). Indeed it has been suggested that their relationship to the British nation state is characterised by 'inferiorization, subordination and oppression' (Anthias, 1990, p. 126). As a result of their racialised status, minority ethnic groups, as part of their daily experiences, encounter racial inequality, racial discrimination and harassment, as well as unequal access to resources. This has persisted across successive generations in what Paul Gilroy terms, the 'changing sameness of racism' (Gilroy, 1987). The accounts by the mothers in the study reinforce this viewpoint and provide many examples of 'racial otherness' and 'ethnic isolation' in relation to their own lives and those of their children.

In order to understand the success of Caribbean mothers in responding to and challenging racism through childrearing and mothering practices, racism must not only be understood as prejudice, emotion or an issue of morality. Racism must also be read as political. Hesse's work (1997) defines racism as a modern form of governance whereby those White groups dominant in western society have, over the course of modern history (the post-Enlightenment period onwards), developed procedures and practices to shape, survey and re-construct the 'other'. Those ethnic groups within this 'other' category are represented as 'deviant' or 'abnormal', whilst the dominant group's own position is re-constituted as 'universal' 'normative' and 'unquestioned'. Since the development of modernity successive western societies have imposed racially divisive categories, what Stuart Hall (1991) terms 'The West and The Rest'. These racialised categories have then been used to entrench, legitimate and manage claims of western superiority and universalism, whilst classifiying 'non-western' groups and cultural practices as 'inferior' and 'other' (Malik, 1996).

In the literature emerging from Britain, the US and the Caribbean concerning mothering and mothering practices by Black and other minority ethnic groups, analysis has focused on understanding how these groups' mothering experiences are constructed and represented as 'inferior' or 'other' by White society (Glenn, Chang and Forcey, 1994; Hill-Collins, 1994). It is suggested that racialised and pathologised images of Black mothers as the 'welfare queen', 'teenage lone-mother', 'baby-mother' or 'Black matriarch' foreground major discussions concerning Black mothering within White western mothering discourses (Sudarkasa, 1997). Thus, a significant aspect of mothering work by Caribbean mothers also involves them challenging the racial construction of Black mothers and the 'normativisation' (Glenn, Chang and Forcey, 1994) of White western (middle class) mothering and childrearing practices.

In my interviews with the mothers they perceive racism as a collective experience that transcends social class and generation differences. For instance, all the mothers felt that they had encountered racism in their everyday lives although the extent that they experienced racism varied, as did the context. These racist encounters are not just confined to overt racial actions such as racial abuse or physical violence. Instead the mothers recognise that racism manifests itself in more subtle 'invisible' and complex ways. Nizinga's comment is one of many viewpoints expressed by the mothers to support this claim:

> I can't really give you a clear-cut example because racism is so subtle that you can't put your finger on it and define it and say this is actually going on, but you know it's there. You just can't articulate it but it's what's going on. It's no use ranting and raving because when you're talking to those people, they want facts. Their idea of racism anyway is name-calling. I can handle that but I can't handle the subtleness, where it is coming from. It did actually make me quite paranoid for a while but I just had to learn how to deal with it. You know, we have it bad, our parents have it bad and our grandparents and great grandparents had it real bad. I don't think it's any worse, it's still just as bad as if we're still stuck on some plantation somewhere, but the situation and circumstances have changed (Nizinga, second-generation mother)

Here racism is experienced as a 'changing sameness'. While its form and expression has transformed over the years, it still continues to inform the daily lives of Black people, and more specifically the lives of Caribbean mothers. The extensive literature documenting the racial inequality Black people continue to experience in British institutions such as, for example, education, social welfare services and the criminal justice system supports these claims of the 'changing sameness' of racism (Madood, 1997).

Throughout history Caribbean mothers, as well as Caribbean people in general, have responded to racial inequality by actively, and in diverse ways, challenging racist practices. Since the Windrush era, where Britain encountered a mass migration of Caribbean people from the Caribbean in order to respond to a labour shortage crisis, Caribbean mothers have been successful in seeking to address racial injustices in their children's and their own lives. Their successes occurred at both an individual and a collective level. For example, during the 1970s, a group of Caribbean mothers collectively organised to campaign for the abolition of Educational Sub-Normal [ESN] schools where Caribbean children were greatly over-represented. Their successful campaign contributed towards bringing about the abolition of these schools (Bryan, Dadzie and Scafe, 1985). Also, in my interviews with the mothers, a first generation mother, recollected her experiences as a factory worker during the 1950s to recount how she collectively organised with the other female workers on the factory floor (many of whom were Caribbean mothers) to successfully lobby management into altering their shift working patterns. Their new working patterns meant that the mothers were now able to take or collect their children from school.

Historically at a collective level Caribbean mothers have also acted as 'community mothers'. Implicit within this understanding of 'community mothering' is that Caribbean women feel and share a collective responsibility for children and other vulnerable members of the Black community, to whom they are not biologically related (Barrow, 1996; Glenn, Chang and

Forcey, 1994; Reynolds, 1999a). Hill-Collins' (1990) study of the Black community in the USA observes that it is common for women who are community workers to use 'family language' to refer to unrelated individuals within their Black community. Her observations mirror my own research examining the experiences of Caribbean women in Caribbean community organisations (Reynolds, 2003). The female workers and volunteers in these organisations utilised a similar language when discussing children and the elderly who accessed the services. So, for example, the women working in the Saturday schools and the mentoring schemes did not have any kinship or biological ties to the children who attending these schools or schemes. Yet, they would often refer to them as 'our children', or 'my children'.

Hill-Collins' (1994) discussion of 'community mothering' and in a broader sense 'community parenting' is particularly useful in understanding how these women's language of ownership represents a moral or cultural obligation to provide care for non-kinship community members. Her work also establishes an interdependent relationship between mothering and wider socio-cultural concerns Black women (and men) have for the Black community. Thus these women regard the range of tasks and duties they perform at localised and practical levels – such as giving up their time to educate Black children in their local community – as beneficial to their local Black communities. Moreover, the community work they perform has been a successful vehicle in socialising and transmitting the cultural values of the community to the next generation.

Childrearing strategies to resist racism

The success of Caribbean mothers is perceived in their childrearing practices and demonstrated in the four strategies they employ to encourage their children to respond to perceived acts of racism. These mothers' childrearing actions are not merely 'coping mechanisms' but rather signify conscious and deliberate acts of resistance. These strategies include the mental and emotional preparation of children for racism; monitoring of the education system; the celebration of Caribbean cultural traditions and Black identities; and the close monitoring and policing of children in the public domain.

Mental and emotional preparation of Black children for racism

A central aspect of Caribbean mothers' childrearing involves the mental and emotional preparation of children for racism. In explaining racism to their children, the mothers present racism as an obstacle that impedes personal advancement or success. The mothers' rationale for representing racism in this form is that racism becomes fixed in the child's mind as an inevitable hindrance in life. However, this should not deter their children from success. Rather societal racism should be used to motivate Black children towards achieving their personal goals and ambitions. For example as one mother states:

> I want her [daughter] to grow up proud of who she is because that way nobody can bring her down. I think making her aware that she has to work a lot harder for what she wants, being aware that there are people out there who will try and stop you from succeeding, that there are people out there who don't expect anything from you, so for her to be aware of it and at all times keep your head up, just be proud and try to be strong (Jamilla, second-generation mother).

And the following comments by a second-generation mother, Nizinga, clearly sum up the attitudes expressed by all of the interviewed when discussing the racism issue:

> I'll tell her not to let it [racism] get you down, don't see it as an obstacle, just get on with it because you can do it (Nizinga, second-generation mother)

It has been suggested that within (White) mainstream society differing types of Black racialised identities are devalued outside of the arenas of sports, music and popular culture (Skellington and Morris, 1992). To compensate for this the mothers look for ways to celebrate their racial and ethnic identities in order to transmit this to their children and re-affirm to their children a high sense of self-worth:

> I remember maybe they [children] had been called a name at school - I had to explain to them that, yes, they were Black and that Black was beautiful. When people try and get brown in the sun they associate it with health, well-being and happiness. I had to show them it was truly wonderful to be a Black person and not a negative thing to counteract the things children would be telling them at school (Caro, first-generation mother)

> I tell her [daughter] she's a beautiful Black princess all the time. I concentrate on all the positive things of being Black (Nizinga, second-generation mother)

The Black Power Movement that established itself in the USA and then Britain during the 1970s influenced the affirmation that 'Black is beautiful' by these mothers. Various commentators have examined the significance of this movement for Black people worldwide (see for example, Davis, 1981). In the context of Caribbean mothers in Britain, what was important about this movement is that the term 'Black' was reclaimed from the dominant discourse in order to reflect a positive racialised identity. Black identities were now celebrated as beautiful and from present era onwards, influenced the mothers' childrearing responses in countering the pathologisation of Black identities within mainstream society.

Parental monitoring of children's education

Caribbean people have a marked history of social exclusion and marginalisation in the UK. Numerous studies have pointed to the way in which racism, 'othering' and 'ethnic isolation' have shaped the experiences of Caribbean people across a range of public spheres. Crucially, Caribbean people highlight the education system in the UK as one of the spheres in which they feel significantly marginalised and encounter racial discrimination. There has been much work addressing the issue of Caribbean children, racism and education. Successive Ofsted reports show that Caribbean children, in particularly young boys, continue to underachieve in schools (Gillborn and Gipps, 1996). Whilst debates attribute this failing to a variety of reasons, (such as, amongst other things, a lack of Black role models in schools, lack of culturally relevant subjects in the school curriculum, a lack of parental involvement, the devaluing of education and learning within Black youth culture), an overriding theme in the debate is that institutional racism and racist practices within the schooling system is a key factor that contributes to Caribbean children's underachievement and it remains a common cause for concern among parents, teachers and policymakers (see Wright, 1988; Mirza, 1992; Gillborn, 1995; Sewell, 1997).

The mothers in my study are themselves very familiar with debates about key issues concerning Caribbean children and the education system. As a consequence one of the mothers' successes has been to develop in their childrearing strategies an increased monitoring of the education system. It is important to note this monitoring differs according to each mother. The mothers' own experiences of education in the Caribbean (primarily first-generation mothers) or Britain (second and third-generation mothers) also influence how they undertake this monitoring. For instance, those mothers who amongst the first minority ethnic children to be educated in Britain in the 1950s and 1960s, as mothers today are very anxious that their own largely negative schooling experiences are not repeated in their children's lives.

For many of these second-generation mothers, primarily from working-class backgrounds, the realities of their own schooling years in Britain were harsh. Racial, and to a lesser extent sexual, discrimination by teachers and pupils combined with limited resources in schools that were concentrated in economically deprived areas meant that their desire and ability for educational success did not match the realities that they faced and it was difficult for them to achieve this success. These mothers own parents valued the meritocractic ideal of education and regarded it as a means to secure inter-generation upward social mobility. However, newly arrived in Britain during the 1950s and 1960s, and lacking direct experience of schooling in Britain, it is not surprising that they did not understand the day-to-day reality of racism that they faced as children at school and how this in turn directly impeded educational achievement.

Not all of the mothers educated in Britain as children during these early years encountered negative schooling experiences. Those mothers who as children came from an affluent middle-class background or went to school in suburban areas, fared better than those mothers who as children were educated in inner-London schools with limited resources. On the whole these women when recollecting their school years remember experiencing fewer incidents of racism and racial harassment by their teachers and generally felt that good relations existed between themselves and the other children.

> My mother was one of few Black teachers working in a school at that time [early 1970s] and that created a bridge between her and the teachers at my school. She wasn't intimidated by asking them questions and she could talk to them on their level. She made them sit up and take note of her and I feel they respected her because she could relate to what they were trying to do with us at school (Anita, second-generation mother).

It could be argued that by sharing a similar middle-class affiliation, the teachers could in many ways relate to these children and their parents and thus judged them as less different from themselves. By seeing Caribbean children from middle-class backgrounds as 'more like us', the teachers were less likely to apply stereotypical characteristics and notions of Black racialised identities to the mothers as children, and to discriminate against them on the basis of their racial or cultural origin. This is not to suggest that teachers never expressed racist attitudes towards middle-class Black children. Diane Reay's (1995) study of the classroom interaction of teachers and children within schools recognises that racism is displayed differently amongst the middle-classes. Racism, Reay argues, is often covert and manifests itself in a taken for granted attitude of superiority towards those perceived as 'others'. In addition, the teachers' often ignore (or claim to ignore) Black children's racialised identity, and instead they adopt a 'colour blind' approach to classroom experiences of Black children. In doing so, Black children's racial and ethnic identities are disregarded and instead they are defined in terms of their closeness in similarity to 'Whiteness' or 'Britishness'.

Not surprisingly, these mothers' own schooling experiences have had a fundamental impact on the way they respond to the education system today and how they choose to educate their children. There appears to be greater pro-activeness on these mothers' part in having direct contact with the teacher regarding the educational affairs of their children. It could be suggested that the mothers' activities, attitudes and practices are part of a wider cultural shift in education towards greater parental involvement and parental choice and consumerism (Ball, 1993; David, 1993). However, this should not diminish the fact that their greater involvement in schools is a consequence of their own schooling experiences.

Britain today is widely acknowledged as a multi-cultural society. In urban areas such as London, it is a common to have diverse ethnic groups in school classrooms. Yet, in the interviews the mothers suggest that there has been little change since their schooling years in terms of many of the White teachers' negative perceptions of, and responses to, Caribbean and minority ethnic children. The mothers' response to this has been to undertake a concentrated monitoring of their children's education in order to challenge and combat any perceived incidences of racism (and also sexism) in their children's schooling. The following quotations provide support this:

> I saw that they weren't moving [my daughter] onto another book, this despite knowing that she had done the reading as I would sit down with her every night to make sure that she was doing it - anyhow I saw that the teacher had moved these other White girls that my daughter plays with onto the next higher level book. So I went up the school and pulled the teacher aside to find out what was going on, after that they moved her to the next level book (Zora, second-generation mother).

> There was this day I picked him [son] up from school. He just started crying, saying that these children at his school kept calling him mud-face, that he's made of mud. We immediately made an appointment with the headmaster to make him aware my son is being racially abused and that he had to deal with this immediately - the long and short of it was that a meeting was called between ourselves and some of the children's parents to talk things through and they got a warning. It brought it home that some things don't change because I was called names, racial names (Tanya, second-generation mother).

These mothers are also keenly aware of their children's curriculum and have greater involvement with their children's school on a day-to-day basis:

> I decided to become a school governor at the school because I felt that I could have a greater role in their education by doing that and my voice would be heard. One of the first things I got placed on the agenda was lack of books in the library that promote positive Black people. It took me a few months to get my way but I kept on raising it at the meetings. I was able to bring more books into the school that were more multi-cultural and that had Black people that the Black children could relate to (Anita, second-generation mother).

Another mother, Michele recollects:

> I remember when she was learning colours and she learnt every single colour except for black, I went down that nursery and said that's the first thing you should have taught her because number

> one, that's what she is and number two, Black is a dominant colour (Michele, second-generation mother).

This incident initially appeared trivial to me but in listening to Michele it was clear that she saw wider underlying implications centring on the issue of racial identity. Michele believes that by failing to teach her daughter the colour 'Black' this devalues her daughter's racial identity, and at a very early age it is training her daughter to believe 'Black' is of secondary importance.[1] These examples of involvement and intervention expressed by the mothers demonstrate their success in putting into place strategies that actively challenge perceived incidents of racism in their children's education.

In addition to greater parental involvement in their children's schooling, some Caribbean mothers are increasingly considering the option of sending their children 'back home' to be educated in the Caribbean. In the study, Cara, herself a secondary school teacher, has had first hand knowledge of racism within the British schooling system and the effects of this on Caribbean children's lives. As a consequence she decided to pursue this option of sending her eldest children 'back home' to the Caribbean. Cara, in talking about the schools in which she has worked, states:

> They are very negative towards the Black children. That really opened my eyes, how some of the teachers are and the negative way in which they perceived our children. They say our kids are really disruptive, they don't want to learn, they're thick, they're slow. It made me think about my own children, what type of education they would receive, that's when we were saying yes, we have to go home [Trinidad]. The children need to have an education where they will be loved and supported (Cara, second-generation mother).

Cara took the decision to return home with her family to her island of origin, Trinidad, during the 1980s, where her eldest two daughters received a secondary school education. During the interview I asked her to address the difference this made to her daughters' education:

> TR: Do you feel your daughters received a higher standard of education, than they would have if you had remained in Britain?

> Cara: Most definitely - education standards are higher in Trinidad, the expectations are higher and the culture of education is something that is accepted. You're not seen as a goody-goody if you're doing it, or talked about, so they didn't have the negative peer pressure to think about. Getting a good education is an accepted norm.

So convinced is Cara of the value of a 'Caribbean' education that she is considering sending her youngest son there to be educated too:

> Cara: I have particular concerns about [my son], being a Black boy, a Black youth, here. I really want him to do the best that he can and my concerns are, if he goes to school here, the kinds of pressure he might have to achieve might be great.

The idea of sending their children 'back home' (to the Caribbean) to be educated is an option being increasingly considered by mothers with school-age children and who still maintain strong family links to their Caribbean island of descent. This option particularly appeals to mothers with adolescent sons. Their views are supported by evidence that indicates Black boys have the highest exclusion rates in schools and from a young age are negatively perceived by teachers as 'hostile', 'aggressive' and 'underachievers' (Sewell, 1997). In addition, amongst both Black and White working-class boys a culture presently exists which identifies academic achievement as effeminate (Mac an Ghaill, 1996; Sewell, 1997). Thus the mothers believe that educating their sons in the Caribbean would free them from racial discrimination and other constraints and reinforce an educational ethos that is commonly accepted in the Caribbean. However, it should be noted that within the Caribbean region, educationalists are also grappling with a similar issue of educational underachievement amongst Black boys. This is further compounded by teacher shortages in many countries in the region, as qualified teachers from the region are migrating to UK, USA and Canada to fulfil teaching shortages in these countries (Caricom, 2003). This suggests that the mothers desire to send their children back home as a means of achieving educational success for their children, especially their sons, is not guaranteed and their views concerning the Caribbean education system is based on a romanticised ideal rather than the actual reality of life in the Caribbean.

Celebration of a 'Caribbean' Tradition and Black Identities

A third strategy utilised by the mothers in their childrearing to challenge racism is to provide their children with a sense of cultural belonging and a collective racialised identity that they can draw strength from in times of difficulties. Across each generation the mothers transmit these Caribbean values and traditions to their children as part of their childrearing. Certain values and traditions such as having well-disciplined children, respect for family members and the local community are valourised and celebrated as culturally distinctive customs:

> Coming to this country, I have never lost my West Indian background or culture. I have brought up my children with the same values I was raised. Things like the respect of elders. Even if you're not related we [West Indians] call everyone aunt or uncle (Dolly, first-generation mother).

> I think that the certain values I grew up with, I look back and I'm glad, Do you know when your parents call you and you don't say 'yeh' or 'what', you've got to say 'yes mummy' or 'yes daddy', little things like that, you had to know respect like that, you had to show respect. That's the way it is in the Caribbean and my parents raised me like that. Also there are little things like you make your bed in the mornings. When you come home from school you have got to take off your school clothes and put on your house clothes. Those kinds of values I want to pass onto my daughter because I think those kinds of values carry you through life and make you a better person (Jamilla, second-generation mother).

Evident in these viewpoints expressed is the mothers' shared belief that respect represents common Caribbean traits. Across many Caribbean societies children's respect for senior members of the family and local community are of paramount importance (Senior, 1991). One mark of 'good mothering' is judged as the ability of Caribbean mothers to rear children that are seen by others to be disciplined, well mannered and respectful to others.

The mothers also insist upon increasing their children's self-awareness and self-knowledge of Black racialised identities within a global diasporic context. This is primarily achieved through the provision of toys, games and books, sculptures and paintings that advance positive self-images of Black identities. This aspect of their parenting represents part of a wider global trend whereby migrant groups are developing and fostering transnational links and racialised identities that transcend national borders and nation states (Goulbourne and Solomos, 2003).

During the interviews it was very common for me to see African masks, sculptures, paintings and other Black cultural artefacts in the homes of second and third-generation mothers:

> I'm teaching my son things now so that he's knows who he is, where he is from, his history, so that he is proud of being Black. I recently bought him a book that is about Black inventors so that he is aware of the important contribution Black people have made to the world outside of the usual images of singing, dancing and basketball. He learns these things at Saturday school, he looks at all the important historical events for Black people here, the West Indies, Africa and America, so he's pretty aware of all the things Black people have had to go through (Tanya, second-generation mother).

Some of the mothers also send their children to Black supplementary schools and Saturday Schools where subjects such as Afrocentric studies, Black history and cultural studies complement the standard teaching curriculum.

Close monitoring and policing of children's activities in public spaces

In public spaces, Caribbean and other minority ethnic groups are highly visible and their actions constantly scrutinised (Hill-Collins, 1999). Not surprisingly, Caribbean mothers are worried when their children enter the public domain. Existing societal gender relations also exacerbates these concerns, determined by Caribbean people's racial positioning in Britain. Therefore, in order to keep their children safe from racial abuse and harassment (and also sexual abuse and harassment) a childrearing strategy involves the mothers closely monitoring and policing their children's activities in the public domain. Gendered relations lead to the mothers monitoring and policing their son's and daughter's public activities in different ways.

In terms of daughters, the mothers' concerns for their daughters' physical safety centre on physical and sexual attacks and harassment. Their concerns are by no means exclusive to Black and other minority ethnic mothers and are shared by mothers of all ethnic groups. In addition to sexual violence and other forms of violence, the mothers also fear their daughters, and sons, experiencing specific racial violence as a result of their racial position in Britain and the construction of Black female sexual identity in western societies. Black women historically have been constructed as 'sexual beings', objects of White male sexual desires (Gilman, 1992). This sexual objectification of Black women, pervasive in western societies, impacts on the way Black mothers, as well as fathers, seek to closely police their daughters' activities as they move through public spaces:

> I worry about my daughter out late at night. It's not that I don't trust her and she's pretty streetwise, but it's not safe especially in this area. Men in cars will be coming to a crawl beside you, checking you out. They assume because you're Black and it's late that you're a prostitute looking for trade. So when she's out late we'll arrange something so she's not walking these streets (Anita, second-generation mother).

A central aspect of this monitoring and control by the mothers, and also fathers, of their daughters' activities and movements in the public domain is also tied up with notions of 'respectability' and the desire to safeguard their daughters 'reputations'. Whilst Caribbean women have high levels of economic activity and autonomy outside of the home (Reynolds, 2001), additional activities that Black women undertake in the public sphere (with the possible exception of church-related activities) are restricted, and the home/private sphere remains their primary location. The mothers' awareness of the way in which Black womanhood and sexual identity is constructed and perceived within dominant discourses further strengthens their concerns about their teenage daughters' sexuality.

The mothers in the study worried less about their male children's physical safety in terms of sexual attack or harassment. However, this does not mean that they worry less about their sons in public spaces compared with their daughters and, if anything, their concerns appear to be greater for their sons. This concern is primarily attributable to two interlocking factors. Firstly, male identities are closely defined by their relationship to the public sphere. The great number of activities they do there combines to make this sphere a highly masculine space. Secondly, in contrast to White males in Britain, Black men's ability to move about freely in this sphere is hampered by the interwoven relationship of 'race', policing and crime. 'Race' and policing is a highly politicised area, with street crimes (such as mugging) represented by the police and media as being intimately tied up with Black male identity (Gilroy, 1987; Runnymede Trust, 1996). On one side, there are 'race' activists, the Black press and academic commentators who cite and criticise the high incidence of police arrest and incarceration of young Black men. They also emphasise the high incidence of police harassment, brutality and the deaths of young Black men whilst in police custody. On the other side, there are mainstream media and public policy discourses that focus on the issue of social exclusion and address the high incidence of crime, civil unrest and public disorder of young Black men in economically deprived areas.

These diametrically opposed debates on Black men, policing and crime means that this relationship becomes fixed in the public's imagination and informs the concerns that the mothers have for their sons in the public domain. The fear of racial attacks and harassment from the police and racist members of the public, along with an increase in Black-on-Black violence, and negative male peer pressure, such as male street gangs, are very real concerns for the mothers.

Several mothers voiced their concerns about the pressure and physical danger they felt that their sons faced in public spaces:

> Now that he's getting older, I fear the call of the streets. Is he going to be continually harassed by the police and arrested for just walking down the street? (Cara, second-generation mother).

> I live in constant fear for my son. Black men are killing Black men and for what? Do you know what really scares me, it's the way these kids are just accepting of it. Violence at school is an everyday thing to them now. I just pray to God it's not my home the school's ringing to say one of my sons is hurt or dead (Joy, second-generation mother).

> I worry about him getting into the wrong crowd and finding himself in trouble. I don't want my son to end up a statistic whether it be a criminal or murder one (Camille, first-generation mother).

At the time of the interviews the racially motivated murder of young Black teenager Stephen Lawrence, of southeast London in 1993, further increased this fear. Since this unfortunate episode there have been more highly publicised cases of violence against young Black men involving Black-on-Black violence.[2] The mothers recognise the fact they cannot confine their sons to home as easily as they can their daughters. As a result, they incorporate strategies into their childrearing that enable them to monitor their teenage sons' activities in the public domain. Although these strategies vary according to each mother, broad patterns exist. These strategies consist of the mothers establishing expected patterns of behaviour from sons when they are out of the home, close monitoring of their sons' friends and activities, and practical advice to avoid problems. The following accounts provide examples of the three main strategies implemented by the mothers.

1. Establishing expected patterns of behaviour for sons:

   > I told my sons that I don't want no police breaking down my door looking for any of them. They knew from the start, that I wouldn't tolerate them getting involved with the police. Once they know how far they can go, what you will and will not tolerate, it keeps them in line. That's it really, that's how I kept my sons out of trouble when they were coming up (Enid, first generation mother).

2. Close monitoring of sons' friends and activities:

   > I try and keep him busy, I have made sure that he has a lot of extra-curricular activities to do when he is at home so he doesn't have time to get into trouble. Also, this way I know where he is and that he's not up to mischief. I have also always made it a point of knowing who his friends are by allowing him to have his friends over for weekends and his school breaks (Camille, first generation mother).

3. Practical advice to avoid problems:

   > We tell them all sorts of things. We have given them some basic rules which I hope will help keep him out of trouble when they're out there. For instance, I say to them no loitering on the streets, just go straight to where you need to go quickly. When they're out shopping they're not to go into shops unless they want something and have the money to pay for it on them. Also to keep themselves close to where shop assistants can see you and never to go into a shop with a large group of their friends (Anita, second-generation mother).

All of these strategies are attempts by the mothers to minimise their sons' visibility and physical presence on the streets. The mothers' fear for sons in public spaces is not just restricted to the Black men's relation to the police, the criminal justice system and racial attacks. It also encompasses male Black-on-Black violence (Runnymede Trust, 1996) which could lead their sons into trouble in the public domain.

Conclusion

Racism is a conceptual tool that helps us to understand how social boundaries are established to include and exclude certain ethnic groups. Yet racism has very real consequences for people's daily lived experiences. For instance, racism has practical consequences for Caribbean mothers in the way that they choose to raise their children in contemporary Britain and to develop childrearing practices. The success of Caribbean mothers has been to utilise their childrearing practices and skills to develop strategies that challenge and resist racism in their children's lives. The four strategies outlined involve the mental and emotional preparation of children for racism; secondly, parental involvement in education; thirdly the celebration of a 'Caribbean' tradition and Black racialised identities; and finally, the close monitoring of children in the public domain. These successes that these mothers have achieved in these areas are by no means exclusive to Caribbean mothers. As racialised 'other' mothers, mothers belonging to minority-ethnic groups have similarly been successful in utilising childrearing skills to employ strategies in resisting racism. As Britain move towards a multi-ethnic society within a globalised world a central commitment of policy makers and the race relations theorists will be to develop a more inclusive society so that Caribbean and minority ethnic mothers can demonstrate childrearing practices that are free from all racial constraints.

Notes

[1] Patricia Williams (1997) in her Reith Lectures also talks about a similar experience in relation to her son's schooling.

[2] In 2001 the death of African young boy, Damilola Taylor, by a group of multi-ethnic youths and in 2002 a spate of Black-on-Black gang shootings in Midlands that eventually lead to the death of two Caribbean teenage girls sparked widespread media interest and public condemnation within Caribbean community and wider society.

References

Anthias, F. (1990) Race and Class Revisited: Conceptualising race and racisms, *Sociological Review*, 38:2, pp.19-42

Ball, S. J. (1993) Education Markets, Choice and Social Class: The Market as a Class and Strategy in the UK and USA, *British Journal of Sociology of Education*, 14:1, pp. 3-21

Barrow, C. (1996) *Family in the Caribbean: Themes and Perspectives.* London: James Currey publishing

Brah, A. (1992) Difference, Diversity and Differentiation, in J. Donald and A. Rattansi (Eds.) *Race, Culture and Difference.* London: Sage

Brah, A. (1996) *Cartographies of Diaspora: Contesting Identities.* London: Routledge

Bryan, B., Dadzie, S. and Scafe, S. (1985) *The Heart of the Race: Black Women's Lives in Britain.* London: Virago

Caricom (2003) *Gender and Migration Patterns in the Caribbean.* Guyana: Caricom

David, M. (1993) *Parents, Gender and Education Reform.* Cambridge: Polity Press.

Davis, A. (1981) *Women, Race and Class.* London: Women's Press Ltd

Gillborn, D. (1995) *Racism and Antiracism in Real Schools.* Buckingham: Open University Press

Gillborn, D. and Gipps, C. (1996) *Recent Research on the Achievements of Ethnic Minority Pupils.* London: Office for Standards in Education, HMSO.

Gillman, S. (1992) Black Bodies, White Bodies; Towards an Iconography of Female Sexuality in late Nineteenth Century Art, Medicine and Literature, in J. Donald and A. Rattansi (Eds.) *Race, Culture and Difference.* London: Sage.

Gilroy, P (1987) *There Ain't No Black in the Union Jack.* London: Hutchinson.

Glenn, E., Chang, G. and Forcey, L. (1994) (Eds.) *Mothering: Ideology, Experience and Agency.* London: Routledge

Goulbourne, H. and Solomos, J. (forthcoming) Ethnicity, Family and Social Capital, in *Journal of Social and Political Studies*

Hall, S. (1991) The Local and the Global, in A. King [Eds.] *Culture, Globalisation and the World System: Contemporary Conditions for Representations of Identity.* London: Macmillan.

Hesse, B. (1997) White Governmentality: Urbanism, Nationalism, Racism, in S. Westwood and J. Williams (Eds.) *Imagining Cities: Signs, Scripts and Memory.* London: Routledge

Hill-Collins, P. (1990) *Black Feminist Thought.* London: Routledge

Hill-Collins, P. (1994) Shifting the Centre: Race, Class and Feminist Theorizing about mothering in, E. Glenn, G. Chang and L. Forcey (Eds.) *Mothering: ideology, experience and agency.* London: Routledge

Hill-Collins, P. (1999) *Fighting Words: Black Women and the Search for Justice.* Minneapolis: Minneapolis press

Mac an Ghaill, M. (1996) *Understanding Masculinities: Social Relations and Cultural Arenas.* London: Open University Press

Madood, T. (1997) *Ethnic Minorities in Britain.* London: Policy Studies Institute

Malik. K. (1996) *The Meaning of Race.* London: Macmillan

Mirza, H. (1992) *Young, Female and Black.* London: Routledge

Reay. D. (1995) Dealing with Difficult Differences: Reflexivity and Social Class in Feminist Research, *Feminism and Psychology: Special Issue on Social Class*, 16: 3

Reynolds, T. (1999a) *Mothering: Reconstructing a 'New' Identity*, unpublished PhD, London: South Bank University

Reynolds, T. (1999b) Re-Defining Black Working Class Mothers, in S. Munt (Eds.) *Cultural Studies and the Working Class: A Reconsideration.* London: Cassell

Reynolds, T. (2000) Black Fathers in Family Lives in Britain, in H. Goulbourne, and M. Chamberlain (Eds.) *Caribbean Families in the Trans-Atlantic World*, London: Macmillan

Reynolds, T (2001) Black mothering: paid work and identity, *Journal of Ethnic and Racial Studies*, 24: 4, pp. 1046-1064

Reynolds, T (2003) Black to the community: Black community parenting in the UK, *Journal of Community, Work and Family*, 6:1, pp. 29-41

Runnymede Trust (1996) *This is Where I Live: Stories and Pressures in Brixton*, London: Runnymede Trust

Senior, O. (1991) *Working Miracles: Women's Lives in the English Speaking Caribbean.* London: James Currey Publishing

Sewell, T. (1997) *Black Masculinities and Schooling: How Black Boys Survive Schooling.* London: Trentham Books.

Skellington, R. and Morris, P. (1992) *'Race' in Britain Today.* London: Sage

Solomos, J. (1993) *'Race' and Racism in Contemporary Britain.* London: Macmillan.

Sudarkasa, N. (1997) *The Strength of Our Mothers: African and African-American Women and Families.* New Jersey: Africa World Press

Williams, P. (1997) *Seeing a Colour Blind Future - the paradox of race - the 1997 Reith Lectures.* London: Virago.

Wright, C. (1988) The Relations between Teachers and Afro-Caribbeans Pupils, in G. Weiner and A. Arnot (Eds.) *Gender under Scrutiny.* London: Open University Press.

Part II

Education and Black Success

Chapter 5

The Influence of Home, School and Community on African-Caribbean Academic Success in the United Kingdom

Susan Hallam and Jasmine Rhamie

Background

The under achievement of children in the United Kingdom has been well documented over the years. Children, in particular boys, have been over-represented in the figures for exclusions from school, poor examination results, Emotional and Behavioural Difficulties (EBD) and receiving statements of Special Educational Need (Fuller, 1980; Taylor, 1981; Mirza, 1992). The situation has changed little in recent years.

Since the 1960s, African-Caribbean children have been labelled and identified as under-achievers (see Taylor, 1981; Tomlinson, 1983b). Research in the 1980's and 1990's reflected earlier findings with pupils continuing to make less progress on average than other pupils (Maughan et al, 1985; Mortimore et al., 1988; Drew and Gray, 1991; Plewis and Veltman, 1994; Gillborn and Gipps, 1996; Ofsted, 1999; Strand, 1999). Recent figures show some improvement from 18 per cent of African-Caribbeans attaining 5 General Certificates of Secondary Education (GCSE) at Grades A*-C in 1989 to 37 per cent in 2000 (DfEE, 2000b). While this is encouraging it has to be viewed within the context of the overall improvement in performance in GCSE Grades A*-C from 30 per cent to per cent. The relative level of under-achievement of African-Caribbeans in comparison with other groups remains (DfEE, 2000b; Fitzgerald et al. 2000; Pathak, 2000).

The data describing the performance of different ethnic minorities are inevitably confounded with other factors that are known to have an impact on achievement in school, for instance, parental education and socio-economic status. In addition, there are important gender differences. At secondary school, boys seem to be at greater risk of under-achievement than girls because of a combination of irregular attendance (Fitzgerald et al., 2000), low teacher expectations, potential conflict with teachers (Gillborn and Gipps, 1996; Wrench and Hassan, 1996) and the high probability of being excluded. Less than 25 per cent of black boys acquire 5 GCSEs at Grade A*-C. They are likely to have GCSEs at grades lower than C or no GCSEs (Pathak, 2000). In contrast, African-Caribbean girls do well at school relative to their male and female working class peers, as measured in terms of average exam performance at GCSE level (Drew et al, 1992; Mirza, 1992), although they may take longer to achieve their long-term educational aspirations. Approximately 60 per cent of Black African males and African-Caribbean females start their degrees when they are aged over 25 (UCAS, 1999). At university, ethnic minority students are less likely (37 per cent) than white graduates (53 per cent) to obtain an upper second or first class honours degree (Pathak, 2000) and they are more likely to be unemployed following completion of their degree (Elias et al., 1999). Racism is clearly implicated here and verified through the studies mentioned above.

African-Caribbean children are over-represented in the figures for exclusion from school. In 1998/9 the overall permanent percentage exclusion rate from school in the UK was 0.17 per cent while the exclusion rates for Black-Caribbean, Black African and Black Other pupils were 0.59 per cent, 0.20 per cent and 0.49 per cent respectively. These proportions represent some improvement from 1995/6 when they were 0.92 per cent, 0.35 per cent and 0.53 per cent respectively. Other minority groups have much lower rates: Indian, 0.04 per cent; Pakistani, 0.01 per cent; and Bangladeshi, 0.07 per cent (DfEE, 2000a). The highest rates of exclusion in 1999/2000 were amongst black pupils of Caribbean heritage, with 46 in every ten thousand pupils of compulsory school age in this ethnic group being excluded. The pupils most highly at risk of exclusion continue to be boys (83 per cent in 2000/2001), those aged between 13-15 (61 per cent) and those of Black Caribbean or Black Other origins with rates of 38 and 40 in 10,000 respectively (DfES, 2002). Despite the Department for Education and Skills encouraging Local Education Authorities (LEAs) and schools to work together to tackle the problem, the relatively high proportion of exclusions continues.

Research focusing on the reasons for exclusion suggests that there may be differences between those leading to the exclusion of white and Black Caribbean and Black Other students. For instance, in Parson et al's (2001) study, following up pupils excluded from primary school, 22 per cent of the pupils excluded were black, over half of these of African-Caribbean origin. The white children were more likely to be eligible for free school meals and statements of special educational needs, to be in public care, have attendance problems and a record of offending. The children who were excluded from black families did not have these social background problems. Osler et al. (2001) reported that some teachers and head teachers believed that there was sometimes differential treatment between ethnic groups, with some white teachers liable to misinterpret the behaviour of certain black pupils. Ofsted (1996) reported that white pupils were more likely to have been traumatised, be of below average achievement and to be excluded for verbal abuse. Black excluded pupils were more often of above average achievement and more commonly challenged teachers' judgements. Given the high proportion of exclusions of black pupils, there is very little research exploring these issues in depth (Gillborn and Gipps, 1996; Kinder et al., 1999; Owen et al., 2000).

While African-Caribbean students' experiences of school vary there is evidence of racist attitudes, low expectations, inappropriate allocation of pupils to ability groups and lack of opportunity to enter high status examinations (Fitzgerald et al., 2000; Rhamie and Hallam, 2002). This is supported by research on selection and ability grouping (Commission for Racial equality, 1992; Troyna & Siraj-Blatchford, 1993; Gillborn and Youdell, 2000; Hallam, 2002). Research exploring successful multi-ethnic schools (Blair et al., 1998) found that schools that facilitated success for minority ethnic groups:

- had head teachers who valued and gave strong and determined leadership on issues of equal opportunities;

- listened to and learnt from students and their parents;

- tried to see things from the students' perspective;

- tried to understand and work with the whole child;

- had clear procedures for responding to racist bullying and harassment;

- worked on strategies for preventing exclusion;

- monitored individual progress;

monitored progress by ethnicity identifying unexpected shortcomings in provision and targeting areas for concern, e.g. setting procedures.

While schools clearly can make a difference, Fitzgerald et al. (2000) showed that 85 per cent of young black males believed that they could have done better at school, citing peer pressure and lack of personal motivation as the main reasons for not working. Most held relatively positive attitudes towards secondary school and felt that a good education would make it easier to get a job.

African-Caribbean success

There has been relatively little research attempting to establish what might promote success in African-Caribbeans in the UK. This is, in part, because some authors and researchers have argued that such a focus might reduce the pressure to tackle failure (Osler, 1997). However, research which consistently focuses only on negative educational outcomes provides an unbalanced perspective of the African-Caribbean community as a whole and reinforces negative stereotypes which, in themselves, contribute to the problem. Further, research drawing attention to under-achievement and the high level of exclusions has been limited in its impact and change continues to be slow. Recommendations made as a result of the research have not resulted in the necessary change in attitudes and practice in schools to bring about an increase in standards. As a result of this, some researchers have turned their attention to African-Caribbean success. For example, MacDonald (2001) provides life histories of 72 black men and women who have been successful in the UK. She argues that this collection provides positive role models for young people and dispels the picture of a black disaffected community involved in crime and unskilled work with success limited to sport.

Early research considering the factors which supported success found that parental encouragement and support, sympathetic teachers with high expectations and the support of the (Pentecostal) church were important (Bagley et al. 1979; Tomlinson, 1983a). Similar findings are to be found in a later report (see Osler, 1997).

Channer (1995), using a life history approach, detailed the experiences of 12 individuals who had been successful in gaining a first degree. The research suggested that associations with the black church provided some but not all black Christians with a 'buffer against racism' (p. 190) but association with the church did not in itself guarantee academic success. Other factors were clearly implicated. The aim of this study therefore was to explore the factors that contributed to the academic success of African–Caribbeans who had continued their education to post graduate level with a view to making positive suggestions about how to promote such academic success in others.

The research

Fourteen professionals were interviewed. With the exception of one health visitor with a professional qualification, all were pursuing or had completed post graduate studies. They ranged in age from 23 - 40 years old. Half were male and all were of Caribbean origin with the exception of one whose parents were Nigerian. The interviews explored their perceptions of their educational experiences. The interviews allowed free expression of their thoughts and feelings regarding their educational success, exploring issues relating to academic qualifications, school experiences, home influences, out of school activities, personal and other miscellaneous factors. The interview data were analysed using a process outlined by Cooper and McIntyre (1993). Four broad categories emerged from the analysis with a number of sub categories and themes. These are set out in the Appendix: Figure 1. The percentage of responses made in each sub-category and in relation to each theme was recorded to provide an indication of the extent to which each applied to across the sample. Home and Individual factors were expressed as having a role to play in contributing to the success of all of the participants. School (86 per cent) and Community (64 per cent) factors were cited by some participants.

Factors contributing to success

Home Factors

All the respondents reported the importance of home influences on their success. Three sub-categories emerged: Parents; the Environment; and Family as Role Models and Mentors (See the Appendix: Table 1). The categories were not entirely independent.

Parental Factors. Parental influence on educational attainment has been demonstrated as important in African-Caribbean success in earlier research (Tomlinson, 1983a; Gillborn and Gipps, 1996). This research identified more specific aspects of parental behaviour which contributed to high levels of achievement. These included Support and Encouragement, Guidance, Goals and Expectations and Knowledge.

All participants reported receiving parental support and encouragement:

> Parents were always encouraging and always supportive... It was just we heard a lot of....you need to be successful, you can be successful that was the philosophy (Lecturer/Teacher, 34 years).

Some parents tutored their children at home and monitored school work.

> When my father was around we had to do homework. He had his own curriculum. We'd come home do his and do the school one as well (Solicitor/School governor, 39 years).

In all cases parents stressed the importance of education. While, the extent of active support varied, even less well-educated parents did what they could to encourage excellence and hard work, driving and motivating their children:

> ... They made me sort of believe that education was important. It wasn't something I could just mess around with because I would regret it in years to come (LLM student, 23 years).

> ... They always pushed me to do better..... I came home with a Maths result, I think I had 99 per cent and my Mum asked me what happened to the 1 per cent. They always wanted me to do better throughout school. There was verbal encouragement. If I finished my homework they would say go back and get more (PhD student, 24 years).

All the respondents were immersed in a value system that sought to encourage, motivate and direct them towards making the most of education.

Parental influence was exerted through guidance, goal setting and high occupational expectations, e.g. lawyer, doctor. Parental determination for their children to do well was a theme that was echoed in many responses:

> I don't particularly think that my teachers were particularly supportive but because I had parents ... I was always sort of guided along the right path from the year nought. You know, my father, my mum would sort of guide me by telling me roughly what would

> be the best educational path to take (Clinical Research Scientist, 26 years).

> My mother decided because she didn't get opportunities when she was young we were going to. So she decided immediately that we were going to do music. She always wanted us to play the piano... so that's the instrument she chose for us and we took to it? (Lecturer/ Teacher, 34 years).

Parents tried to understand the British education system and what they needed to do to best support their child's progress through it taking account of their personality, abilities, strengths and weaknesses:

> My mother's a teacher at *** University and she tracked my progress and said that it seems that you're weak in Economics, ...so she got me a private tutor for Economics (Lecturer/ Counsellor, 40 years).

One respondent related the experience of her parents having to decide which of two secondary schools to send her - selective or non-selective:

> They had to sum up what sort of individual I was in terms of what I could cope with - always playing catch up or whether or not I needed to feel King Pin. I think my parents quite rightly decided that I needed to be at the top. That I could sustain that rather than feeling I was floundering at the bottom (Educational Psychologist, 31 years).

Other parents were aware of the difficulties inherent in the educational system for black children and attempted to overcome them. For example, some were reluctant to allow their children to become involved in extra-curricula sports activities because of the way that they perceived the system, as tending to steer African-Caribbean children into non academic areas:

> I think my dad, particularly, was kind of clued in on, you know, the way in which the educational system sort of funnels black kids or pigeon holes black kids at an early age. And also he was determined that I would not fit in. He was very good like that (Clinical research scientist, 26 years).

While most parents trusted the education system they were committed to playing their part in negotiating their way through it to help their children.

Environment. An environment encompassing a sense of belonging, and a loving, supportive, stable and secure home was cited by almost all respondents (93 per cent) as being crucial to their success:

> Even though I went to live in Jamaica with my grandmother as a child I still had a fairly secure childhood in terms of feeling that somebody loved and appreciated me (Doctor, 30 years).

The term 'general upbringing' was used by a number of respondents to summarise everything about the home and parents, their philosophy and the way they were brought up. Four respondents could be considered to have had an advantaged, and in some ways, privileged upbringing. The schools they attended, the area they lived in and in the whole family lifestyle were essentially middle class:

The influence of home

> We were very fortunate. We were that very new middle class in a way because my parents had professional occupations. We had our own home. We were living in a very nice area. We had the luxury to be able to go on holiday and when you've got those factors it does contribute to how you see your life (Lecturer/ Advisory Teacher, PhD student, 40 years).

> I think with sort of black churchy middle class kind of families there is this thing to push your kids towards the profession that kind of thing. A career in computers is honourable so is law, medicine and that sort of stuff. But that's the background that I was coming from (Clinical Research Scientist, 26 years).

Often the parents were not employed in professional occupations neither were they financially able to send their children to fee paying schools but they saw education as a way of helping their children to rise to something better. In referring to her parents, one respondent said:

> they hadn't had formal education and they used to say to us: 'We hadn't any schooling but you are having schooling so you should be able to do quite well' (Teacher/ MA student, 26 years).

Parents also provided resources, including books and encyclopaedias, other learning materials and finances to pay for private tuition and educational and culturally enriching trips. Parental occupation itself did not emerge as important. However, 'general upbringing' was referred to as encompassing parental philosophy and child rearing practices.

Family as Role Models and Mentors. Relatives were important as role models and mentors:

> I used that as a great encouragement to think that if they [parents] didn't have schooling and they could do so well then I've got this opportunity that I could... And also my parents used to tell us about their siblings who had gone off to different universities and your uncle's a doctor and your aunt's a doctor... And they used to come to visit us and we had that challenge to know that we had relatives who were quite academic and we should do the same (Teacher/ MA student, 26 years).

For some the modelling process was direct with parents themselves involved in studying:

> I saw my parents working full time and I also saw them studying full time as well. So seeing that in your own environment, I think that can act as very strong motivating factors. I saw them working and I saw them studying. Both at the same time and I saw my Mum raise a family as well, as well as doing all the housework and stuff (Health Visitor, 38 years).

Having academically successful family members served to inspire some respondents, spurring them on to success by making them aware of what was possible.

Individual Factors

The second largest category to emerge from the data comprised themes relating to the characteristics of the individual. These were classified into five sub categories: Motivation; Confidence; Awareness; Talent; and Deportment and Behaviour (see the Appendix: Table 2). Table 2 also sets out the percentage of responses in each category.

Motivation. As illustrated in Table 2, self-motivation was reported as important by almost all respondents (93 per cent). Some were extrinsically motivated, having clear external goals; others were intrinsically motivated and enjoyed studying for its own sake. Self-discipline, a desire to do well, strength and determination were recurring themes. Some of the respondents attributed their self-motivation to internalising the demands of their parents:

> By the time I got to my O levels, up until that point, it was my parents that motivated me ... because you couldn't come home from school and play out... You came home from school you changed your clothes and you did your homework and when you finished you watched a bit of television. We've grown up with that... So by the time I had finished my GCE's I didn't need to be pushed I knew what I had to do (Lecturer/Advisory teacher, PhD applicant, 40 years).

> I think my own motivation has developed from an extension of my parents, because I think when I became a teenager I used to hear my mum's little voice: 'You should be studying' and then I began to take that on as a sort of self-corrective mould for myself (Teacher MA student. 26 years).

The desire to do well and having high expectations were also viewed as being internalised through experiences at home:

> If they (the parents) are pushing you to be the best you can and do the best you can then you're not satisfied... there is the sort of person who says go on how can I do more, how can I advance. You're never satisfied. I think that's what I got from them (PhD student, 24 years).

Goal orientation emerged as a theme from more than half the respondents (71 per cent). Comments referring to the hope that there will be rewards at the end and to the single mindedness that enabled the goals to be realised.

> I saw people around me messing around. I knew that I didn't want to be a part of that crowd. I knew that it meant being odd to certain people. But I was prepared to live that oddness to get what I wanted (Educational Psychologist, 31years).

> It was never a major hassle for me to go and sit exams and stuff like that. I wanted to be a doctor I liked studying and I got on with it (Doctor, 30 years).

Confidence. The respondents had confidence and determination that they could succeed:

> I'm working extremely hard... and I consider every single day how I have to strive... It makes you stop and think before I actually put my head on the pillow, you can do it, you can reach it (Research Scholar, 32 years).

Some believed that this derived from internalising parental values, aspirations and beliefs about what was possible.

> My parents would say...you can do anything you want to do. It was having that belief that made you say, 'Yes, if I really put my heart into it, I can do it.' (Lecturer/Advisory Teacher, PhD applicant, 40 years)

Awareness of self and circumstances. Respondents reported that they could step outside themselves and see their circumstances taking account of the wider picture. They were able to recognise their own vulnerable position as African Caribbeans and the negative stereotyped perceptions that white society often had of them. They also recognised the importance of school and the education system and what was needed to successfully negotiate it:

> I was shrewd enough to do enough that I needed to pass an exam. For example, I would put in the effort needed to 'get by' (Solicitor / School Governor, 39 years).

Talent. Some indicated that they were perceived as being more able and that this affected the way they were treated in school:

> Because I was perceived as being bright the teachers didn't give me an attitude like they gave my other friends. They would be a lot more helpful. The teachers were very supportive of me. They thought I was different or exceptional compared to the others so they always gave me a lot more time. (Solicitor / School Governor, 39 years).

Deportment and behaviour. Two respondents commented on the importance of speech and behaviour which conformed to accepted school norms in helping to set them apart from other black children, breaking teacher's stereotypical perceptions. These individual characteristics, often developed through home influences, were clearly important in determining the opportunities which were made available within the educational context.

School Factors

Respondents' perceptions and assessments of their own schools reflected key determinants of effective schools cited by the Office for Standards in Education (OFSTED, 1995) (see the Appendix: Table 3). Table 3 also sets out the percentage responses in each category.

School Ethos and Type of School. Issues raised in relation to school ethos were often focused on the relative emphasis placed on academic success. This was sometimes attributed to the type of school attended, e.g. fee paying or selective, where there was perceived to be a stress on academic excellence with teachers concentrating on the academic progress of students.

> It's just the teaching is good. They encouraged all the girls into believing that they can achieve and do things... certainly at *** you have to excel in everything, even games (LLM Student, 23 years).

Although, high expectations are an acknowledged feature of effective schools (Mortimore et al., 1988; Tizard et al., 1988), two respondents described the low expectations they observed when starting school in the UK having arrived from the Caribbean. Such comments have been echoed in other studies (Channer, 1995; Osler, 1997).

> I remember the first day I went to school (in the United Kingdom) ... It was totally unbelievable and there were kids in the secondary school who just about knew their tables, stuff that we learnt in the Caribbean when we were 6 and 7. It took me a while to adjust downwards because I was very much up there in the Caribbean and in the end I had to level down in terms of what I learnt. I slowed down in my learning (Solicitor / School Governor, 39 years).

Teachers. The sub category Teachers included the themes of high expectations, support and encouragement, and teachers' skills. Most respondents had some supportive and encouraging teachers.

> My teachers, they had the belief that you can do well, not all of them, but one or two (PhD student, 24 years).

> I had a music teacher who was brilliant. He took me as his own and I guess I was his glimmer of hope and of course the PE teachers were all right. But in regular classes where I was pretty good like Chemistry and Biology the teachers were rather blasé (Minister of Religion, 36 years).

One respondent who wanted to be a teacher described problems getting her Mathematics O level which at that time was necessary for teacher training. She described:

> I remember saying to him 'the Maths is too hard, I'll be a nursery nurse instead. He looked at me and said 'What! No way, you keep on with the Maths. You've got the ability to make a really good teacher. You will get the Maths before you leave.' And that just motivated me so much. I always remember him for that. (MA Student. 36 years).

The descriptions of teachers referred to as 'good', 'excellent' or 'brilliant' were tempered by descriptions of others who were perceived as uncaring, unsupportive, hindering examination and career aspirations and in some cases being racist:

> I wanted to do O level in History ... and she absolutely refused. She would not allow me to do the O level ... I wanted to do both because you could do both in those days. She was a teacher that I never liked and I knew that it was simply because I was black that she didn't think that I would be able to do it. And that was one thing that I picked up on. As it happens I got a grade 3 but I went to sixth form and did the O level later in November the same year and passed with a grade B. I felt that I had proved her wrong (MA student, 36 years).

> In some cases, in state schools, parents paid entry fees for external public examinations when teachers refused to enter their children. Where parents were paying school fees or the pupils attended

selective schools such hindrances to academic progress were not in evidence and teachers were overwhelmingly described as supportive.

School Organisation. School organisation had two main themes, ability grouping through banding, streaming or setting and extra curricular activities. The organisation of the school in terms of placement of students in ability groups emerged as an important factor. Some respondents described being moved to higher groups after initial inappropriate allocation.

> They had me in the C class at school and I kept coming first, second or third in all of my classes and they moved me up and I was often hanging in there with the best of them. I even got much higher overall grades than some of those in the A class (Health Visitor, 38 years).

> When I came they kind of assessed you and put you in a class that was appropriate to your level and they put me in the middle of the year and by the end of the year I had jumped through three classes and got a little pen. It was a kind of a 1A 1B 1C 1D and it wasn't streamed in the sense that you were in one class for everything rather different classes for different subjects (Doctor, 30 years).

African-Caribbean pupils are often placed in low attaining classes (Hallam, 2002). Some progress rapidly upwards through the system, others do not and experience a lack of academic challenge and stimulation.

Most respondents were involved in extra curricular sporting activities, although parents sometimes limited engagement with sport emphasising academic work.

> I did enjoy music. And I did enjoy drama. I was always in the school productions. We put on lots of musicals. We had a very strong music department. So I was always involved in music. I did do a bit of sports but I stopped as soon as I started my O levels, because my parents … said they did not send me to school to be an athlete. So it was fine to do it as part of a sports day or whatever but nothing to take up that seriously…. (Lecturer / Advisory Teacher / PhD applicant, 40 years).

Other common activities included music and chess. Participation in subject oriented clubs was enjoyed to a lesser degree.

Community Factors

Community factors were less frequently raised in the interviews. They included Church and Related Activities; Music Tuition and Activities; Community Projects and Cultural Activities; and access to Role Models and Mentors. A breakdown is provided in the Appendix: Table 4.

Church activities. The church sub category represented the respondents' participation in church-organised clubs such as, the Boys Brigade, Cubs and Scouts, Brownies and Girl Guides and Pathfinders (a mixed boy's and girl's club). Religious belief emerged as a theme as well as active regular involvement in church programmes. Nine (64 per cent) of the respondents had some Christian church involvement while growing up. Six were actively involved in church programmes, for three (21 per cent) involvement was restricted to the Boys Brigade or the Brownies. These activities provided opportunities to develop self-confidence and self-knowledge in and of their abilities - for instance, through arranging youth services in the church, reciting Bible texts or poetry before the congregation or performing musically.

> I've been fortunate in that I think my own sort of charisma and confidence that I've had through doing things in church that kind of thing has inspired me to go on and do something (Clinical Research Scientist, 26 years).

Religious involvement included concepts such as the Christian work ethic. At least one respondent attributed success to this:

> We were brought up as Seventh Day Adventists and the principles behind Christianity which ... is the work ethic: do well, don't cause trouble, you know this kind of thing. You go to church, you behave yourself and sit still, you listen to what is being said. You discuss when its time to discuss, you read and study before you go to church. All these things help towards helping you succeed in your own life (Health Visitor, 38 years).

Other themes that emerged related to the engendering of self-belief and self-worth. A small number of respondents attributed their success to God's will, guidance and blessing, others to a strong supportive atmosphere in church, which also provided opportunities to experience success through working on projects and for awards; developing self-discipline and a work ethic and enabling the respondents to experience praise for their accomplishments:

> My church, it fostered a strong supportive atmosphere that encouraged me to go for the mark. It is amazing how the church fulfilled that. It did it in more ways than one (Minster of Religion, 36 years).

Music Tuition. Several participants reported receiving private music tuition, usually piano, often outside school which involved taking national graded music examinations. Two respondents regularly performed publicly in a brass band or at a music school. Active participation in music seemed to encourage self-discipline and also provided an environment where there was clear evidence of success.

Community Projects and Cultural Activities. Participation in sports, youth clubs, visits to the Caribbean and visits to local cultural sites such as, museums, libraries and art galleries were frequently mentioned. Just under half of the respondents had visited the Caribbean. This was beneficial as it provided positive role models of black people at all levels of society.

> It was great to see blacks who had achieved and each time you turned on the television there were black people on the television. It was brilliant. Yes, I loved it (Lecturer/Advisory teacher/ PhD applicant, 40 years).

> Black people having these wonderful big houses, even with pools. I remember that I thought it was great (Health visitor, 38 years).

In the UK, one of the participants became involved in setting up a youth club for African-Caribbeans because of older siblings who were playing leading roles in their development. His sense of achievement and ownership came with his involvement:

> I helped set up community projects like the *** youth club, running the community centre for kids and so on. Black kids at that time had nowhere to go to so it was a bit of an innovation to have somewhere for black people to come to and do different projects like the education project looking at history in schools and things like that (Solicitor/School Governor, 39 years).

Role Models and Mentors. Role models were to be found in the church, in older friends and, as reported above, during visits to the Caribbean.

> I think that going to the mainly Afro-Caribbean church we had a lot of fairly well qualified people like a lot of nurses, teachers, skilled people there. I think it was good to see black people with jobs. Owning their own homes and driving their own cars. That was always there in the background. I think that was probably helpful (Health Visitor, 38 years).

> We had a chap who was a friend of the family. He was struggling to do O and A levels (national academic examinations) although he was quite a few years older than us. He was very encouraging and tried to give us focus as children (Minster of Religion, 36 year).

Role models within the community created a sense of confidence in, and awareness of respondents' own abilities. They fuelled an awareness of the possibilities for success and played their part in spawning aspirations.

The evidence presented above suggests that a range of interacting factors contributed to the academic success of the participant African-Caribbeans. Examination of each individual case suggested two possible models of success: a Home-School based model and a Home-Community based model.

The Home School Based Model

The Home-School Based Model of Success (see the Appendix: Figure 2) shows the home, child and school grouped together as one. The school, effective with high academic expectations, is closely linked to the home and the child. There is a common purpose, shared language, culture and values. All pursue the same goal, that of academic success. Involvement in the community is important and is engaged in to provide a wider range of experiences, but it is not central to success. A sense of purpose and achievement is fostered in the school and home and internalised by the child. The child, having the major influences of their life in harmony and united in purpose, is able to succeed academically. The experiences of four of the respondents seem to be described by this model.

The Home Community Based Model

Figure 3 (in the Appendix) outlines the Home Community Based Model of Success. Here the community and home together provide the child with a 'sense of belonging', security and acceptance while emphasising the importance of achievement and success. The community is pivotal in providing the child with opportunities where he or she can experience success. The school is not a part of this circle. Its influence is separate and directly focused on the child. The child's experiences at school vary depending on the support and encouragement or lack of it of individual teachers who may respond to particular characteristics in the child. In this model, the school despite having low expectations, does not deter the child from success as s/he has experienced it outside school. The child takes from the school what s/he needs to achieve the goals which have been formulated by influences outside school. In this model, the parents and representatives of the community who have been influential in the child's life, share the wider society's perspective of what constitutes success. The experiences of the majority of respondents fit within this model. The success of these children within the school system appears to be due to their experiences of learning outside of school. Such activities as preparing and studying to gain badges in church organised clubs, preparing presentations for church services, planning and following through a community project from start to finish and the discipline and practice necessary for competence as a musician, appear to help develop skills that are useful in school. Alongside these learning experiences comes the confidence and self-worth that engenders self-efficacy in relation to other tasks. The rewards and positive feedback received serve to ignite a desire to continue in the same vein. The successes experienced in the supportive and caring environment of home and community (and sometimes church) provide evidence of what is possible and promote motivation to persevere at school.

Issues arising from the research

In response to the findings of the research, two models are presented that might act as starting points for exploring the way that home, individual, school and community factors interact in different ways to contribute to academic success in African-Caribbean children. However, the small number of participants means that the results and conclusions drawn must be treated with caution. No claims are made that the models can account for the achievement of all academically successful African-Caribbeans. Indeed there may be those who have shared similar experiences to those of the participants but who have been unsuccessful academically.

The Home School Model outlined in Figure 2 suggests that where African-Caribbean children attend schools where expectations of academic success are high for all pupils they respond to this ethos and succeed academically. However, most African-Caribbean pupils attend inner city state schools (Pathak, 2000) where there has been a tendency for academic expectations to be low and resources to be inadequate. The model outlined in Figure 3 presents a scenario where African-Caribbean children are enabled to succeed despite low expectations in school and mixed responses to them by teachers. Supportive, achievement oriented community activities may, in conjunction with a supportive, education focused home and motivated child, work together to provide a strong network that enables the child to succeed in school and remain focused on the goal of achieving despite the obstacles. This model is particularly important because African-Caribbeans often live in inner city areas characterised by poverty and high unemployment and we know that socio-economic status is one of the most powerful predictors of educational success. Children from lower income families face exceptional obstacles en route to success irrespective of their ethnicity and the values of their parents (Roberts, 1980). The evidence presented here suggests that local communities can provide a 'sense of belonging' and opportunities to be successful which can demonstrate to young African-Caribbeans that it is possible for them to succeed in spite of the obstacles.

In the examples cited, support was provided by church and youth clubs. However, many black communities have set up supplementary schools which may in the future be instrumental in supporting academic attainment in young black people. While these are often portrayed as being a response to mainstream educational exclusion and poor practice in some schools, they are also places where blackness is the norm - places where African-Caribbeans can develop the sense of belonging which seems to be important in achieving educational success (Mirza, 1997; Reay and Mirza, 1997).

Other opportunities for enhanced self-esteem through the demonstration of achievement and receiving praise for it were in evidence in relation to music tuition. Involvement with music may also have encouraged self-discipline and inculcated habits of independent study. In contrast, sport, which might have been expected to play a similar role, was perceived by some parents as a distraction from academic work. Given the outstanding success of many black athletes this is interesting and worthy of further exploration.

Successful academic role models were perceived as being of great importance. These included family members, friends of the family, members of the church attended, or those observed in visits to the Caribbean. Such successful role models are not available in the immediate environment of many African-Caribbeans.

Overall, in the UK, there are relatively few examples of African-Caribbeans whose success has derived from high levels of education. This is reflected in education itself where there is a lack of ethnic minority teachers, head teachers (TTA, 1999), governors and chairs of governors (Scanlon et al., 1999) and in higher education where there are few lecturers and almost no personnel in senior positions from ethnic minorities (HESA, 2000). In schools, a number of projects have been set up where young African-Caribbeans are supported by an older successful mentor (Kane, 1994). While there is anecdotal evidence of the success of these projects, there is no hard data (Pathak, 2000). There is a clear need for high status African-Caribbean academic role models. This is an issue that requires the attention of the academic, educational and race relation communities.

The development of the home community model of success does not lay the burden of responsibility for academic achievement solely at the door of the home and community but makes an expressly critical indictment of some schools and the role of some of the teachers within them. That racism has been a feature in the interpretations of specific events in the school experiences of some respondents necessitates a re evaluation of the role played by schools in the under achievement of pupils. Due to racism, black people, no matter how motivated, are often denied the opportunity of an adequate level of education (Mirza, 1992; Gillborn, 1995). The findings underscore the need for effective schools, with high expectations, to become the norm rather than the exception. While educational performance overall has improved in recent years in the UK, academic achievement in the African-Caribbean community in comparison with other groups has not. To address this, schools need to examine their policies and practices, and ensure that they hold high expectations for *all* of their pupils irrespective of ethnicity.

While gender differences were not the key focus of the research, the sample itself, which included equal numbers of male and female participants provided evidence that males can achieve high levels of academic success within the UK education system providing that the conditions are appropriate. Generally, however, African-Caribbean males are over-represented in figures for exclusion from school and their under-achievement is more marked than that of their female counterparts. African-Caribbean girls are more successful educationally. This seems to derive from their active striving to be included within UK society, accessing available educational resources and through these creating opportunities for upward mobility. This contrasts with the male perspective which Mirza (1997) suggests assumes that racial equality can only be achieved through confrontation, mobilising in protest, riots, local politics and community organisations. She suggests that within the male African-Caribbean community, there is a perception that academic success is a form of collusion. The evidence reported here did not indicate gender as a differentiating factor. The factors mediating success were common for male and female participants. All demonstrated considerable determination to succeed. Male participants, although it was not explicitly stated, had rejected the notion that educational success was negatively associated with 'conforming' or 'colluding' with the mainstream and perceived it as desirable. This being so, raising the achievement of African-Caribbean boys may require interventions aimed at engendering and sustaining positive attitudes towards academic success and making their educational experiences more positive. While the evidence suggests that they have a positive attitude toward education in general (Fitzgerald et al., 2000) their reported negative experiences of school, particularly with some teachers, combined with strong peer pressure tends to lead to resistance and ultimately exclusion. Educational opportunities are then further damaged and negative attitudes towards society's values reinforced (Pathak, 2000). Addressing this will require schools to demonstrate that they are actively tackling racism, monitoring the progress of ethnic minorities (OFSTED, 1999) and enriching the curriculum so that it caters for and includes all pupils (Blair et al., 1998). There also needs to be a genuine demonstration that the educational achievement of African-Caribbeans will be rewarded in the employment market (Owen et al., 2000); that racial discrimination will cease; and that the UK is a truly multicultural society where equality of opportunity is a reality. This level of change will take time.

The research reported here constitutes one starting point for the continuing analysis of what can contribute towards promoting the academic success of African–Caribbean children. While acknowledging the need for schools and the wider education system to rid themselves of prejudice and racism, it also acknowledges that there is much that parents and those in the African-Caribbean community can do to support young people and celebrate their success. There is also a role for the research community in developing understanding of those factors are of paramount importance in promoting the academic achievement of young African-Caribbeans, providing evidence which can guide productive ways forward.

Notes:

1. Editor's note: This chapter is a much expanded version of an earlier paper entitled An Investigation into African-Caribbean Academic Success in the UK, *Race, Ethnicity and Education*, 2000, 5: 2, pp. 151- 70.

References

Bagley, C., Bart, M. & Wong, J. (1979) 'Antecedents of scholastic success in West Indian 10 year olds in London'. In G. Verma and C. Bagley (Eds.) *Race, Education and Identity*. London: Macmillan

Blair, M. & Bourne, J with Coffin, C., Creese, A. & Kenner, C. (1998) *Making the difference: Teaching and Learning strategies in successful multi-ethnic schools, DfEE Research Report No 59*. London: DfEE

Channer, Y. (1995) *I Am a Promise: The School Achievement of British African-Caribbeans*. Stoke On Trent: Trentham Books

Cooper, P., & Mcintyre, D. (1993) Commonality in teacher's and pupil's perceptions of effective classroom learning, *British Journal of Educational Psychology*. 63, pp. 381-399.

Department for Education and Employment (2000a) *Statistics of Education: Permanent Exclusions from maintained schools in England, Issue No 10/00*. London: DfEE

Department for Education and Employment (2000b) *Youth Cohort Study: The activities and experiences of 16 year olds: England and Wales*. London: DfEE

Drew, D. & Gray, J. (1991) 'The black white gap in examination results: a statistical critique of a decade's research', *New Community*. 17, pp. 159 172.

Drew, D, Gray, J. and Sime, N. (1992) *Against the odds: The education and Labour market experiences of young black people, Employment Department, Youth Cohort Series Report, No 19, June.* London: HMSO.

Elias, P., Mcknight, A., Pitcher, J., Simm, C & Purcell, K. (1999) *Moving on: graduate careers three years after graduation.* Manchester: Higher Education Careers Service Unit/ DfEE

Fitzgerald, R. & Finch, S. (2000) *Black Caribbean Young Men's Experiences of Education and Employment, Research Report 186.* London: DfEE

Fuller, M. (1980) 'Black Girls in a London Comprehensive'. In M. Hammersley & P. Woods (eds.) *Life in School: The Sociology of Pupil Culture.* Milton Keynes: Open University Press

Gillborn, D. (1995) *Race and Anti-racism in Real Schools.* Buckingham, Open University Press

Gillborn, D & Gipps, C. (1996) *Recent research on the achievements of ethnic minority pupils.* London, HMSO

Hallam, S. (2002) *Ability Grouping in Schools: a Literature Review.* University of London: Institute of Education

Higher Education Statistics Agency (HESA) (2000) *Resources of Higher Education Institutions 1998/99.* Cheltenham: HESA

Kane, L. (1994) Mentoring for black students: improving equality of opportunity, *Education and Training.* 36, pp. 18 24.

Maughan, B., Dunn, G., & Rutter, M. (1985) Black pupils' progress in secondary schools: Reading attainment between 10 and 14. *British Journal of Developmental Psychology*, 3: 2, pp. 113-121

Mirza, H. (1992) *Young, Female and Black.* London: Routledge

Mirza, H, S. (1997) Black women in education, in H.S. Mirza, (Ed) *Black British Feminism.* London: Routledge

Modood, T. & Shiner, M. (1994) *Ethnic Minorities and Higher Education: Why are there differential rates of entry?* London: PSI Publishing

Mortimore, P., Sammons, P., Stoll, L., Lewis, D. & Ecob, R. (1988) School Matters: The Junior Years. Wells: Somerset: Open Books

Office For Standards in Education (1995) *Characteristics of Effective Schools.* London: HMSO

Office For Standards in Education (1999) *Raising the Attainment of Minority Ethnic Pupils.* London: HMSO

Osler, A. (1997) *The Education and Careers of Black Teachers.* Buckingham: Open University Press

Owen, D., Green, A., Pitcher, J. & Maguire, M. (2000) Minority ethnic participation and achievements in education, training and employment, Research Report 225. London: DfEE

Parsons, C (1996) Permanent exclusions from school in England, trends, causes and responses, *Children and Society*, 10, pp. 177-186.

Pathak, S. (2000). *Race Research for the Future: Ethnicity in Education, Training and the Labour Market.* London: DfEE

Plewis, I, & Veltman, M. (1994) *Where Does All the Time Go? Changes in Infant Pupils' Experiences Since the Education Reform Act.* London: University of London, Institute of Education

Reay, D. & Mirza, H. S. (1997) Uncovering genealogies of the margin: Black supplementary schooling, *British Journal of Sociology of Education,* 18: 4, pp. 477-499.

Roberts, K. (1980) Schools, Parents and Social Class. In M. Craft, J. Raynor, & L. Cohen, (Eds.) *Linking School and Home.* London: Harper and Row Publisher.

Scanlon, M., Earley, P., & Evans, J. (1999*) Improving the Effectiveness of School Governing Bodies, Research report 111.* London: DfEE

Spinelli, E. (1989). *The Interpreted World: An Introduction to Phenomenological Psychology.* London, Sage

Strand, S. (1999) Ethnic group, sex and economic disadvantage: associations with pupils' educational progress from baseline to the end of Key Stage 1, *British Educational Research Journal,* 25:2, pp. 170-202.

Taylor, M. (1981) *Caught Between: a review of research into the education of pupils of West Indian origin.* Windsor: NFER Nelson

Teacher Training Agency (1999) *Initial teacher training performance profiles.* London: TTA

Tesch, R. (1990) *Qualitative Research.* New York: Falmer Press

Tizard, B., Blatchford, P., Burke, J., Farquhar, C. & Plewis, I. (1988*) Young Children at School in the Inner City.* London: Lawrence Erlbaum Associates

Tomlinson, S. (1983a) Black women in higher education: Case studies of university women in Britain. In L. Barton & S. Walker *Race, Class and Education.* London: Croom Helm

Tomlinson, S. (1983b*) Ethnic Minorities in British Schools: A Review of literature 1960-1982.* London: Heinemann Educational Books

University And Colleges Admissions Service (1999) *Statistical Summary 1998-9.* Cheltenham: UCAS

Wrench, J. & Hassan, E. (1996) *Ambition and marginalisation: A qualitative study of underachieving young men of Afro-Caribbean origin, DfEE Research Series No 31.* London: DfEE

Appendix

Figure 1. Success Factors

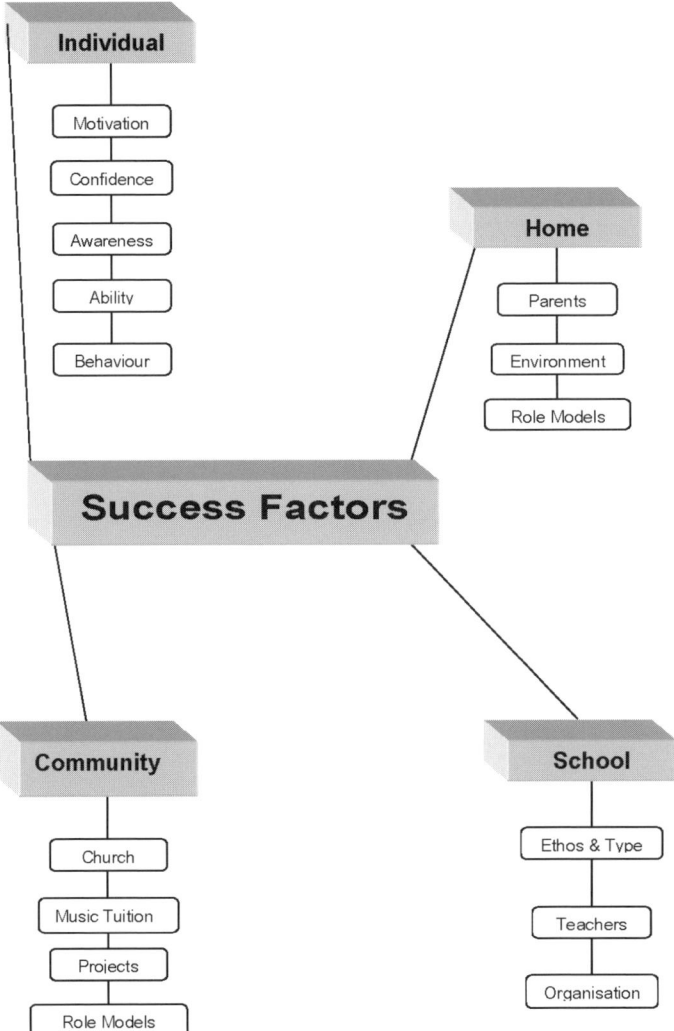

Appendix

Table 1: Home factors: sub-categories and themes

	% of Respondents referring to theme
Parents: Support and Encouragement	
- motivating and encouraging	100
- sacrificing time and interests to be involved in the education of the respondent	93
- emphasising the importance of education and schooling	86
- taught at home or tutors provided	71
- encouraging and monitoring school and homework	71
- supportive of respondent	71
- supportive of school	57
- pushing respondent to do better	21
- acting independently, not solely relying on teachers' assessments of respondents	14
Parents: Guidance, goals and expectations	
- high expectations	86
- guiding educational path with clear goals	43
- determination to see the respondent through education	21
Parents: Knowledge	
- knowledge and understanding of the education system	43
- knowledge and understanding of the respondent	21
Environment	
- providing resources, security and loving support	93
- general upbringing	36
- 'middle class' upbringing	29
- disciplined and strict environment	29
Family as Role Models and Mentors	
- parents as mentors and role models	43
- academic relatives and siblings	43
- relatives as mentors	7

Appendix

Table 2: Individual subcategories and themes

Individual Factors	% of Respondents referring to the theme
Motivation	
- self-motivated	93
- goal oriented and focused	71
- strength, determination and will power	50
- desire to do well and work hard	50
- enjoy studying	21
- self-discipline	7
Confidence	
- self-belief, confidence and faith in oneself	71
Awareness	
- aware of the education system and the importance of schooling	57
- feeling loved and appreciated	7
- awareness of black culture and stereotypes	21
Talent	
- natural ability	14
Deportment and behaviour	
- good speech and behaviour	14

Appendix

Table 3 School sub-categories and themes

	% of respondents referring to the theme
Ethos and type of school	
- Positive atmosphere	64
- Ethos: academic excellence	36
- Very good state school	21
- Fee paying or selective school	14
- Primary schooling in the Caribbean	14
Teachers	
- Supportive and encouraging	64
- Abilities	35
- Expectations	14
School organisation	
Banding and streaming	29
Extra-curricula activities:	
- Sports	71
- Music/drama	50
- Extra English and Maths	21
- Chess clubs	14

Appendix

Table 4 Community Themes

	% of respondents referring to the theme
Church	
- Regular, active involvement in programmes	43
- Religious beliefs	36
- Clubs	36
- Sense of belonging and support network	29
Music Tuition	
- Tuition	64
- Additional band or music involvement	14
Community projects and cultural activities	
- Positive experiences of the Caribbean	43
- Visits to libraries, museums, art galleries, etc.	14
- Sports	14
- Youth clubs	7
Role models and mentors	
- Within the church community	36
- Older friends	29
- From the Caribbean	21

Appendix

Figure 2 Home-School Based Model of Success

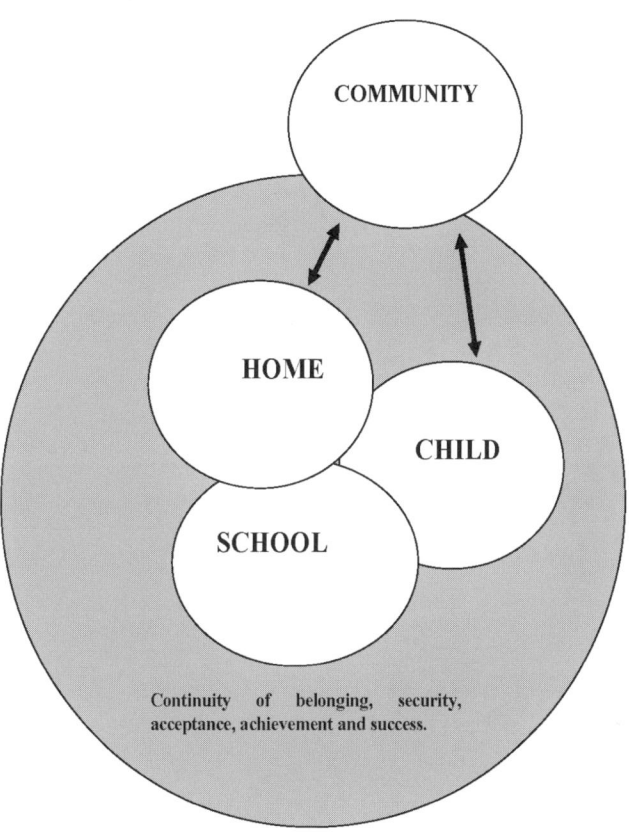

Appendix

Figure 3 Home-Community Based Model of Success

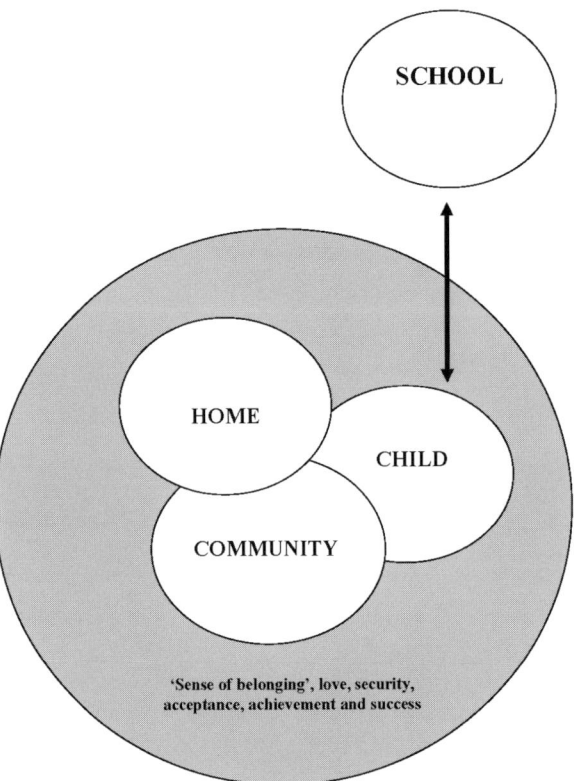

Chapter 6
Syble's successful children

Doreen McCalla

> There was an old lady who lived in a shoe
> She had so many children she didn't know what to do

Some of you may know the famous nursery rhyme from which this quotation is extracted. It describes the life of a radical, old lady. She was radical because first, she had hundreds of children and second, they all resided, not in a house, but in an enormous shoe. Of course, this nursery rhyme is fictitious but the story I am about to tell you is not. So let's begin! Once upon a time...

Preamble

This is the story of Syble's successful, African-Caribbean children. More will be said about Syble Morgan and her children[1] below. But for now, let me say that this story is about the apparent educational and employment success of some of the children who attended a Black[2], British, inner-city, community nursery that was established in 1976 by Syble Morgan - the first Head for eight years. It focuses on the influence that the nursery and Syble have had (and are having) on parents and workers. The success of the children (and their parents) is particularly poignant since they are Black and working-class and thus more susceptible to racial discrimination and social exclusion. How far have the nursery and Syble contributed to the success of the past children, now adults, parents and workers? What are the perception and experience of the nursery by present parents and workers? What impact is the nursery having on the lives of its present children? Is the success of its children indicative of their views, some acquired from Syble and other staff at the nursery, and experiences of citizenship and identity in the British setting? These questions are posed and discussed throughout this case-study.

The data comes from 'small-scale', empirical research conducted in the year 2000-2001. The fieldwork was undertaken over six months. A sample of participants relating to the nursery was derived from Syble's personal contacts and 'snowballing'. Fifteen in-depth individual and group interviews were conducted, fieldnotes collected of the setting and diary-entries made from testimonials/stories by academics and professionals at a nursery seminar held in November 2000. Group interviews comprised of between three and seven people. The sample is small-scale because insufficient fieldwork time prohibited, first, the searching out of participants and second, the contacting of others as some were many past pupils living far away from the nursery location both within and outside Britain (McCalla, Grover and Penn; 2001 McCalla, 2002c).

Before focusing on the success of Syble's children, I wish to first mention the role Syble played in the life of the children by asking, who is Syble? I will then show, in the second section, existing knowledge in nursery education and provision. Third, I shall consider the evidence of success discovered by this study and fourth, examine the nursery's contribution towards the children's success. Finally, the story concludes with recommendations arising from this research and a summary of the relevant arguments. Apart from references to ideas that relate to the children's success, the essay does not elaborate on the nursery's operation in detail; that is what it does and how it does it. This is discussed in McCalla, Grover and Penn (2001).

Who is Syble?

Like the old lady who lived in a shoe, there is an African-Caribbean Black woman called Syble Morgan, who immigrated to England from Jamaica in the 1960s. She was 'sick and tired' of being 'sick and tired' of Black educational underachievement, racial hostility in Britain generally (see Coard, 1971; Stone, 1981; Troyna and Stone, 1986; Wright, 1992; Gilborn and Gipps, 1996; Gillborn, 1997; Blair et al, 1998) and racial discrimination in state, early years provision in Handsworth, Birmingham. So as a result, with the support of members of Harambee - a Black organisation which owns the nursery, she started Marcus Garvey Nursery in the locality for African-Caribbean pre-school children (McCalla, Grover and Penn, 2001). Syble believed that not only were schools and early years' providers discriminating against Black children but were also failing to meet the children's and parents' cultural needs. Thus the Marcus Garvey Nursery aims to meet the cultural needs and values of African Caribbean children (their parents and its workers) while simultaneously providing for their social and educational requirements. See figure 1 .

Marcus Garvey Nursery thus sought and continues to seek to:
•focus on Black, African-Caribbean philosophy and awareness which is reflected in practice.
•meet the cultural and social needs of the children who attended. This was to be done through the nursery's day-to-day focus on Black culture and identity in all its pursuits, such as, Black play activities and the provision of African-Caribbean food. It was hoped that these early cultural inputs and a focus on positive discriminatory practices would better prepare Black children for later life by combating educational underachievement and social exclusion.
•provide full day care from 7.30am to 6.30pm for 40 children aged 2-4 and provide pre-school education that would include bilingualism.
•provide training and support for African-Caribbean parents, especially in parental skills.
•employ an all Black workforce from management to ancillary staff.
•provide a homely, culturally-sensitive environment in which the local community can socialise.

Figure 1: Ethos of Marcus Garvey Nursery

Syble hoped that this early cultural input and focus on positive discriminatory practices would better prepare Black children for later life through combating Black educational underachievement (Morgan, 1986, McCalla, 2002a; McCalla, Grover and Penn). Syble Morgan states that the original nursery was set up to be:

> ...accountable to us, Black people in the community, to determine our own needs and to set our own policies for meeting those needs. ... It is important to note here that although our management committee and our staff are Black, we have had White children at our nursery (Morgan, 1986 pp. 69-70).

Thus, Marcus Garvey Nursery specifically serves the needs of the African-Caribbean children and the local Black community unlike no other pre-school service in Handsworth (McCalla, Grover and Penn 2001). In this, it is similar to the Black supplementary schools in London (Reay and Mirza, 1997 - reprinted in this book) in which a 'Black only' space is provided and where Black women play key roles.

Syble's children comprise of three distinctive but connected groups: (1) the past and present children of Marcus Garvey; (2) the parents of these children and (3) the former and current workers of the nursery. These three groups span almost three generations of people involved in the nursery. They are Syble's children because they either appreciate the significant contribution she has made in shaping their lives and/or respect her dedication and sacrifice in setting-up and managing the only Black-led nursery at that time (incidentally, the nursery has remained functioning as a Black nursery after Syble's departure and to the present day) and/or acknowledge the importance of the nursery in terms of the Black, cultural values it promotes (McCalla, 2002a; McCalla, Grover and Penn, 2001).

The direct impact of Syble on the children, parents and workers that is, her immediate (or personal), face-to-face involvement with those who attended or were involved in the nursery during Syble's Headship, is astounding. The study identified several incidents where Syble's significance through the nursery) contributed to social inclusion and civic engagement (McCalla, Grover and Penn, 2001).).

> And the support we had there, especially Mrs Morgan. For me, she was a mother figure. I was young and a little bit confused... She was very good and we remained friends. We have all gone into various directions but every time we come here we know we can call on her. So it was a good support network for me as a young mother as well as for my children... I had quite a few problems and I was able to go to her (Cassandra, mother of adult children who attended the nursery).

This parent was not only given the support, in what is a friendly atmosphere, thus enabling her to gain emotional and psychological stability in her youth, but this stability, in turn, equipped her to be educated and eventually acquire professional employment - an area further discussed below. A former Harambee committee member also shares similar sentiments concerning Syble's contribution to the development of the Nursery:

> ...we went around to Mrs Morgan ...and asking come and sit on this committee please, and she would give up her time and her evenings and her weekends. Oh my God, she's amazing (Committee Member).

Similarly, Syble's indirect effect that is, her future (or later) and long-term influence on the past and present children attending the nursery, is also significant. Years after her departure, her legacy lives on. 'Hot knowledge' (Ball and Vincent, 1998) or the good reputation heralded throughout the community about the nursery was a crucial factor in a father's choice of pre-school care and education for his daughter who, at the time of research, was attending Marcus Garvey Nursery.

> I don't want to lose links with the nursery because this is very good, and I'd like to see it continue... people know about this, because it's been here so long. Years. ...I can't remember how we found out about it. I think somebody just mentioned it. It was word of mouth, yeah, it was word of mouth... it was when it was coming to nursery time, I wanted to send her to a nursery that was predominantly Black... I heard good things about it [the Nursery].

Before discussing the apparent success of the children the limited evidence on Black success in the UK will be explored.

Black success in context

The focus on the success of Syble's children is significant in terms of advancing present knowledge on the study of African-Caribbean achievement in education and employment in England. Carrington (1986) points out the overwhelming success of Caribbean children in sports education. Studies by Bagley, Bart and Wong (1979), Fuller (1980), Mac an Ghaill (1988, 1994), Mirza (1992, 1995), Channer (1995), Rhamie and Hallam (2002,) and Hallam and Rhamie (ch. 5 in this book) also demonstrate the educational success of Black youngsters in England. With the exception of Channer which takes a life-history approach, calling for participants to recall their experiences from schooling, these studies give a snap-shot account of success at a specific moment in time, invariably during schooling and higher education. In contrast to these studies which have concentrated on examples of Black success from a selective small group of youngsters in schools and post-schooling this study focuses on pre-school setting and demonstrates success in significant numbers from a single, educational establishment taking, in part, a life-history (or longitudinal) approach.

With regards to employment, Small (1994) points out that African-Caribbeans in England, like their North American equivalents, are found to succeed in careers such as sport and music and in specific fields, excel and dominate their White counterparts. Nonetheless, in other areas of employment, African-Caribbean success is generally below that of other ethnic groups (see also Berthoud 1999; Pathak 2000).

Although there is some evidence of African-Caribbean education and employment success, this is sporadic especially when compared with studies that portray Blacks and, in particular African-Caribbeans, as failing. Recent research shows Black youngsters as disproportionately represented in various forms of social exclusion (school expulsion, unemployment, imprisonment and institutional psychiatric admissions) (See Owen et al. 1991; Graham and Bowling 1995; Audit Commission 1996; 1999; Gillborn 1997a; 1997b; Parsons et al., 1996; Blair et al. 1998; Pearce and Hillman 1998; Social Exclusion Unit 1998; Weekes and Wright 1998; Wright, Weeks and McGlaughlin 2000; DfEE 2000). Others point to Black educational underachievement being explained by low intelligence and IQ (Verma and Bagley, 1979), a failure of ethnic minorities to assimilate and lose their cultural and linguistic identification in order to progress (Mullard, 1982) and Black pupils' low self-esteem and feelings of negative self-worth (Stone, 1981; Mirza, 1992). More recently, the blame for Black underachievement is firmly laid at the doors of schools for failing to practise ethnic diversity (Gillborn and Gipps, 1996). The ongoing, government Youth Cohort Study (DfES, forthcoming) of 30,000 teenagers in England and Wales shows African-Caribbean students' GCSE grades in 2002 below that of Whites and Asians with 36 percent of Black students gaining five or more A-C grades compared with 52 percent of Whites and 52 percent of Asians respectively. Given the insufficient evidence of African-Caribbean success in England, the findings in this study are all the more significant and necessary - a further indication and reason for recognition and praise of the children's success and the nursery's input towards it.

Evidence of Black success in England

Measuring education and employment success

The account presented here is a development of my preliminary referral to the children's educational and employment success elsewhere (see McCalla, Grover and Penn 2001). Success here is assessed in terms of 'value-added' that is, the net-gain in educational and employment success from a state of deprivation (or disadvantage) to success. Stated differently, the level of actual achievement given a participant's starting position. Assessing value-added success was classified under five social factors. See Table 1 below.

Table 1: Social factors for assessing value added success

Factors	*Details*
Ethnicity	Participants are Black and thus susceptible to experiencing racial harassment, discrimination, underachievement and social exclusion.
Social Class	Significant proportions of participants are/were of working-class origin although due to upward social mobility and success their working-class position is questionable.
Poverty	Some participants are/were on very low-incomes, welfare benefits and/or receiving student grants/loans. None of the participants in the sample were currently unemployed although there were occasional references to non-employment (temporary or short-periods of unemployment) by people who were involved in or attended the nursery in the 1970s-1980s. Previous unemployment is also noted during this period. Non-employment was often the result of either completion of an employment contract or pregnancy and childcare directly after the birth of a new baby. (Marcus Garvey cares for children from ages two to five). Reasons for full-employment from the sample is due to participants' willingness either to migrate globally (mainly to North American) and regionally (primarily to Southern England) for employment or to start their own business in England.
Family Composition	Majority of single-parent families, headed mainly by women. This does not mean that these mothers valued education less favourably than conventional families comprising of married, heterosexual couples. These parents (largely mothers) were highly concerned about their children's educational well-being and future success and that of themselves. Nevertheless, some of these matriarchal households were poverty-stricken resulting from absent fathers who should be contributing to the financial (and social) well-being of the families but were not fulfilling these responsibilities, leaving the mothers to struggle and compensate for any shortfall by taking low-paid jobs.
Housing and Geographical Location	Social and material bereft in Handsworth, Birmingham remains infamous as in the 1970s although much urban regeneration has occurred since then. It is among this landscape of urban decay that Syble's children were educated and cared for (and still educated and cared for) in the Marcus Garvey Nursery.

As shall be demonstrated from the findings below, some, but not all, of Syble's children started from a position of 'multiple deprivation'and social exclusion and were prone to a 'cycle of deprivation' especially those attending the Nursery in its infancy that is, in the late 1970s to 1980s. The study found that although still somewhat deprived, children born in the mid- to late-1908s/1990s were substantially better off than the children before them. Nonetheless, the transformation from social inclusion and civic engagement is remarkable, thus demonstrating the important role the Nursery plays in countering social exclusion.

The sucess of past and present children

The success of the past children, now adults, is telling. Some have attended or, at the time of investigation, are attending Universities and colleges. Courses of study include a variety of subject specialisms such as, media studies, social care, business and law at different levels ranging from degrees and professional qualifications to GCSEs and NVQs[3]. Others are schoolteachers, accountants, finance clerks, nurses, chemists, fashion models, fashion designers, computer technicians and lawyers (McCalla, Grover and Penn 2001). The following two quotations are between former workers at the Nursery who converse about the success of ex-pupils:

> Dennis: Toyah McKenzie. She's a dentist.
> Syble: Toyah McKenzie. Toyah is the daughter of the woman that used to cook for me…
> Dennis: … she has set up her dentist practice on Quinmel Road
> Tibsey: A young, Black woman with drive.
> Syble: A young, Black woman with drive.
> Dennis: With drive, with education.

And:

> We mobilise all the young people and people like Leroy are now a solicitor (Dennis, former committee member).

Incidentally, two of the former students who attended the nursery have returned and are employed as nursery nurses. Roslin is one such example:

> Roslin: Well, I'm a nursery nurse and I work at Marcus Garvey Day Nursery, Monday to Friday, go college on a Wednesday, completing my NVQ level 2 in early years and doing health and beauty…
> DM: You attended the Marcus Garvey Nursery… when you were about 2 or 3?
> Roslin: Yeah…
> DM: …Did any of your friends attend Marcus Garvey Nursery?
> Roslin: Yeah…
> DM: What are they doing now? …
> Roslin: …two of them are doing Business Administration…. Couple of them are doing Health and Social care… Leisure and Tourism, Hair and Beauty.

The comparative level of educational and employment achievement of some of the children may not appear particularly striking or exceptional. Roslin, aged nineteen at the time of investigation, again points out the comparative success of some of the pupils who attended Marcus Garvey with others who did not:

> DM: So what are these doing? These people who never attended the nursery.
> Roslin: Well some of them are executives and… lawyers, doing all them big courses.

It must be pointed out, however, that if the children's race and thus vulnerability to racial discrimination, working-class status, poverty and the like, are taken into account, Syble's children are successful. Their success is all the more important since some of them experienced racism from teachers after leaving the Nursery during schooling (see Wright, 1992; Gillborn and Gipps, 1996 on teacher racism in schools). A former pupil gives an account of her experience of racism at secondary school:

> DM: You stayed there for a year. Why did you change school?
> Delonie: Cause I kept on getting into trouble…The only reason I kept on getting into trouble, you know, I was always in trouble with one particular teacher…And then it's just like they put me on report and everything and they were just watching me.
> DM: Were these White teachers?…
> Delonie: Yeah, they were White teachers but I felt …like I was a target. You know what I mean?
> DM: …So this was in year 7?
> Delonie: Yeah.

Having experienced a traumatic period after this incident and some problems adjusting to her new school, Delonie eventually settled into schooling. On leaving school with GCSEs she embarked on a career in care-work:

> When I left Brightground Girls, I went to Thomas College and I did a year there, in Health and Social Care. But then after, I …worked with elderly people. …And then I decided I would work with children because when I used to do my placement at the nursery. I used to enjoy it (Delonie, former pupil).

Delonie's experience demonstrates that educational and employment success has not eradicated racial encounters for these children as confirmed in McCalla (2002a). Despite their success they are presented with racism occasionally or day-by-day at school, and as mentioned below, in employment and wherever they go in Britain. Nevertheless as mentioned above, apart from possessing immense confidence to withstand a certain degree of external opposition, these children have learnt to develop their own coping strategies to deal with specific situations. These strategies are family, church, community, solitude/isolation and detachment (Channer 1995; Rhamie and Hallam 2002; McCalla, 2002a) and/or as, Ray, a voluntary worker demonstrates below, Black solidarity amid White majority presence.

Parents of present pupils also express their pleasure over the level of progress achieved by their children after attending the Nursery. A parent whose child has recently entered primary school makes the point echoed by most parents:

> …when he started at school, the staff found him to be advanced. You know, it's like you're a Black child, you're not supposed to know that much. Your level of learning isn't supposed to be here…because those tend to be White children. They're [White children] assumed highly intelligent, therefore a Black child … should be lagging behind.

Similar observations were noted by a former Nursery worker:

> They would get to school and initially they would be used as monitors because they were far in advance of the other children and I think what we were trying to do was to encourage the parents to explain to the teachers that they [children] can do more. And sometimes what tended to happen was that, because the children weren't being challenged, they became destructive which then had an adverse effect because there were issues of children, very young, being labelled and how that labelling carried on from infant school, through the junior school, though the senior school…

How these children will fare beyond primary school remains to be seen since a recent large-scale survey by Gillborn and Mirza (2000) of British school children demonstrates that children of African-Caribbean origin generally do well in primary school. However, the study showed their progress falling off significantly in secondary school in relation to their earlier achievements and in comparison with other minority ethnic groups. Nonetheless, if the success of Syble's adult children is anything to go by, some of these younger children may also succeed.

Before discussing the success of the parents it is worth noting that anecdotal evidence suggests that not all of Syble's children may have succeeded. There may be some educational failure and wastage as Syble and a former assistant manager acknowledge and recall:

> We had successes, well of course in everything there are some children who did not turn out how we expected them to (Pearl).

And:

> Now when I meet the parents in the streets, the children that were there, the ones I've met anyway – maybe the ones I don't meet aren't doing so good – but quite a few of them have made it to University, and the others that haven't gone to University are in good jobs. So I know it works. I know. I know (Syble).

In spite of this anecdotal claim, no incidences of educational or employment failures were found in my investigation. More research would be required to ascertain evidence of underachievement. However, a more significant point to be made here is not whether there are failures or not - there may well be - but from the evidence presented it can be inferred that the success of Syble's children as a group (and as individuals) is extremely rare. Moreover, even if failure is to be found among the successes, this does not take anything away from the success of Syble's children, as it is extremely unusual to identify so many success-stories in a single nursery comprising Black working-class children. The revelation of such a high proportion of success is, in itself alone, evidence of success. Furthermore, the nursery is successful so long as it continues to encourage success and achievement for its children. It has never ceased to do this. As mentioned above, nationally and statistically African-Caribbeans are disproportionately represented as underachieving and failing. Since this is the current situation, the question then to be asked is why have these children from Marcus Garvey succeeded while other African-Caribbean children have not? What is notably significant about Marcus Garvey that has made the difference? The answers possibly rest with issues that I shall address when discussing the nursery's contribution to the children's success in the next section.

Finally, before addressing the success of parents, and then workers, it must be noted that the Nursery's aims, and Syble's original aims for setting up the Nursery as noted in the figure

1, have now been accomplished and realised. Time-allowance - at least twenty years - was required to fulfil an unrelenting vision and for it to come to 'maturity'. A 'quick-fix' was uncalled for here. The evidence demonstrates that Syble's patience has paid off. Her wait was not in vain.

The success of parents

Wilma, whose now adult children previously attended Marcus Garvey when Wilma was an unemployed single mother, demonstrates the education and employment success of parents generally. After working at the Nursery as first, a volunteer cook and then a nursery nurse:

> …I went to college to do my social work then went into [social work] fieldwork and been doing fieldwork in [name of 3 localities]…and now [I'm] a manager.

Calvin whose primary-school aged daughter also attended Marcus Garvey is another example:

> My daughter used to go here from when she was two. Myself, I'm a social worker by profession, but I also run a voluntary organisation. I'm a founder member of a voluntary organisation called [name of organisation].

Former committee members reminisce on even more stories of parents' educational and employment success. Unlike the parents already mentioned, these parents were residents of the hostel that was also owned by the Harambee Organisation:

> There was this girl that was at the hostel and when she started having children she came here [Nursery] with them… I don't know what it [course] was, but I know that she was on a course at Thomas College (Syble).

And:

> Committee member: Angel…
>
> Syble: She was one of the first ones, who came and worked with me here, then she went to MEB [the West Midlands Electricity Board] and then she went to be a social worker.
>
> Committee member: She is unique actually. Through the hostel, through the nursery and now to social services.

Then:

> Rachel that you met at High Road Nursery, her mother [worked at the Nursery and went on to nursing]. Now Rachel was … a baby at the time (Syble).

Unlike the original children (now adults) who attended the nursery as pupils, who sought various types of professional-sector employment, many of the past and present parents identified in the study eventually settled into numerous social care professions, primarily social work. This is probably because most of these parents received their initial training in care-work at the nursery. Their training is in keeping with what seems to be part of a national trend. Recent data that relate to higher education show a disproportionate presence of African/Caribbean students on social work and related courses (Reay et al. 2001; Rhamie and Hallam 2002).

This study at Marcus Garvey reveals that the initial training proved decisive in determining the parents' career trajectories. More importantly, the training received at the Nursery profoundly contributed to the social inclusive process of many parents (Grover, 1999). The socio-economic saving to society over twenty years from apparent social exclusion to social inclusion is undoubtedly evidence of success (McCalla, 2001) – a point which is developed more thoroughly below.

This study has also showed that these parents, predominately Caribbean immigrants, succeeded later in their life-course compared with their children born in the UK. In other words, unlike their British off-springs who left school with formal qualifications that prepared them for professional employment, these Caribbean immigrants' educational and employment success occurred only after gaining no or limited qualifications, experiencing periods of unemployment and the occupation of low-paid, unskilled labour. We now know from recent studies referred to above, that racism was an integral factor resulting in their underachievement. The difference in cultural identity across generation-lines, which is discussed below, may also have some bearing on the difference in educational success (and employment attainment) within and at specific timeframes/ages between Caribbean immigrants and Caribbean Britons. Could British patriotism and Caribbean identity be responsible for racism and ultimately their late achievement? It may well be due, in part, to these factors. Nonetheless, this does not explain why, albeit later in their lives, Caribbeans are now succeeding and second, Black Britons are also experiencing racism and underachieving, which is especially noticeable among African-Caribbean boys/men (see Sewell, 1997). Furthermore, these parents have a mandate to Britain through their British citizenship despite their expressed Caribbean identity (see below). Notwithstanding this, a more credible explanation of later success compared with their children may lie in a combination of, first, a previous lack of awareness of racism in the education system and how best to counteract its effects and, second, values in relation to identity/race and education. Syble succinctly portrays parents' former ignorance of institutional racism in schooling during the late 1960s-1970s:

> When our children complained about the treatment they were receiving from school some of us parents did nothing because we did not realise what was happening to our children in the '70s. We did not realise that schools were failing our children until it was too late. They had already left school with no qualifications. But we were determined we had to do something for the next generation (Fieldnotes).

For many of the children, now parents of Marcus Garvey, it was too late for school education. Nonetheless, it was definitely not too late for education *per se*. Their new found knowledge of racial injustice in education and confidence to reverse their life chances propelled them into social action which took the form of social solidarity and the revaluing of education-acquisition for themselves and their children. It was not that these Caribbean parents devalued education *per se* because education was greatly valued in the Caribbean. However in Britain, education for immigrants was restricted by racism and these Caribbeans needed to relearn to value education as an immigrant in a racially unjust society. The best way to defy the impact of racism was to educate themselves and network from within the Black[4] community. This is what they did and still do in the twenty first century when necessary.

For all the parents in the study, education has proven invaluable to employment success and deprivation-relief in Britain. Their Caribbean identity has not hindered their progression. However, how much of this identity has had to be compromised to move on/ up requires further investigation. Nonetheless, thirty years on, promotion prospects and job security within White mainstream employment remains extremely problematic for some. In order to move on, these Caribbeans have to move out. They exit for employment either within the Black community itself, self-employment and/or through emigration to the Caribbean or North America. Carol, is an example of one person thinking about migration:

> The level of racism here is too much... I have worked within the caring field for the past twenty odd years, both as a residential worker, as a field social worker and now as a Project Manager for an organisation, where I oversee their childcare. My next aim will be to move to the Caribbean and give some of those skills that I've developed... into the community out there.

The only real and promising option available to some of these Caribbeans is migration to relieve displacement and rekindle a real sense of belonging. However, in the case of these successful Black people, migration is the Caribbean's gain and Britain's loss. For having been educated and trained in Britain, these people will ultimately benefit the Caribbean from an exodus from Britain of essential knowledge and skills – a type of brain-drain.

The success of workers

The workers identified here are either previous or present workers at the nursery. They differ from the parents and children mentioned above (who, in some cases, also worked or presently work at the Nursery) in that their children have never attended Marcus Garvey Nursery nor have they ever attended the nursery as pupils or are they parents themselves. It is because these workers share the Nursery's values' or adopted its beliefs through their employment at and encounter with it, that the Nursery has attracted them. Coincidentally, many of these workers also reflect the success and idiosyncrasies of those who attended or attend the Nursery. As the saying goes, 'birds of a feather flock together'.

Workers identified in the study can be classified into three distinctive groups: first, paid nursery nurse workers; second, Harambee governors and committee members who are or have been directly involved with the Nursery and third, volunteers. Grace, a former assistant Nursery manager who is now a social worker and Tammy, currently a nursery nurse at Marcus Garvey at the time of investigation, typify the success among the group of wage-earning nursery workers:

> I saw the job ... in one of the local papers [in Liverpool] that it was advertised...And I applied and I got it and the rest is history. And I worked there [Birmingham] for eleven years...I have now gone on to pastures new. I worked here [Marcus Garvey] for about two years then I moved to another local authority nursery on the other side of the city and from there I went on to do my social work training and am working as a social worker now... I think that I had given time to that Nursery and I needed to see if there were other children out there who needed the kind of support that I had given to

> the children at Marcus Garvey and to bring in some ideas because I think … Black children were using local authority nurseries but I didn't know what sort of cultural input was there [in the local authority] and I thought that I needed to spread my wings as well. The opportunity came and I took it (Grace).

And:

> I've been [permanently] employed say 3 months but before that I was employed on and off for 3 years – like voluntary… When I was at school I wanted to be in childcare and before I decided I thought I'd just go on work experience. So the school organised it for me to work here. [When] I was here on work experience I decided that I wanted to do it… I started my GCSEs in year 10, and then when I moved up to year 11, my art teacher … said that … I could start progressing and doing A level while I was doing my GCSEs… While I was doing my GCSEs, I was doing A level Art and then I had like the year just gone to finish them [A levels] off. So I guess I was doing GCSE and A levels at the same time (Tammy).

As the data demonstrates, Grace's and Tammy's contact with Marcus Garvey occurred at different periods in their career trajectories. Irrespective of their differing contacts with the nursery, their educational and employment success and the general progression is evident. Tammy's educational achievement is particularly good since one of her A levels was taken in year 11 while also studying for her GCSEs at a inner-city multi-racial school that performs below average in the national and regional GCSE league tables.

Educational and employment success is also found among Harambee members. As pointed out in McCalla, Grover and Penn (2001) all members presently on the committee have either professional or managerial employment. Similarly, the study found that former members now occupy professional and/or managerial jobs in local government, other public-sector organisations and the private sector as opposed to their previous employment in manual or semi-skilled occupations. Dennis, a former committee member, exemplifies this upward social mobility.

> DM: What are you doing now?
> DENNIS: Personally, I went to University after the five years and became a solicitor. And I came back and was Chairman of Harambee for about 5 more years… I was a solicitor when I was Chairman.

Finally, the study revealed success among the Nursery's volunteers, some of whom gained invaluable work experience to develop a career in social care and/or education. Others capitalised on the social, interactive and disciplinary skills that could be gained through this opportune encounter at the nursery and which proved useful in acquiring paid work in other professions. Ray is a prodigy of this experience.

> I got a job doing silver service, but when it's the summer holiday, it's a bit quiet so I haven't really got any work going at the moment, so I thought I might as well come in [to work at the Nursery] and get some experience. … I want to be

an accountant from ages ago … I used to go to Queen Elisabeth Grammar… I've got 4 A's, 4 Bs, 3 Cs and a D, GCSEs … I stayed in the sixth form at Queen Elizabeth. I did that for a year but then … I needed a change of environment, and the subjects I was doing English, Maths A levels. So I'd rather go to college and do things like accountancy and business studies and then, you know I can see my career coming to reality if I do subjects like that with what I want to achieve… [At school] I was the sport captain for 5 years. I was captain of the basketball team and the rugby team.

As in the case of Tammy who is roughly the same age as Ray, Ray's educational success is quite clear : achieving GCSEs and now doing 'A' levels. However, by contrast, the disparity in their life-course could not be more different. Ray attended a highly prestigious, Birmingham grammar school, possibly unknowingly, traded on conventional Black stereotyping as a sports achiever; at the time of research, he is employed as a part-time waiter at an expensive, local restaurant; he is currently a volunteer at Marcus Garvey and wants to venture into an accountancy career. In addition, he is the child of parents who are themselves both working and arguably successful too. Furthermore, by contrast to most participants in the study, Ray also lives with and was reared by both parents:

DM: Your father's a (interrupt)
RAY: He's an electrician and does computing.
DM: … Do you live with your mother?
RAY: Yeah, I live with both my mum and dad.
DM: What does your mother do?
RAY: My mother did childcare first then she went on to look after the
mentally ill at Bryant Cross Hospital…. now she's got her own business in
travel and she's been doing that for the last 5 or 6 years.

Furthermore, whilst a significant proportion of the participants experienced some form of racism, whether in schooling as demonstrated by Delonie, or later in life, Ray seemed not to have, so far, faced racism.

DM: Queen Elizabeth is a predominantly White school. As a Black male, how did you feel in that environment?
RAY: At first I thought I would come against some racist element, but there wasn't really that much… the teachers told me that so many people looked up to me in school.

Ray's inexperience of racism could partly be explained by his popularity[5] on the one hand as pointed out by his teachers, and Black solidarity on the other:

DM: Were there any other Black children?
RAY: Yeah. In my year there were seven. Seven of us out of 120. We all just stuck together really. We all got through school together. We didn't stay together and go against everyone else, but you know, we helped each other through and that.

In turn, Ray's popularity and group support could have contributed to his educational success in addition to the fact that he did not face any other real problems such as those experienced and Tammy:

> When I got to like third year, things started to get a bit rocky, because there was like problems at home and stuff [bereavement] and I took a lot of time out of school... And then, when I got to year 10, I thought 'forget it, just do what you have to do basically and I came out with the grades that I wanted... I just dedicated myself to my work. I knew that if I didn't do it, that no one else was going to do it for me. My whole attitude just changed. From those few things that had happened to me... I had to grow up like quick time... I had no choice really. It just happened that way.

Oblivious to general problems and racism at school, whether is Ray's good fortune is likely to be sustained in his later life more generally and education and employment specifically is an open question. McCalla (2002a) demonstrates that it is possible to escape racism in school only to face it in employment and in higher education. Ray may not be well prepared should he later encounter racism. He states:

> Other people have experienced enough and have told their stories and how... they coped with it. I'll learn from other people's experiences. I just don't know if I come across it. I'm just not going to take any notice really and just get on with what I'm doing.

Ray's success is achieved from a level of marginal disadvantage by comparison to other participants in terms of schooling and social background. The value-added to achieve success in his case is arguably less than others who have, in some instances, succeeded amid multiple deprivations. He is, in many respects, an 'exception voice' (McCalla, 2002a).

The Nursery's contribution to the Children's success

The analysis so far has focused on the educational and employment success of Syble's children. However, the contribution made by the Nursery towards this success has yet to be discussed. Thus I now turn my attention towards this area.

It must be pointed out that it is difficult to ascertain the exact factors responsible for the children's success, whilst acknowledging that the values encouraged at the Nursery may have significantly contributed to their success. For the children who formerly attended the Nursery (as pre-school children and their parents as support-workers and volunteers), how much of their social, cultural and intellectual development can be put down to their experiences at Marcus Garvey? According to David et al. (1992) and Ball (1994) high quality early years' education and care have a great impact upon the life chances of pre-school children, thus one of the reasons for this investigation into pre-school influences on the later life of Syble's children. The Nursery has consistently attracted a certain type of employee and volunteers that is, those people who share the social and cultural values of the nursery. This leads therefore to the fact that Marcus Garvey is consistently reproducing itself. More importantly, if these workers had attended Marcus Garvey as pre-school children, parents or originators then the acquisition of success could be clearly related to the Nursery. However, many of the recent workers did not have prior contact as noted above. It therefore follows that whilst the Nursery has contributed invaluably to the children's success, and no less so to the workers who have gained useful life-skills through their work at the Nursery, it follows that there are also other factors responsible for the children's development. Family-ties, Church-association, and/or Black solidarity also impact on the life-course and attainment-levels of the children (Channer, 1995; McCalla, 2002a; Rhamie and Hallam, 2002) and these must also be taken into account in the analysis of the research findings.

The Nursery's contribution to the success of Syble's children is largely seen in terms of two main factors: one, its sustained development and reinforcement in the children of a positive sense of self, and two arising from the first, its high expectations for the children.

Reinforcement of a positive sense of self

A notable and significant observation of the stories of Syble's children (and Syble too) is their positive sense of self. The children's sense of self is constructed on ideas relating to citizenship and their strong self-awareness of racial and cultural identity - ideas which, in all cases, are derived, in part, from their involvement with the Nursery. Since the concepts of self-identity and citizenship are significant and convoluted and superimposed one on the other, I shall consider them simultaneously in relation to the children's views and experiences that is, abstract theory shall accompany practical and actual illustrations that are grounded in data derived from the children's stories.

The grounded identity formation in this study is about individual perception encouraged and expressed in public and private spaces within and between cultural groups or communities and how individuals act upon that perception. Cultural identity publicly expressed is paramount to group and individual existence and survival, well-being and success. Others' definitions of individual identities is therefore of lesser importance in this conceptualisation. As sincerely, pellucid and succinctly put by Syble when referring to a conversation with a White professional:

> We have our own culture and although you don't think much about it, it's our culture and when you lose your culture, you lose yourself and I don't want my children losing themselves;

and Collette, one of the Nursery managers in Marcus Garvey's history:

> [we] make sure that...they're painting their faces, because we do that a lot. I don't think a child can go through the Nursery at all before having that experience of talking about themselves, painting themselves.

Active recognition and appreciation of the cultural values within and between cultural commonality and difference and national unity and divergence are also significant; so too, is an acknowledgement that we all, as human beings, belong to the human race, despite our distinctive phenotypes. Thus individuals, within and between groups, are not judged by their colour but by their character (Feinburg, 1998[6]; McCalla, 2002a).

The creation of a communal world of diversity[7] is possible through continued partnership where spaces in which communities meet within and between groups are stablished and where self-identification is voiced and awareness of total citizenship rights and responsibilities (see below) are developed beyond the collective space. The Nursery provides a physical meeting ground for Syble's children. It is safe and familiar - a home-from-home, community environment (McCalla, Grover and Penn, 2001).

Although starting from a position of community and group association, the Nursery systematically attempts to recognise and promote individual identity within the group. It is from this position of individual awareness that exceptions or monocultures within and between groups are identified. Monocultures are seen where specific individuals may not comfortably subscribe to, fit in with and accept all community-norms and stereotypical conventions (see McCalla, 2002a). Ray's general life-course and inexperience of racism typifies a monoculture of sorts. This self-identity formation which recognises exceptions is novel and moves beyond the homogeneous, racialised and/or genderised group and specific, ethnic and/or gendered community conceptualisations of identity forwarded in the last twenty years. (See Bhabha, 1984; Balwin, 1985; Gilroy, 1987, 1993; Ramdin, 1987; Spillers, 1987; Grewal et al., 1988; Childers and hooks, 1990; Parmar, 1990; Silvanandan, 1990; Brah, 1992; 1996; Hall, 1992; Mirza, 1992; 1997; Bakare-Yusuf, 1997). Whilst these studies have usefully charted the development of multiracial membership in 'Black Britain', their primary, and in some cases sole, focus on collective group association is at the expense of identifying monocultures.

Feinberg's (1998) and McCalla's (2002a) advocacy of cultural and racial identity publicly expressed resonates with the Nursery's values in another sense. It is an attempt to avoid assimilation that is, in this instance, hegemonic imposition of the majority identity on minority identities. Hegemonic imposition, whether consciously or unconsciously administered, is likely if expression of cultural identity is preserved for the private domain under the guise that matters of identity are personal and private.

As in the case of self-identity, the Nursery's contribution to success of Syble's children in promoting a positive sense of self is demonstrated through its values of citizenship defined in terms of political, civil and social rights and responsibilities. Political rights grant individuals' voting-access in the democratic process and permit active engagement (or at least, taking an informed interest) in public affairs. Civil rights enable protection and security by the law and social rights are concerned with basic public services and the organisation of collective-action (Marshall, 1950; 1981; Roche, 1992; Turner, 1990; 1993). Ideas of individual choice amid collective responsibility, duty, equality and entitlement (Driver and Martell, 1997) are also encapsulated within this political, civil and social scenario. In other words, from a collectivist stance, social and racial communities are citizens when they can actively and freely engage in all aspects of that society because they are part of that society by birth or through legal acquisition. Thus, the Nursery teaches Syble's children that personal identification (citizenship as identity, Carrington and Short, 1997) should not prohibit individual liberty to totally engage in the political, civil and social society.

The marketised, consumerist and post-fordist connotation of citizenship, prevalently encouraged during the 1980s to early 1990s (Saunders, 1993) is not intended here. So whilst the consumer citizenship ideal is an advantageous and seemingly trendy option made available only to those able to compete in the consumer marketplace, it is not for those unable to do so. It assumes a social, economic and racial-level-playing field and thus the capacity of all individuals, whatever their social class or racial grouping, to complete on equal terms since compensatory measures are unavailable to those who cannot.

Although individuals are entitled to political, civil and social rights and responsibilities through citizenship, failure to understand societal cultures and systems could prohibit access to benefits. So instead of focusing on consumer citizenship which would only be beneficial to some and not all of Syble's children, the Nursery emphasises knowledge and understanding procurement, through education, in order to articulate and access citizenship entitlements. Only then can the children, in turn, be accountable and responsible to society (McCalla, 2002a).

> I do think that a certain level of education does give you the monopoly to manoeuvre yourself so you can live (Syble Morgan).

In this section, Syble's children shall be identified in terms of British-born and Caribbean-born. This demarcation is made to reflect the two differing self-identity and citizenship expressions between Syble's British-born and Caribbean-immigrant children.

Syble's indigenous children.

Ray provides an example of expressions of personal identity:

> Successful and [a] Black person who has achieved... That's how I see myself. That's how I would like people to see me... I say I'm British but with Caribbean origins... I don't deny my origins... I'm proud that my parents are Jamaican.

Ray clearly identifies himself as successful, racially Black, culturally (and nationally) British but with Caribbean heritage/roots derived from his parents. His cultural identification as British is further clarified and reinforced when he discusses his taste in music and literature.

> DM: Do you read...Black, cultural books or anything?
> Ray: Not really.
> DM: ...Are you into cultural music?
> Ray: Such as?
> DM: Reggae or...hip-hop?
> Ray: I can listen to it to a certain extent but after a certain time it gets on my nerves ...I listen to things like Hip-Hop and R and B. I don't listen to country music or western music...[and] not really regga.

Ray's taste for Rhythm and Blues (R and B), Hip-Hop and Soul, as also highlighted by others in the study, is characteristic of younger indigenous Blacks who are seeking to establish their identity and, thus, purpose in British society. He abhors the taste in music traditionally preferred by his parents' generation of Caribbean immigrants, that is, Country and Western. Ray confidently proclaims how he would like others to perceive him - a level of confidence witnessed by all participants.

Although certain of her cultural identification as British, Tammy, a nursery nurse, is, unlike Ray, unwilling to definitively define herself in racial terms since she is of mixed-parentage and mixed racial origin (see Ifekwunigwe, 1997), preferring, by and large, to leave this open to others' recognition and racial classification:

> Tammy: I come from a lot of different cultures. I've got White in me. I've got Asian in me. I've got Chinese in me... People are going to say, 'what are you? Where do you come from?' And sometimes I'm stunned... Continental, I think...
> DM: You see yourself as Continental, yeah?
> Tammy: I say I'm British, but if they say, what colour are you, I say, 'Well, what you see is what I am'. ...It takes too long for me to say 'well, I'm half this, I'm quarter this, I'm quarter that'. There's no point. I was raised as a Black child. I was raised in a Black environment.

Being less assured of racial position seems to be typical of children of mixed parentage (Ifekwunigwe, 1997) as Beverley affirms - a mother whose child (Saline) attends the nursery and who is of Asian and African-Caribbean parentage:

> She looks around the nursery she sees children that are…quite dark, and she will mix with everybody… she looks at herself and sees that she is paler than a few of them, but at the same time, she sees somebody else who might be paler than she is…

Nonetheless, despite the uncertainty about racial identification portrayed by both Tammy and Saline, through Beverley, Blackness seems to be accepted as the most dominant race in both situations. The acceptance of Blackness as the prominent racial identity, is essentially premised from the community association and interaction of the child and/or, in the case of one-parent families, the parent who has the greater involvement and influence in child-rearing of the child in question. For Tammy this was her Caribbean-born and bred, Black father and for Saline it is Beverley.

> DM: does your child give you any indication by something she says or things she does that she … recognises who she is?
> Beverley: I think more definitely with the language… she should be able to express herself as she wishes. … Saline …has strong Black influence…I suppose my daughters can both identify with me, as I identify with my mother, so I don't know if that's got anything to do with it.

Although racial identity is important to the participants, the quotations above demonstrate that it is less significant in terms of who defines an individual when compared with cultural (and national) identity. This is especially noticeable for people of mixed-parentage. Syble's indigenous children are not only assured of their cultural identities so as to express them confidently in public spaces but also believe it is their right to define themselves. However, in terms of race, the data suggest that the option to define another is left open; permissible to others since individuals' phenotypes are either obvious to self and others, as in Ray's case, or dubious to others and/or self, as in Tammy's and Saline's situation.

A poignant point about identity formation that has been gleaned from the study of Syble's indigenous children is the awareness and articulation of racial difference and 'shades of Blackness' by very young children. Beverley's reference to Saline is one such example. Until now, this was revealed only in studies of school-aged children and older youths (Mac an Ghaill 1988; Wright 1992; Mirza 1995; Weekes 1997; Wright, Weeks and McGlaughlin 2000) and thus it is an area for further research with pre-school children.

The Nursery's Caribbean immigrants.

Whereas all participants who were British-born identified themselves as culturally British although acknowledging Caribbean cultural influences on their lives, their parents and other acquaintances, in complete contrast, all Caribbean immigrants constantly referred to their Caribbean/Black heritage, folklore and immigration. This sense of belonging to the Caribbean and identifying themselves as solely Caribbean is apparent by these Caribbean immigrants despite their numerous years as residents in England between fifteen to forty years and irrespective of exposure to British culture over this period.

> When we were talking about the confidence thing … I think that also goes way back beyond just the nursery for me because again, it was about where I was coming from, where we had a very close-knit family in Jamaica. There was a lot of support within my family. Our goal was to make sure we helped

each other and enable each other to do things … And I think because of that supportive network and having the goal and the target …[when I]… came to this country, which I didn't want to, when I came here it was about making myself a better person, to return or to help the others… I am very proud of where I am coming from and what I do or what I used to do [in Jamaica] … (Enid, mother whose children attended the nursery).

And:

> I am an immigrant from the Caribbean who has lived in this country for the last fourty years (Syble Morgan).

High Expectations for Syble's Children

Apart from developing a positive sense of self in the children, the Nursery also has high expectations for them especially with regards to educational and employment achievements. This high expectation coupled with an active promotion of the social and cultural values in practice, acted as a definite self-fulfilling prophecy in that, Syble's children succeeded because they were encouraged and believed they would succeed.

> I think one of the things we found, is that we would encourage our children to do the 3Rs, learn to read and write (Pearl, assistant manager).

This high expectation for the children has resulted in their educational and employment success and a constant striving by them to pursue goals beyond their present attainment. It has simultaneously led to their unwillingness to settle for less than their full potential. Whilst this striving is commendable, it could equally be viewed as undesirable if it leads to unrealistic goals or unnecessary frustration in the children as they attempt to achieve high standards, as Tammy demonstrates:

> I decided to do A level Art and Design because I had the talent and I thought there's no point making it go to waste and plus I had a good grade in my GCSE for Art… I think I could have done better. Even though I got good grades, I still think I could have done better.

It is possible that Tammy could have done better if her social circumstances had been different, that is, if she had not also been suffering the bereavement of her mother prior to her final examination year. As this essay demonstrates, Tammy's examination performance was outstanding. Given the period situation surrounding her examination it seems apparent that Tammy is, needlessly, too hard on herself or, more positively, simultaneously shows her extremely high standards.

Although the Nursery valued educational attainment, it is important to note that it was more concerned with encouraging excellence in whatever area an individual demonstrated a talent or gift and where their individual personality and character could best-perform.

> We took them on at age 2. And I would say … none were allowed to fail. Even if they weren't able to do the alphabet, they were able to do something. We looked at the individual child and what they were good at and tried to

> develop that because not all children are academically minded. So in that sense, even if it was just to get the children to socialise that was something. It wasn't all about they must do this; they must do that (Pearl, former assistant manager).

In addition to valuing individual talent, the Nursery was active in preparing Syble's indigenous and Caribbean children for life, beyond the nursery, for school, college, university, employment and society; by equipping them with the necessary life-skills.

> I think our main ethos at the time was ... to encourage the children to achieve and to get on with life and to give them sound grounding (Nursery worker)

And:

> One of the big things that we looked at was what was expected of a Black child going into school (Pearl, former Nursery worker).

Furthermore, McCalla, Grover and Penn (2001) point out the significance of Marcus Garvey as a community nursery in attempting to combat social exclusion. From its origin to the present day, Marcus Garvey sought to prepare future parents to engage in the formal economy as citizens in society. This was made possible through the strong parent-support network at the Nursery, the encouragement of parents to get involved in the Nursery either as employees or volunteers; and by enabling and encouraging parents to engage in the formal labour market and education. Put succinctly, the Nursery positively reinforced high expectation for the children and sought to value their interests.

The impact on the children of reinforcing these two factors that is, promoting a positive sense of self through self-identity and citizenship formation and high expectations for the children, has not only culminated in their success but may also be responsible for creating in them some very noticeable, aesthetic characteristics, which the next subsection focuses on.

The significance of reinforcing a positive sense of self and high expectations

What is interesting from the children's life-experiences is their overwhelming confidence, motivation, proficiency, ambition, keenness to take opportunities when they arise and ability to set and achieve realistic, high standards for themselves and others. In turn, they are willing to transfer knowledge and skills to others. The evidence from the study would suggest that the reinforcement of a positive sense of self and the instilling of high expectations derived from the social interaction, care and education acquired at the Nursery, directly (and indirectly) correlate with and are plausible factors in the children's later development. Said differently, the manifestation of a Black only (or majority) space, specific cultural knowledge, values and practices and positive Black role models could have formed the basis for the children's life-course. The Nursery's input, along with other factors such as family-ties, church and community-association (Rhamie and Hallam, 2002) could also be responsible for traits of immense confidence in the children (McCalla, 2002a; McCalla, Grover and Penn 2001):

> For my daughter, [a] very strong-minded person. She knows what's out there.

> She knows what we are up against as Black people but she doesn't let that prevent her. Self-esteem, self-confidence, things like that, that was developed at an early stage. And with the input from the nursery and the support I got and the determination I've got, all those contributed to what her and my son, what they are now. But I don't think if I didn't have that support network that I would probably look at things differently (Enid, mother of now adult children who attended the Nursery).

And:

> I wanted my daughter to go here, because one, I wanted her to go to school amongst African-Caribbean children. Secondly, I wanted her to understand and be grounded firmly in her culture and her roots. And I think this here nursery offers that. And also, have made her very confident. So there's a lot of things about her personality that I think, the nursery has enhanced and made stronger (Calvin, father whose daughter recently left Marcus Garvey for primary school).

Similarly, apart from self-identity, it was in this nursery setting that Syble's children learnt about citizenship and later acknowledged their citizenship rights, entitlements and responsibilities to Britain and how to obtain, fulfil and maintain them. Both the indigenous and Caribbean children identified themselves as British citizens, albeit from birthright in the indigenous children's case and through immigration legislation in the Caribbean children's case. Since they belong to the United Kingdom they expect equality of access, opportunity, integration and participation in Britain so as to accomplish their full potential, despite their colour. The essay however, demonstrated that in reality this was not always the situation they experienced. Racism was essentially responsible for this.

So to the End! And they all lived happily ever after?

This essay has revealed the phenomenal educational success of mainly working-class children, their parents and workers (Syble's children) who attended a Black-majority, community nursery in Birmingham. It demonstrated that the nursery's reinforcement of a positive sense of self and high expectations for the children seemed to be primarily instrumental in educational and employment success. With regards specifically to self-identification, there were distinctions in terms of cultural and national identities between indigenous and immigrant Caribbeans although sharing the same racial group that is, Black. Those born in Britain viewed themselves as British whereas, those who migrated from the Caribbean remained loyal only to a Jamaican identity. Despite this distinction, participants were unashamed of their racial, cultural and national identities and acknowledged their potential to achieve. However, despite the efforts of the Nursery, the study showed that success was also dependent on community support, personal determination and hard-work and, for some, faith in God. This was because success occurred amidst social deprivation, in many cases, working class disposition and racism. Due to these factors, the period of success in the life-course of Jamaican immigrants (often first and second generation) and British natives (second and third generation) varied, with Jamaican achievement occurring later in their life-cycle and Britons' attainment is often realised during and soon after compulsory schooling.

In spite of success, a number of questions are begged and remain essentially unanswered. How far are people of African-Caribbean descent, as referred to in this paper, citizens of Britain? To what extent are they treated justly socially and integrated in the British context? The study revealed that both Jamaican immigrants and British natives either experienced or were prone to experiencing racism. However, British natives mainly fared better than Jamaican migrants. This is possibly because Britons played the identity-claim and nuance cards to fight for, challenge and secure their citizenship rights and responsibility. Irrespective, both national groups acknowledge racial injustices in the British system which attempted to fail them. This acknowledgement was and still is useful to the participants as a means to continued success. For Blacks, in this case Caribbean, cannot simply put their eggs all into one basket. These Caribbean successfuls were prepared to use what they had already achieved to consider and pursue educational and employment options.

The fact that there is some evidence of educational and employment success of people of Caribbean origins as portrayed in this account does suggest that racial tension in Britain may be subsiding, albeit gradually, and that the acceptance of different races is indeed improving substantially especially since the late 1960s-1970s. Nonetheless, the success of the participants in this study is exceptional and should not be viewed as the norm or used as an excuse for complacency with regard to efforts towards sustained social integration and cultural diversity. For whilst these participants may have succeeded, national statistics on education continue to demonstrate the over-arching level of African-Caribbean educational underachievement, especially with regards to African-Caribbean boys.

Recommendations and further research

The significance of the findings from this study to ameliorate our understanding in racial and ethnic studies generally, Black success specifically, and existing public and educational provision are many. Thus I highlight the following areas requiring future attention:

- The importance of using this and other similar research to encourage Black achievement as a means to reversing the self-fulfilling prophecy and perpetuation of African-Caribbean educational and employment underachievement, especially among African Caribbean males;

- The need for further studies into Black success and the possibility of an emerging African-Caribbean middle-class in the United Kingdom (McCalla, 2002a).

- To carry out investigation into racism in pre-school settings and among pre-school workers and children;

- To use this and other similar studies to aid in the continued development of school and pre-school curricula, especially with regards to issues of self-identity and citizenship;

- The need for more research into the impact of early, cultural education and care on childhood development.

Notes

[1] As agreed by participants, Syble's actual name and the real name of Marcus Garvey Nursery are used.
However, the identity of other participants and settings has been changed for the sake of anonymity.
[2] Here 'Black' refers to people of African-Caribbean descent.
[3] GCSE is the acronym for General Certificate of Secondary Education and NVQ stands for National
Vocational Qualification taken by post-16 years in England and Wales. GCSEs are primarily academic qualifications whereas NVQs are more practical and vocational in nature.
[4] Here I have used Black rather than Caribbean so as to include Black Caribbean/Britons and other racial groups also.
[5] Although racially different, as Kevin is White, like Kevin in McCalla (1998), and McCalla (2001b). Ray also engages in extra-curricular activities thus enhancing a balance between formal studies and vocational activities.
[6] Although Feinburg's (1998) account is particularly useful here in terms of helping to construct theory, it must be noted that his work is based solely on abstract theory which is illustrated with practical examples. It is not based on an empirical investigation.
[7] Feinburg's identity formation is constructed within an American liberal framework which focuses firstly, on individuals, then on individuals as a subset of the whole group. Identity as referred to here is premised on a collectivist ideology. In other words, identity at the community/group level commences from the position of *the whole*.

References

Audit Commission (1996). *Misspent Youth ... Young People and Crime*. London: HMSO
Audit Commission (1999) *Children in Mind: Child and Adolescent MentalHhealth Services*. London: HMSO
Bagley, C.; Bart, M. and Wong, J. (1979) Antecedents of scholastic success in West Indian 10 year olds in London, in G. Verma and C. Bagley (Eds.) *Race Education and Identity*. London: Macmillan
Bakare-Yusuf, B. (1997) Raregrooves and raregroovers: A matter of taste, difference and identity, in H. Mirza (ed.) *Black British Feminism: A reader*, London: Routledge
Ball, C. (1994) *Start Right: The Importance of Early Learning*. London: Royal Society of Arts
Ball, S. & Vincent, C (1998) 'I heard it on the grapevine': 'Hot' knowledge and school choice, *British Journal of the Sociology of Education*, 19: 3, pp. 377-400
Balwin, J. (1985) Princes and Powers, in J. Balwin (Ed.) *The Price of the Ticket: Collected Non-Fiction 1948-1985*. London: Michael Joseph
Berthoud, R. (1999) *Young Caribbean Men and the Labour Market: A Comparison with Other Ethnic Groups*. York: Joseph Rowntree Foundation
Bhabha, H. (1984) Of Mimicry and Men: The ambivalence of colonial discourse, in *October*, 28, Spring
Blair, M., Bourne, et al. (1998) *Making the Difference: Teaching and Learning Strategies in Successful Multi-Ethnic Schools*. London: DfEE
Brah, A. (1992) Difference, diversity and differentiation, in J. Donald and A. Rattansi (Eds.) *Race, Culture and Difference*. London: Sage and Milton Keynes: Open University Press.

Brah, A. (1996) *Cartographies of Diaspora: Contesting Identities*. London: Routledge.

Carrington, B. (1986) Social Mobility, Ethnicity and Sport, *British Journal of Sociology of Education*, 7:1.

Carrington, B. and Short, G. (1997) Citizenship and nationhood: the constructions of British and American children, in M. Leicester, C. Modgil and F. Modgil (Ed.) *Values, Culture and Education: Political and Citizenship Education*. London: Cassell

Channer, Y. (1995) *I am a Promise: The Schooling Achievement of British African Caribbeans*. Stoke-on-Trent: Trentham Books

Childers, M. and hooks, b. (1990) A conversation about race and class, in M. Hirsch and E. Fox Keller (Eds.) *Conflicts in Feminism*. New York: Routledge

Coard, B. (1971) *How the West Indian Child is Made Educationally Sub-normal in the British School System*. London: New Beacon

David, T., Curtis, A. and Siraj-Batchford, I. (1992) *Effective Teaching in the Early Years: Fostering Children's Learning in Nurseries and in Infant Classes*. UK: OMEP

Department for Education and Skills (DfES) (2003) *Youth Cohort Study*. London: DfES

Driver, S. and Martell, L. (1997) New Labour's Communitarianisms, *Critical Social Policy*. 17:3, pp. 27-44.

Feinburg, W. (1998) *Common Schools/Uncommon Identities: National Unity and Cultural Difference*. New Haven: Yale University Press

Fuller, M. (1980) Black girls in a London comprehensive, in M. Hammersley and P. Woods (Eds.) *Life in School: The Sociology of Pupil Culture*. Milton Keynes: Open University Press

Gillborn, D. (1997a) Young, black and failed by school: the market, education reform and black students, *International Journal of Inclusive Education*. 1, pp. 65-87.

Gillborn, D. (1997b) Racism and Reform: new ethnicities/old inequalities, *British Educational Research Journal*. 23: 3, pp. 345-360.

Gillborn, D. and Gipps, C. (1996) *Recent Research on the Achievement of Ethnic Minority Pupils*. London: HMSO

Gillborn, D. and Mirza, H.S. (2000) *Educational Inequalities: Mapping race, class and gender*. London: OfSted

Gilroy, P. (1987) *There Ain't no Black in the Union Jack*. London: Hutchinson

Gilroy, P. (1993) *The Black Atlantic: Modernity and Double Consciousness*. London: Verso

Graham, J. and Bowling B. (1995). *Young People and Crime*. London: HMSO

Grewel, S., Kay, J., Landor, L., Lewis, G. and Parmar, P. (1988) *Charting the Journey: Writings by Black and Third World Women*. London: Sheba

Grover, C. (1999), *Childcare in the Community: Community Nurseries in England*. London: Daycare Trust

Hall, S. (1992) New Ethnicities, in J. Donald and A. Rattansi (Eds.) *Race, Culture and Difference*. London: Sage

Ifekwunigwe, J. (1997) Diaspora's daughter's, Africa's orphans? On lineage, authenticity and "mixed race" identity, in H. S. Mirza (Ed.) *Black British Feminism: A Reader*. London: Routledge

Mac an Ghaill, M. (1988) *Young, Gifted and Black*. Milton Keynes: Open University Press

Mac an Ghaill, M. (1994) *The Making of Men: Masculinities, Sexualities and School*. Milton Keynes: Open University Press

Marshall, T. (1950) *Citizenship and Social Class*. London: Pluto Press

Marshall, T. (Ed.) (1981) *The Right to Welfare and Other Essays*. London: Heinmann

McCalla, D. (1998) *Benign and Malign Definitions of Conflictual Power in School Sector Decision Making: Theory and Practice*, Ph.D. Thesis. London: King's College London

McCalla, D. (2001) Multiculturalism for identity and citizenship/multicultural education in american state schools, review essay, *Pedagogy, Culture and Society*. 9: 3, pp. 427-430

McCalla, D. (2002a) The academic and the community meet: two, black female voices, *International Journal of Inclusive Education*. 6: 2, pp. 165-183

McCalla, D. (2002b) A theoretical theory of benign power in schools: A preface, *Discourse: Studies in the Cultural Politics of Education*. 23: 1, pp. 39-57.

McCalla, D. (2002c) On collaboration and metamorphosis: Social research with education leaders for social justice and social change, paper presented at *British Educational Leadership, Management & Administration Society* conference, 20-22, September. Birmingham

McCalla, D., Grover, C. and Penn, H. (2001) *Local Nurseries for Local Communities: The History of Neighbourhoods and their Prospects*. London: National Children's Bureau

Mirza, H. (1992) *Young, Female and Black*. London: Routledge

Mirza, H. (1995) Black women in higher education: Defining a space/Finding a place, in L. Morley and V. Walsh (Eds.) *Feminist Academics: Creative Agents for Change*. London: Taylor and Francis

Mirza, H. (1997) Introduction, in H. Mirza (Ed.) *Black British Feminism: A reader*. London: Routledge

Morgan, S. (1986) Practice in a community nursery for black children, in A. Shama, J. Cheetham and J. Small, (Eds.) *Social Work with Black Children and their Families*. London: Batsford

Mullard, C. (1982) Multicultural education in Britain: from assimilation to cultural pluralism, in J. Tierney (Ed.) *Race, Migration and Schooling*. London: Holt, Rinehart and Winston

Owen, D., Harrison, G. et al. (1991) Ethnic factors in voluntary and compulsory admissions, *Psychological Medicine*. 21, pp. 185-196

Parmar, P. (1997) Other kind of dreams, in H. Mirza (Ed.) *Black British Feminism: A reader*. London: Routledge

Parsons, C., Castles, F. et al. (1996) *Exclusion from School: The Public Cost*. London: Commission for Racial Equality

Pathak, S. (2000) *Race Research for the future: Ethnicity in education, training and the labour market*. London: Department for Education and Employment

Pearce, N. and Hillman, J. (1998) *Wasted Youth: Raising Achievement and Tackling School exclusion*. London: Institute for Public Policy Research

Ramdin, R. (1987) *The Making of the Black Working Class in Britain*. Aldershot: Gower Publishing

Reay, D. and Mirza, H.S. (1997) Uncovering genealogies of the margins: Black supplementary schools, *British Journal of Sociology of Education*. 18: 4, pp. 477-500.

Reay, D., Davies, J. David, M. and Ball, S. (2001) Choices of degree of degrees of choice? Class, 'race' and the higher education choice process, *Sociology*, 35, pp. 855-874

Rhamie, J. and Hallam, S. (2002) An investigation into African-Caribbean academic success in the UK, *Race, Ethnicity and Education*. 5: 2, pp. 151-170

Roche, M. (1992) *Rethinking Citizenship*. Cambridge: Polity Press

Saunders, P. 1993 Citizenship in a liberal society. in B. Turner (Ed.) *Citizenship and Social Theory*. London: Sage, pp. 57-90

Sewell, T. (1997) *Black Masculinities and School: How Black Boys Survive Modern School*. Stoke on Trent: Trentham Books

Silvanandan, A. (1990) *Communities of Resistance*. London, Verso

Small, S. (1994) *Racialised Barriers*. London Routledge

Spillers, H. (1987) Mama's baby Papa's maybe: An American grammar book, *Diacritics*. 17, Summer

Social Exclusion Union (1998) *Truancy and School Exclusions*. London: HMSO

Stone, M. (1981) *The Education of the Black Child: The Myth of Multiracial Education*. London: Fantana

Troyna, B. and Stone, M. (1986) *Racism, Education and the State*. London: Croom Helm

Turner, B. (1990) Outline of a theory of citizenship, *Sociology*, 24: 2, pp. 189-217.

Turner, B. (1993) (Ed.) *Citizenship and Social Theory*. London: Sage

Verma, G. and Bagley, C. (1979) A critical introduction, in G. Verma and C. Bagley (Eds.) *Race, Education and Identity*. London: Macmillan Press

Weekes, D. (1997) Shades of Blackness: young Black female constructions of beauty, in H. Mirza (Ed.) *Black British Feminism: A reader*. London: Routledge

Weekes, D. and Wright, C. (1998) *Improving Practice: A whole school approach to raising the achievement of African Caribbean Youth*. London: Runnymede Trust

Wright, C. (1992) *Race Relations in the Primary School*. London: David Falton

Wright, C., Weekes, D. and McGlaughlin, A. (2000) *'Race', Class and Gender in Exclusion from School*. London: Falmer Press

Chapter 7

Uncovering Genealogies of the Margins: Black Supplementary Schooling

Diane Reay & Heidi Safia Mirza

Introduction: a continued tradition of racial activism

Black supplementary schools, that is extra schooling organised and run by and for the community outside of mainstream provision, has been in existence for over 40 years—for as long as the Black community has constituted a significant presence in the UK. The schools are organised mainly on Saturdays (hence are also sometimes called Saturday schools), but can be held on Sundays and even on weekdays after school. The schools are to be found in church halls, vacant school rooms, community centres and even the homes of teachers and activists. As the term 'supplementary' suggests, such schools have been officially regarded as an addition or 'supplement' to the mainstream. However the analysis of Black supplementary schools in educational and social research resists popular conceptions of these schools as additional or complimentary to the mainstream. Often described as 'grassroots educational movements', they are viewed primarily as places of resistance to racism and for the struggle to succeed (Stone, 1981; Dhondy (et al., 1982; Tomlinson, 1985; Chevannes & Reeves, 1987; Mac an Ghaill, 1991; Dove, 1993; Channer, 1995).

Chevannes and Reeves argue very strongly that supplementary schooling is a collective strategy of the Black community to combat the inadequate education available to Black children (Chevannes & Reeves, 1987, p. 149). In a similar vein Maureen Stone theorises supplementary schooling as grassroots activism:

> reminiscent of the kind of activity amongst working-class socialists in the late-nineteenth and early-twentieth centuries. There is no comparable contemporary English working-class equivalent to the West Indian Saturday schools. Unable to influence the school system, the West Indian community has devised its own response ... the Saturday school. (Stone, 1981, p. 238)

The similarities of impulse and purpose between socialist Sunday schools of the early twentieth century, which began in Scotland in 1895 and spread south through England (Steedman, 1990; Green, 1990) and Black supplementary schools, which were established in Britain since the 1960s are evident. Both have sought to teach pupils about their culture and history and both have focused on teaching educational skills that it was felt were not being provided elsewhere. Both have been largely uncharted in official records. Most significantly, both demonstrate local grassroots resistance of the working classes to forms of education which are imposed rather than negotiated.

In mapping a genealogy of counterschool grassroots movements we have a history which stretches back over 100 years, from socialist Sunday schools in the past, to Black supplementary schools now. Though middle-class educational reform had secured the demise of working class socialist Sunday schools by the late 1940s—within 40 years of their establishment—the Black grassroots educational counter movement still appears to be evolving forty years after its inception.

Ironically the ambiguous status of Black supplementary schools has meant that they have been for the most part left alone. The schools are not seen to represent a 'critical mass' in terms of numbers and voice. What is regarded as their fragmented, localised, contingent formation is not perceived as constituting any threat to the mainstream. As funding through local authority or the voluntary sector has always been small, unreliable or resisted these schools' self-sufficiency and genesis in community activism has placed them outside the local authority gaze. For the most part these schools rely on parental contributions and community donations.

Black supplementary schools also do not threaten mainstream legitimacy through the demand for religious or racial separatism. These small grassroots, local, often community based schools, are not regarded in the same light as the voluntary aided separate religious 'ethnic' schools movement. Unlike established Muslim, Jewish or Seventh Day Adventist schools the supplementary school is based on a philosophy of inclusion rather than exclusiveness. A notable characteristic of these Black schools is that no matter if the school's orientation is Methodist, Evangelical, Pentecostal, Rastafararian, or Afrocentric (rooted in Garveyism), other children, including White working class children and children from other dominations or ethnic backgrounds, are welcomed. Their open community membership means that these schools place themselves outside of the contentious discourse for separate religious 'ethnic schools'. Black supplementary schools are in that sense an anomaly within 'ethnic education'.

However while the Black educational movement is seen as spontaneous and progressive in the literature, it is also described essentially as a reactive response to mainstream educational inequality and marginality. Our thesis is that Black supplementary schools should be seen as more than simply a response to exclusion and evidence of good practice. In their presence and praxis these schools embody an evolving organic critique of mainstream educational 'lacking'. In mapping Black supplementary school's hidden history, in revealing their other world, what emerges is a picture of collective Black educational agency that challenges taken-for-granted assumptions embodied within mainstream educational rationale. In the words and actions of the heterogenous Black female educators involved in these schools, we find evidence of a radical Black agency from which has evolved a unified collective consciousness.

The Study

Our study was a small scale six-month project which focused on the work of Black supplementary schools. The aim of the study was to interrogate the assumptions inherent within the dominant discourse of Black underachievement by moving toward an understanding of positive Black educational motivation. To achieve this the study focused on the work of Black women educators who were also mothers and activists involved in these schools. Though the complex and seemingly contradictory nature of their activism was the primary preoccupation of our analysis, an important contextual objective of the study was to establish if there was a significant presence of Black schools within our given locality, London.

No one knows the number and size of this 'other' educational market. There exists no official records or national survey of such schools. To establish a basis for arguing that these schools can constitute a social movement, we attempted to build up a local database of Black supplementary schools, concentrating on the several London boroughs where 58.7% (290,968) of the population in the UK are known to live. Official funding records held by community information officers, library records, and local authority education departments yielded little information. Even national organisations, such as the CRE (Commission for Racial Equality) knew little about where to find Black supplementary schools. Personal Black social networks and tracing advertisements in the Black press were more fruitful in terms of building a picture of this hidden grassroots provision.

In six months we uncovered the presence of 60 supplementary schools across 15 boroughs in Inner and Greater London. Of these schools, 48 were concentrated in the 7 Inner London boroughs of Brent, Lambeth, Southwark, Lewisham, Kensington and Chelsea, Hackney, and Haringay, where the population makes up over 20% of the local population. We found 12 schools in Lambeth alone. The average size of the schools were between 30-40 pupils. However some schools had as few as 15 children and others as much as 90. One of our study schools even had a waiting list of 400 pupils! The age range of pupils catered for was anything between 3-18 years old, though the average age of most schools was 5-16 years.

In our small scale study of Black supplementary schools, we believe we only scratched the surface. Even by the time the study ended, through personal and social networks and word of mouth we were hearing of more and more schools everyday. Some times there would be several on one council estate or in one neighbourhood. They appeared to spring up 'unofficially' in houses, community centres, and unused school rooms. These schools appeared to be a growing rather than declining phenomena.

The main purpose of the study was to collect qualitative data on the work of Black women educators in order to move toward an explanation of the strong presence of positive educational motivation within Black community. To gather qualitative data we visited two supplementary schools, one in London, Colibri, and one in a provincial city, Scarlet Ibis. We also carried out in-depth interviews with seven of the Black educators involved in four supplementary schools- the two study schools and a further two schools, Community Connections and Ohemaa, both of which are sited in London. In addition, eight mothers whose children attended the supplementary schools were interviewed.

Our study then, is a small-scale, intensive, investigation into an under-researched area of educational practice. Our findings are necessarily tentative and exploratory. However, we have tried to draw out the main themes that emerged from the study and, in doing so, hope to contribute to better understandings of complex strategies for attaining Black_educational success.

Black Educators: a genealogical approach

Teaching at the grassroots, whether in socialist Sunday schools in the past or supplementary schools now, has been largely overlooked in academic writing. Grace's comment in the late 1970s is just as true today as it was 20 years ago: 'the teachers of the working-class have few written histories which document their philosophies and aspirations, struggles and achievements' (Grace, 1978, p. 2).

Black educators working in supplementary schools have a very different relationship to their pupils' education from their mainstream counterparts. Henry Giroux conceptualises committed inner city teachers as transformative intellectuals. (Giroux, 1994). However, his analysis underestimates the contextual constraints under which they operate in a period in the 1990s which has seen the triumph of a new ascendent capitalism (Cole & Hill, 1995; Goodson, 1995). Even then we cannot assume that more than a small minority have a commitment to social change. Under such wider societal conditions it seems that 'mutually reinforcing moments of pedagogy and politics as primary to the practice of representing as an act of resistance and transformation' are far more likely to be found in supplementary schools than state schools (Giroux, 1994, p. 49). Similarly it is supplementary schools rather than their mainstream counterparts which provide opportunities for students 'not simply to discover their hidden histories but to recover them' (Giroux, 1994, p. 50).

Foucault's genealogical method is about the retrieval of counter memories. Genealogical practice:

> transforms history from a judgment on the past in the name of a present truth to a 'counter-memory' that combats our current modes of truth and justice, helping us to understand and change the present by placing it in a new relation to the past. (Arac, 1986, p. viii)

Foucault did not clearly articulate a theory of genealogy, making a genealogical approach difficult to operationalise in empirical research. As Mitchell Dean states 'Foucault left us no extended methodological statements on genealogy (Dean, 1994, p 14). In very simple terms perhaps genealogy can be best summed up as a critique of dominant discourses which draws on knowledges and ways of thinking that are marginalised and/or stand outside the mainstream. This fits in with Barry Smart's understanding of genealogy as:

> a more committed position which questions and criticises the effects of power associated with the scientific hierachisation of knowledge. (Smart, 1992, p. 55)

While such a definition suggests it is problematic to build up a genealogy of supplementary schooling, the discourses of Black educators working in such schooling could be utilised to critique and challenge, for example, dominant discourses on 'race'. Genealogy, therefore, presents a different version to traditional history. Its critical stance in relation to mainstream versions is exemplified in genealogy's attempts:

> ...to reveal the historicity of qualities and properties which either have been thought to lack a history or to have been neglected (Smart, 1992, p. 57).

As Dean asserts genealogy displaces the search for ultimate foundations with a 'form of patient criticism and problematisation located in the present' (Dean, 1994, p. 20). It is in Black grassroots organisations such as supplementary schools that we find consistent and concerted efforts to problematise Whiteness, in particular the Whiteness endemic in our educational system.

Stephen Ball sees a methodological affinity between educational ethnography and genealogy (Ball, 1994, p. 3). In our work we have highlighted the connections between recording the perspectives of Black educators in supplementary schooling and genealogical method. Although in no way would we claim our research constitutes a genealogy. It clearly does not:

> Historical research is thus very important in Foucault's conception of genealogy: by documenting the discontinuities of history, he dispels the shadow of a monolithic, transcendent culture from which marginalised groups and individuals must wrest the rights to their identities. (M E Bailey, 1993, p. 105).

Our research is not historical, our data reaches back over 20 years unlike the centuries which Foucault's genealogies spanned. However, we are attempting a similar process of uncovering subjugated knowledges:

> (Genealogy) locates many discontinuous and regional struggles against power both in the past and the present. These voices are the sources of resistance, the creative subjects of history. (Sawicki, 1991, p. 28)

Black educators demonstrate that there are different versions to the hegemonic discourses on 'race' and education which either objectify Black people or homogenise their experience under an all-embracing conceptual framework (Gurnah, 1992).

In his own work Foucault used genealogical method to problematise metanarratives (Foucault, 1977, 1981). He examined existing grand theories for their power effects. As Jana Sawicki points out genealogies 'serve less to explain the real than to criticise other attempts to grasp it' (Sawicki, 1991, p. 53). As such she asserts Foucault's genealogies operate not as theories but rather as mechanisms for criticising theories. Genealogies function as challenges to the taken for granted, normative assumptions of prevailing discourses. We have tried to take a broadly genealogical approach to Black educators' narratives by using their accounts to present a different version to the prevailing discourses on 'race' and education.

Uncovering the views and perspectives of Black educators could be a contributory part of a project to map out what has been left out of generally accepted knowledge about the relationship between 'race' and education. It is in this specific sense of 'suppressed perspectives', namely, inserting the views of Black educators into existing discourses on 'race' and education, that a genealogical method seems appropriate. The relevance of Black educators' understandings for any genealogy of 'race' and education becomes even more apparent when we read that for Foucault genealogical research is concerned with:

> the insurrection of knowledges that are opposed primarily not to the contents, methods or concepts of a science, but to the effects of the centralising powers which are linked to the institution and functioning of an organised scientific discourse within a society such as ours. (Foucault, 1980, p. 84)

Foucault developed his genealogical methodology in order to explore:

> the union of erudite and local memories which allows us to establish a historical knowledge of struggles and to make use of this knowledge tactically today... what it really does is entertains the claims to attention of local, discontinuous, disqualified, illegitimate knowledge against the claims of a unitary body of theory that would filter, hierarchies, and order them in the name of some true knowledge. (Foucault, 1980, p. 83).

It is such erudite, local, memories Charity, a mother and teacher at Colibri sees the importance of preserving even as they slip from memory:

> It is very special that sort of commitment and it's important the history of the school doesn't get lost because then there'd be no account of all the struggles to set it up and keep it going in those early years.

A Gendered Social Movement

Of the 60 schools in our research over 65% of the teachers were women. Where men ran the school, women's daily work as teachers and carers was clearly the majority input. Mac an

Ghaill writes that in the Black education movement. 'It is important to emphasise that Black women were at the forefront of the implementation of these strategies of resistance.' (1991, p. 134). Similarly Black women writers, Bryan *et al*. argue, 'For Black women challenging education has been part of a wider struggle to defend the rights and interests of the Black community as a whole … education struggles have been central to our political development' (1985, p. 59)

It has been argued that such conscious forms of female collective action should be recognised as constituting a new social movement (Mirza, 1997). An analysis of female collective action offers a new direction in the investigation of Black social movements where for too long Black female agency has remained invisible. In the masculinist discourse of 'race' and social change, the assumption has always been that the struggle against racist exclusion is contested and fought over in the masculine arena of the streets riots, rebellion and violent confrontation characterise the struggle of the (male) youth in the city (Solomos & Back 1995). In privileging such an analysis the subversive and covert transformative action of women is rarely valorised as an act of social change. Black women struggle for educational inclusion in order to transform their opportunities and so in the process subvert racist expectations and beliefs. In our study the women collectively opened up transformative possibilities for their community through their pragmatic recognition of the power of education to transform and change the hegemonic discourse (McLaren, 1994; hooks, 1994).

All four schools, Ohemaa, Community Connections, Colibri, and Scarlet Ibis had been set up primarily by women. Both Verna and Maxine talk in terms of 'themselves and a few other mothers getting together'. Charity, who had worked as a full-time coordinator at Colibri was adamant:

> 'It's mainly the women who are the ones who are involved in education in this country. Within the Afro-Caribbean community it tends to be mainly women. In my family that was the case and at Colibri it was mainly women who came and that was fine. Obviously, there were a few fathers who were involved and there were a couple of men who were on the committee but it was mainly women.

Kathleen Casey has documented the commitment her sample of Black women teachers in the US made to the (re)construction of communal meaning for Black people (Casey, 1993, p. 153). There were similar processes at work in the narratives of the six Black women educators we interviewed. They expressed a powerful sense of outrage at existing racial inequalities, but one which was fused with an agenda for change which they had begun, and continued, to translate into action. Their dedication to (re)construct communal meanings of being Black was awe-inspiring. Two of the women had life threatening illnesses yet still maintained their commitment to, and involvement in, supplementary schooling. As one of them commented:

> I have to stop for my own sake. I need to look after my own health and try and recover. Also to do more things that are for me. You have no idea how many creative writing and poetry workshops I have missed because they are all at the weekend. My work has been on the ground with children, doing my bit here and it has been rewarding, very rewarding. Children have gone through the school that others have given up on and they are doing very well. Matthew who was so very, very difficult when he came, could not sit down for more than thirty seconds I see him now on his way to college. Perhaps it is alright you know, that this is a stage. The school has done a great deal for a number of children. I can see the fruits of my

> labour. Even if I don't find someone to take over perhaps it is enough what I have done. (Verna)

Encapsulated in her query is a sense of doubt; that in a social context in which she recognises so much needs to be done to combat racism, there is still a need, even after 16 years involvement, to play an active part. There are powerful resonances in her account with the accounts Black American women teachers gave of 'raising the race' (Casey, 1993, p. 152). Both incomcorporate an acceptance of personal responsibility for the well-being of one's people, and especially for the education of Black children.

It is in their praxis; the combination of theory and action (Weiner, 1994) in these women's narratives that we see the seeds of a genealogical analysis (Foucault, 1981, 1991; Dean, 1994). Using their accounts we have tried to make visible the wider aspirations and struggles against racism of Black communities in Britain.

'Giving Back': the rehabilitation of 'old fashioned' values

Helen frames the motives of Black educators in terms of 'giving something back'. Black educators themselves often used language of commitment, community and continuity that seems out of place with the educational jargon of the 1990s. They too often conceptualised both their own involvement and the later involvement of young Black people who had attended Saturday school as 'giving back':

> I always received a lot of encouragement as a child myself. I went all the way through to university and I know how very important it is to give encouragement to children and that is why I kept my involvement so long. (Helen)

> I really wanted to do Saturday school because so much was given to me when I was a child. I had so much positive input I wanted to give some of it back. I also wanted to challenge this Government's views on community—that community isn't important. (Verna)

> All the young people who work here as volunteers they've all attended a supplementary school and have all come in through the supplementary school system. They have kept that commitment and they all want to give something back. (Maxine)

This theme of 'giving back' was even extended to current pupils:

> I think you need a special period in the day when you allow the child to give something back. (Verna).

The concept of giving back presupposes a community to give back to. It also presupposes that that community has given you something. Verna talks of what 'a joy it has been to be involved in Saturday school', while Rose talks other involvement as 'a gift'. This discursive construction of reciprocity between community and individual is positioned in stark contrast to mainstream schools' relationship to the Black working-class communities that make up a sizeable proportion of their catchments:

> I don't know where the local school thinks it is-not on Highway estate that's for sure When schools have nothing to do with the local community, you know are totally outside the local community-somehow, I don't know how but they are not in touch. They are

> simply not in touch and I don't know how that has happened but it has. There is no real contact with parents apart from talking down. (Rose)

The Organic Nature of Supplementary Schooling

It is out of these discursive constructions of reciprocity, community and continuity that understandings of supplementary schooling as organic can be built. Casey describes her Black women teachers as 'the organic intellectuals of their people' (Casey, 1993, p. 153). In a similar organic vein Maxine uses the metaphor of a tree to explain how her supplementary school has flourished:

> One of the most positive things about the school is its instilling of community continuity. It puts out branches and they make it stronger. We have mentors, older children working in the school to help the younger ones. But beyond that we have ex-pupils who come back to help.

Black educators' narratives demonstrate the ways in which supplementary schooling grew out of Black grassroots demands rather than as impositions from above. Scarlet Ibis supplementary school was set up after a small scale research project asked:

> forty families, mainly Caribbean but some mixed race, about why they thought Black children were underachieving. After that myself and a few of the Black mothers got together. (Verna)

Talking about the inception of the same supplementary school, Rose, who had also been involved at the very beginning, said:

> The school grew out of local demand, you know. I think that's a very good thing. They asked the parents what they wanted and they wanted Saturday school.

> I got involved because of a need that my children had. I felt that the system was not operating to a high enough standard to enable my children to realise their potential ... So I decided along with another couple of parents I would tutor my children at home. Then these parents and me set up this school which I have been involved in for over 16 years. (Maxine)

Charity's narrative on how Colibri was started includes similar themes of activism, community and commitment:

> There was a group of about six parents, who like myself as a Black teacher, were dissatisfied with what was happening to Black pupils. They felt if they had been in the Caribbean their children would be much further on academically and they decided something had to be done, schools weren't doing anything so it had to be them. I really wish someone had had the time to chart the enormous amount of work they put in those first few years. It was immense. The school started off in someone's front room on Saturday mornings. The parents doing all the teaching themselves to start with and it was very much focused on what was their main concern; their children

not being able to read and write properly. Then these parents found the group of children grew from 10 to 15 and soon it was 20 and at this point it was unmanageable running a Saturday school in someone's front room so they petitioned the council for accommodation and finally got one of the council's derelict properties. They spent their spare time shovelling rubbish out of the room, tramps had been living there, doing building, repair work, getting groups of parents together to decorate. They pulled together and did all this work themselves, used the expertise they had to get the school on its feet.

This activism stands in contrast to the prevailing discursive construction of the working-class, whether Black or White. Dominant discourses paint a picture of apathetic masses, the inactive and the uninformed; parents who need to be cajoled or persuaded to even hear their children read. The Government White Paper 'Choice and Diversity' locates the problem of 'indifferent' parents as being 'at its worst in our inner city or large housing estate areas' (DES, 1992, p. 6). While official discourses are locating indifference within working-class communities, both Black and White, in the accounts of Black educators we find counter memories of industry, commitment and sustained grassroots activism among Black communities in inner cities and council estates. Supplementary schools provide a different version to orthodox accounts which position Black people as passive victims or pathological actors. They tell tales of effective Black agency.

We have found in earlier research that the majority of White working-class parents were acting to little effect because the ways in which they tried to compensate for inadequate education were individualised and unsupported (Reay, 1996). In contrast there is a collectivist element in Black agency. Maxine and Nadine talk in terms of responding to their own children's unmet needs in relation to the state system. However, in both cases there is not an individualised course of action but a strategy (setting up a Saturday school; getting involved in one) that is a much more collectivised, community based response:

> I wanted Saturday school to be free and open, mainly for the local community. (Verna)

The use of community in the discourse of Black educators operates as a challenge to the consumerist individualism of the 1990s. The term 'community' has a very chequered history. It has often been used by left wing academics in both a mythical sense and as a mechanism of nostalgia (Seabrook, 1982; Hoggart, 1957). In both the media and academia it is seen as an absence in working-class life in the 1990s; a glue that held working-class life together in the 1940s, 1950s and 1960s but which has progressively come unstuck under the right-wing, free-market hegemony of the 1980s and 1990s. Across the political spectrum it is used to represent a commonality of values and interests; one that stresses the importance of civic duties and consequently is far more focused on conformity than any form of empowerment. Alternatively, it is used in an apolitical and pluralistic sense in much postmodernism.

However, it exists in a very different sense not only in the discourse of Black educators but, more tellingly, in their praxis. They put it into practice!—Ohemaa, Community Connections, Colibri and Scarlet Ibis are community schools in a real sense that mainstream schools have never managed to achieve. Helen, a White mother living on Highways Estate, who sent her child to Scarlet Ibis Saturday school, said:

> What I like about Saturday school is how committed the teachers are; committed to giving something back to the community they've come from. You don't get that with the White working-class made

good. The Black families on the estate haven't given up, they have still got their drive and their sense of community and I really like that. You know, it's also about what I was talking about earlier, giving something back. Rose wanted to put something back and so did the other teachers, there was a guy too who had been to university—it's this idea that you get qualified and then you actually come back and help—use your qualification to help the people you've come from, like I said White people don't do that. (Helen)

Challenging the Normative Assumptions of Whiteness in Mainstream Schooling

Writing of an innovative girls' comprehensive David Gillborn states that its people's education programme was 'helping many working-class students (of diverse educational backgrounds) begin critically to deconstruct taken-for-granted assumptions about '"race", racism and racists' (Gillborn, 1995, p. 151). However, such curricular input is far from the norm in mainstream schooling. As Omar, Aisha's son commented 'The best thing about Saturday school is Black studies. We learn a whole lot of things we don't get told about at Milner primary'. All too often, in the public sphere, Black people are starved of images of themselves (Gates, 1988).

Interestingly, the failure of mainstream schooling to realise Black pupils' potential is sometimes linked in the accounts of Black educators to lack of small group work and individual attention as well as to the absence of any recognition of Black culture:

> For some teachers we are seen as a criticism of mainstream because we do find time to do the individual work to get children reading and writing when mainstream hasn't. (Rose)

> Things are getting worse, much worse in schools. Class sizes are going up when they need to come down. Extra support is being eroded, our children can't get the help they need. I am saying this as a primary school teacher. (Paul)

However, Verna has a different analysis:

> None of these arguments made that much sense to me apart from the fact that Black culture and history and literature were not portrayed in the content of the education and Saturday school was set up to counter that.

While Brenda states emphatically:

> White bias is everywhere in education, everywhere except in Saturday school, that is.

The aspect of 'race' that has been consistently overlooked and taken-for-granted in western societies is Whiteness (Frankenberg, 1993). However, as Brenda's words illustrate, Whiteness is not taken for granted in supplementary schools. They provide discursive sites where assumption of Whiteness as normative are subverted. If, as Judith Butler writes, genealogy works towards disrupting normative categories (Butler, 1990) then a genealogical method can be used to subvert the normalisation of Whiteness and offer some vision of alternatively racialised worlds. It is in supplementary schooling that we find the genesis of both approaches.

Supplementary schools provide a context in which Whiteness is displaced as central and Blackness can be seen as normative.

'Fitting in': disrupting the normative through dialogue

The problematic interface between supplementary and mainstream schooling is only touched on in the literature on supplementary schooling. The little that exists suggests a separation between the two and an avoidance of dialogue (Clark, 1982; Dacosta, 1987). Clark and Dacosta both suggest that a major impetus for this separation comes from parents, many of whom do not wish the children's mainstream teachers to know that they attend Saturday schools:

> It has always been my wish to make contact with schools, but some parents did not want the schools to know their children were receiving help. Clark, 1982, P. 25)

Our research found relationships differ from borough to borough, even catchment area to catchment area. A number of Saturday schools are sited in state schools and colleges, some are funded by their local authority, while yet others seem to be largely invisible to official networks. Attitudes about the relationship with mainstream schooling differ widely within the supplementary school movement:

> We see our role as supporting and complementing schools (spokesperson for Keen Students Supplementary School, *Caribbean Times*, 2/7/94).

Valentino Jones, who teaches at the Josina Machel Supplementary school, also talks in terms of complementing mainstream provision (Jones, 1986). A counter view is put forward by Ama Gueye. She sees supplementary schooling as the only educational means through which Black communities can maintain any distinct cultural heritage (Gueye, 1988, p. 2). While many of the qualified teachers working in supplementary schools are employed by the state sector, varying degrees of mistrust permeate the supplementary/mainstream relationship which must place such teachers in a conflictual position. Sally Tomlinson, writing about a Saturday school, states that:

> This latter organisation particularly, was mainly known to teachers by hearsay rather than actual contact, and some anxiety was expressed that the organisation was 'teaching Black power'. (Tomlinson, 1984, p. 39)

'Black Power' certainly fits into the racialised discourses of local politics that Solomos and Back write about (Solomos & Back, 1995).

A clear recognition of the 'threat' supplementary schooling might be seen to pose to mainstream, and evidence of attempts to alleviate mainstream fears, were there in the accounts:

> The Chief Education Officer and the council had got onto this feeling that we might be doing something threatening to schools, you know. We actually faced a bit of hostility, opposition. (Verna)

As a consequence a number of Saturday school educators talked in terms of trying to 'fit in'.

> We have tried to fit in and I'd say now that our relationship with the children's mainstream schools is very good. (Nadine)

However, alongside examples of 'fitting in' there were challenges to mainstream understandings of supplementary schooling:

> Black Power is such a distortion, you know, if Black Power means self-confidence, positive self-esteem, then all children need it. More than that we all do. Empowerment is something we all need, White as well as Black, to see it as a threat is to misread what empowerment is about. It is something we all need, not just a few. I don't think that's how those parents saw it 15 years ago as Black Power. I think they wanted something they were entitled to as parents—you know their children realising their potential. If that's what empowerment is the sooner we all get it the better. (Charity)

There was a further rationale for fitting in; to counter criticisms of doing things so differently children's learning would actually suffer rather than benefit:

> That's another reason for getting into their mainstream schools. It's important to go and see what methods they use so that you don't confuse the child. For instance, maths to make sure to do it the way that they do in school. I often question some of the methods they use in school but say for instance they use bricks for counting then we make sure we have them for children at Saturday school to make sure we don't confuse them. (Rose)

and:

> Education must be in context and so we didn't want to be doing things too differently to what was going on in school. We had to address this as that was a criticism of the Saturday school so we had to ensure we were in tune with their mainstream school curriculum and we worked with the parents on that to give us that information. You know, 'what books were they using?' (Maxine)

A third motive for fitting in is that only then can supplementary schools have any impact on mainstream provision:

> I think we have convinced the school that they need to get at, to address the culture of Black children in some way (Verna)

So fitting in enables an educative role in relation to mainstream schooling:

> In our time we've done an awful lot of talks in schools about our curriculum, about what we do, about the ideas we have for integrating Black children' culture. (Verna)

Nadine talked of regularly going into children's ordinary schools:

> Mostly I suppose it is to talk about our children here, to give some feedback, talk about problems they're having or look at what help they need, but I also go in to do Black history in schools, like with Black history month I go into about 3 or 4 schools to talk in assemblies or to classes. Then I will go in to talk, well it's mainly to the Head but sometimes deputies or classteachers, about Ohemaa or Windrush, about what we do here.

Rose describing the relationships she had built up with the local primary schools said:

> Well it's talk and more talk (laughing). I used to go into schools a lot. I think it is important from the point of culture, you know, to go

> in. Different schools celebrate different things. Well before I got ill I would go into one school for Martin Luther King day to talk to all the children. Then the primary school has a Caribbean week and I would go in to sing Caribbean songs. Have you heard of Anansi? Well I used to go in to tell Anansi stories and Rosa Parks, You know? I would tell them stories about Rosa Parks so there was a whole lot of Black culture that I'd do in school.

It is evident from the accounts of Black educators that supplementary schooling has to juggle complex, and at times contradictory, positionings in relation to mainstream education. The strong elements of empathy, inevitable degree of identification and desire for dialogue are undercut by supplementary school staffs advocacy role vis a vis pupils and also their parents. In last resort they are there to put the child and parents' case:

> On balance I'd have to say my contact with the local primary schools hasn't really been positive. There have been problems for the children with racist incidents now, in their mainstream schools. So have been into schools to talk to Headteachers with their parents mostly. There are schools where our children are called monkey and no one is doing anything about it and some of our mothers are nervous, you know, about going into school to talk to teachers. So I will go into school and say to the Head 'What does your bullying or your anti-racist policy say?' But it is not just parents, children will bring up racist incidents, especially at circle time and if they do I always take it up. You know go in to ask the Head 'How do you deal with a child who continually runs amok, calling Black children monkey, being racist?' (Rose)

Black educators' narratives raised many issues around racism in state schooling. There were subtleties of racism rarely mentioned in mainstream accounts:

> Last year Alex had a young White male teacher who set up weekly meeting to talk about Alex's problems in the classroom. We talked endlessly about Alex's problems but nothing really changed. I don't think it was so much a case of him being racist more of being frightening of being seen as racist, you know. He seemed to give Adam a free reign in the belief, you know, he was being a caring teacher. But Alex was learning nothing except how to get away with murder. I kept telling him 'He needs to be made to learn'. He kept killing him with kindness. So we did talk plenty but no one got anywhere. Alex just did what he liked. (Marilyn)

Paul Gonnolly writes of similar misguided anti-racism in which the Afro-Caribbean boys in his research school were encouraged and valorised for their sporting prowess while their disruptive, work avoiding strategies in the classroom were overlooked (Connolly, 1994). As Charity points out:

> Its a question of mundane everyday racisms. You know there is an endless stream of stories of putting your hand up and never getting noticed. Children getting really despondent because they have tried really hard with a piece of work and got just the same mark, the same comment as a piece they haven't worked anything like so hard on. (Charity)

Positive Model of Home School Relationships

Claudette Williams describes the relationship between Black educators and Black parents in supplementary schooling as symbiotic (Williams, 1995). This symbiosis infuses the parent-teacher relationship. Supplementary schools operate with a very different home-school interface to mainstream; one in which the parent remains the expert on their child despite the schooling context:

> We have spent a lot of time persuading parents how important and educative learning through dance and drama is. However, at the end of the day we have to go with what the parent wants. There is one little boy whose mother insists that he only do Maths and English. I always feel sorry for him when the others go off to do some creative work. But his mother insists so that is that. (Brenda)

Brenda paints a very different picture of parental involvement to that existing in mainstream schooling where Black and White working-class, and even some middle-class parents, lose their expert status in relation to their child once they enter the school gate. Black educators articulated a very keen awareness of the problematic relationship Black parents had with their children's mainstream schools:

> Our parents feel very strongly they are not listened to. The education system has a very long history of keeping parents out. In the 50s and 60s parents had virtually nothing to do with schools. We have come a long way down the road. I think it's part of that history, you know, 'We're the teachers, we know best'. It's partly to do with class but it is also because whenever they see Black parents opening their mouths they see them as creating discord or problems so I can understand the feelings of being fobbed off or not listened to. I think schools need to give more space to parents, to listen to their views. I think there needs to be more links between the home and school. Teachers do not know enough about the context of children's lives and about parents' lives. They need to know and then be able to use that. So I think the relationship between parents and teachers isn't a happy one and it hasn't been for years. It needs developing, it needs encouragement, there needs to be the space for it. (Verna)

This awareness informed their own interaction with parents. Conflicts and tensions where they do exist seem to be played out through dialogue rather than the feelings of being 'fobbed off' and not being heard that Black and White working-class mothers recounted to their tales of mainstream involvement. (David *et al.*, 1997). However, this is not to deny shades of some of the recurrent tensions between parents and mainstream teachers; namely the construction of parents as a conservative bulwark against innovative practices of educators. Such a view is there in what Brenda, Verna and Nadine say;

> We don't want the situation our parents find in school where they keep on being fobbed off. Here we are very much governed by the parents and what they want. You know they are telling us they don't get listened to in ordinary schools so it is really important that we are seen to listen. But that does cause problems with what we can offer in terms of the curriculum because while the staff here

> would like to give more time to Black studies, parents are telling us to concentrate on the basics 'to make that your first priority', so in a way there is a conflict, but not really because we have to go with what the parents want. We don't want to make the mistakes of children's ordinary schools so we really prioritise listening to parents. (Nadine)

and:

> Although I have spent a lot of time explaining why we work in the way we do, I suppose the parents could disapprove, in some ways Saturday school is not what they expect. I have a very strong philosophy of child centredness. I have always been very committed to supporting the child. In our society children often don't have a voice. I suppose parents might have expected Saturday school to be more formal, I mean we work in groups there is no sitting in rows but I believe in working in ways which are best for the child so there is a strong focus on three Rs but also on making the work really interesting for the child, starting from where the child is and integrating things around culture and history. (Verna)

However, there was no uniform parental view among the Black mothers interviewed as to what supplementary schools should teach. Charity, Mona and Yvonne see the focus on basics as the main reason for their child's attendance, Anna, Jumi and Ellen see Black history and cultural studies as just as important an aspect of such schooling while for Aisha it is the most important thing supplementary schools can offer:

> Those very things that tackle the identity of children and address their vulnerability as Black people, I think there's going to be less and less of that as the National Curriculum develops because the Government see it as a threat and see it as politics so those teachers who go on doing it are seen as subversive. I think that's the reason they have put this emphasis on parents because they see parents as coming in and taking over from those sort of teachers, teachers who are political. It's an appeal to White parents. That's why I've sent Omar to Saturday school.

For Aisha sending Omar to Saturday school is a response to the increasing ethnocentrism of the National Curriculum. However, as stated earlier Jumi, Anna and Yvonne, place equal importance on Saturday schooling's emphasis on formal pedagogy. Jumi's account reveals the tensions in competing demands. Jumi spoke of the importance of recovering Black history for Tamara in the light of her own experience of being kept ignorant by the British educational system:

> I didn't even know who Marcus Garvey and Malcolm X were, can you believe it, all through school in Hackney and I didn't find out about them until I was grown up.

However, Jumi also has a more pragmatic agenda:

> Tamara needs individual help, she doesn't get it at Milner but they've promised me she'll get it there. I really want them to get down to the three Rs with her.

Any examination of the importance of supplementary schooling as a source of counter discourses needs to unpick the complexities of a seemingly conservative educational stance—the insistence of Black parents on the importance of formal pedagogy and the three Rs and how it relates to transformative aspects of supplementary schooling. Anna commented vehemently of her daughter's primary school:

> I think there's too much faffing around. I think they should take teaching the basics by the horns and get on with it.

She commented later:

> Saturday school is about both those things. Her getting some help with the basics is important, but it is also about positive self identity. She is having individual tuition now, I'm paying a teacher I know to come round once a week so Saturday school isn't just for basics cos I'm tackling that anyway. I think being exposed to Black role models and Black history is just as important.

Anna's explanation exemplifies the two significant, yet apparently contradictory, strands motivating Black parents. There is the transformative impetus of the Afrocentric curriculum of many Saturday schools. This is increasingly apparent when counterposed to a history national curriculum in which the focus is upon:

> political, constitutional and military history rather than social or cultural. School history is envisioned as a poetics of power played out as a soap opera of kings queens and courtiers, as spectacle and personality. Emotion, identification, remorse and empathy are to be exercised and instead we have history as reconstitutive moral force and as a celebration of oppression and violence (Ball, 1994, p. 39).

When set against such 'curricular fundamentalism' (Ball, 1994, p. 39) in which the pasts of both the colonised and the working-classes are ignored (Ball, 1994, p. 46) the potential for powerful oppositional stances, increasingly precluded in mainstream provision, becomes clear.

Challenging the Stereotype: supplementary schooling and child centred education

Supplementary schooling is often depicted as very formal with a heavy focus on the 3Rs. A teacher in the school adjacent to one of the supplementary schools commented that 'it concentrates on drilling children' while another teacher asserted 'It's all 3 Rs with a bit of Black history thrown in'. Neither had visited the school. However, there is a different way of viewing supplementary schooling. Such a view depicts the curriculum offer in supplementary schooling as a pedagogic challenge to the progressive methods of inner city state schooling where Black and White working-class children all too often were encouraged to feel good about knowing very little (May, 1994). Instead a concentration on the 3Rs can be reinterpreted as a necessary counterbalance which ensures the focus on Black culture and 'feeling good' is combined with a pedagogy underpinned by high expectations and high standards. Rather than 'drilling children' supplementary schooling is re-attempting the failed project of progressive state education with a locally constructed curricular solution. The potentiality of supplementary schooling lies in its message that a combination of relevant curriculum and high standards is possible.

Often in Black educators' accounts relevant curriculum was described in terms of child centredness. Verna, Rose Nadine and Maxine all talked in terms of their practice as childcentred. Maxine explained about her school's interactive maths class for children who needed more support. Learning was based on the children's everyday world:

> We use all the things children like, like Reebok and Nike, Porsches and BMWs. We actually apply maths to everyday life in a way that's fun.

She asserted:

> If you are really serious about helping children realise their learning potential then you keep trying different ways. No matter what the experts say, children have different learning styles, so you can't just use one, you have to keep trying until you find one that suits the child. We are very conscious of that here. We think it is important to match teaching styles to the child's learning needs.

While Rose and Verna both described a curriculum offer which was just as grounded in creative arts as in Maths and English:

> The older children have written their own stories, prose and poetry, plays that they have then performed on stage in front of an audience. You know we have done so many things and concentrating on that the academic side but as well we do a lot of art and craft, especially for carnival. We always are making things or cooking something for carnival. They make all their own costumes. (Verna)

However, although there are strong overlaps, what we have here is a different variant of child centredness to progressive mainstream education. For Black educators a good mainstream school would encompass Black studies as integral to a child centred approach. Talking about the vagaries of anti-racist provision and its dependence on whether local authorities see race relations as an issue, Verna commented:

> I say beyond all that, that it is the child who is important, that it is important for the child to feel good about him/herself. To be able to see themselves in toys and books or whatever. I think policy just isn't child focused enough. I have a very strong philosophy of child centredness. I have always been very committed to supporting the child. In our society children often don't have a voice.

and:

> We are very child centred so there's lots of group work. (Rose)

However, sometimes child centredness is correlated with the empowerment of Black pupils:

> We always have a session which is about giving children a voice ... We teach them to speak, to develop a voice that can be heard ... We tell them to be proud of what they are, to be strong about speaking out. I think perhaps that is the most important thing we do, helping them develop a voice that gets heard because it is easy for Black children not to be listened to in school, to be thought of as a nuisance when they say something. I think in Saturday school it is quite clear that they are expected, entitled to speak out. (Rose)

Encoded in these women's texts on centering the child are far-reaching criticisms of mainstream schooling. Their words inscribe the lack of respect for the Black child and his/her culture in state schooling. Their pedagogic response aims to overturn the processes of silencing and marginalisation by restoring the child to centre stage. We would suggest that in these four supplementary schools, Black children can find 'really useful knowledge' (Johnson, 1979, 1988) which allows them 'to step outside the White hermeneutic circle and into the Black' (Gates, 1988, p. 258). British state schooling, despite a recent history of multi-cultural initiatives (King & Reiss, 1993; Tomlinson & Craft, 1995), still operates with predominately taken-for-granted assumptions of Whiteness as normative. Black supplementary schools provide a space to challenge such assumptions, as Verna asserts:

> You need to give them a fair representation of the world. It is not a cosy little White world in the back of beyond. Open it out we are all in it together. Give them a fair crack of what the world is and the world is multi-cultural. (Verna).

Beyond normative assumptions which centre Whiteness, Rose, Maxine and Verna's focus on the child as the pivot of educational practice has to be set in a contemporary economic and political climate in which children of all ethnic backgrounds are discursively constructed as products. Supplementary schooling challenges such constructions of its pupils while seemingly buying into the dominant discourses of traditional pedagogy with its focus on the 3 Rs and 'back to basics'. The prevailing educational climate is one in which a mainstream female primary headteacher from an ethnic minority background can comment, without any sense of irony, that:

> one of the worst things about the educational changes is that with this hugely expanded brief of financial manager, personnel officer, site manager, you know, all these additional roles, you can hardly ever get into the classroom anymore ... and the worst thing about the lack of contact with children is that it makes your job so difficult because it is so essential to be able to gauge how your teachers are coping, to know whether they are covering the National Curriculum adequately.

In a discursive context in which children are viewed from the top echelons of educational hierarchy increasingly as a mechanism for judging teachers, supplementary schooling is still operating with a different conception of the child. It may seem a strange proposition to suggest that supplementary schooling with its focus on formality and concentration on 3 Rs enshrines a resistance to the fading away of child centredness. However, as Charity points out, the view of supplementary schooling as very formal is a stereotype perpetuated by people who have no involvement in them:

> I think there is a stereotype and I think it is just that a stereotype. I think inevitably when Saturday schools are first set up there is a focus on parents' preoccupations, which is 'why can't my child read and write properly?' I think Saturday schools start off tackling what they see as the most urgent problem so they often do have a 3Rs focus at first but I think most of them evolve. Of course also there are many different types of Saturday school just as there are many different mainstream schools and some inevitably are better than others. However, I think they do develop a curriculum that is far more sophisticated and complex than a simple focus on 3Rs. That is certainly what has happened at Colibri ... We try and provide what we think is the best balance taking all the different needs into account.

> You know we have decided that this curriculum is the fairest balance that we can achieve. (Charity)

This fair balance constitutes a very different version of what education is about to the hegemonic version that is taken for granted by increasing numbers of teachers in mainstream schools.

Black Achievement: against the conceptual tide of ' "Race" and underachievement

In Mac an Ghaill's research on Black supplementary schools a Black teacher makes the point that 'for twenty years policy makers have been concerned about Black underachievement in schools. If that is true why have they never used voluntary schools, where young Black people are academically successfully, as a model of good practice.' (1991, p. 134) Indeed, if a genealogical analysis of Black supplementary schools offers the possibilities for, and provides evidence of Black academic achievement, we must then ask the question 'why has the idea of Black educational underachievement persisted in the dominant discourse about the Black community for over 30 years?'

Though over time the explanation has changed, the theme of Black underachievement has remained constant. In the 1960s the underlying rationale informing educational directives was that Black underachievement could be explained by differential intelligence and IQ (Verma & Bagley, 1979). By the 1970s the debate shifted to that of assimilation. Then it was being argued that ethnic minorities needed to assimilate and lose their cultural and linguistic markers in order to progress (Mullard, 1982). In the 1980s the multicultural education programmes stressed that underachievement was caused by low self esteem and feelings of negative self worth among Black pupils (Stone, 1981; Mirza, 1992) Most recently, towards the end of the 1990s, the latest Government review of 'race' and underachievement by OFSTED suggests that by not recognising cultural differences between pupils, schools can reinforce and encourage racist practises. The authors of the study assert, 'Failure to address ethnic diversity has proved counter-productive at the school level. Where schools have adopted "colour-blind" policies, for example, inequalities of opportunity have been seen to continue.' (Gillborn & Gipps, 1996, p. 80)

In an about turn, it appears the debate has moved from a position where it was claimed equality rests on achieving sameness (cultural assimilation), to a postmodern position where equality rests on recognising difference (ethnic diversity). Such a philosophical stance in the 'race' and underachievement debate, while on the surface appearing progressive, has implications for the future education of young Black people both in mainstream and supplementary schools. As Black women indicated in their statements, to emphasise that there are differences between racially 'marked' British born pupils adds fuel to the ideological drive towards selective schooling. It openly invites in the notion of different or 'special' needs for different or 'special' pupils. It welcomes into the classroom the natural justice of the market place, which quietly, on the basis of 'choice' does its work by sifting and sorting out those who are less able from those who are more able. The Conservative Government's call for increased ethnic monitoring to redress the problems raised by ethnic diversity (Guardian 6.9.96) sets in motion a legitimate mechanism for sifting and sorting until quite naturally there will be a return to 'special' schools, 'sinbins,' 'sink schools', or 'no go' schools for problematic Black pupils.

The Black educators have already sensed the pressure to use Black supplementary schools as 'special' schools for 'special' pupils. Local authority rationalisation of funding and new terms and conditions for eligibility to funding emphasise selectivity and the 'down sizing' of supplementary schools in any one area (Sewell, 1996). It was not surprising in this political climate of 'contract culture' to find three of the four Saturday schools we visited deliberately avoiding direct funding by the local authority. A Black equal opportunities officer working within one of the London boroughs in which fieldwork was carried out confirmed from her insiders position the problematic future for Black supplementary schools:

> While raising Black educational achievement is clearly important, there is evidence of worrying reworking of how supplementary schooling is seen, even by the sympathetic within local educational hierarchies. Supplementary schooling as a vehicle for entitlement and empowerment has slipped off the agenda to be replaced by a construction of supplementary schooling as a means to climbing educational league tables. (Equal Opportunities Advisor)

How Black supplementary schools can be used to enhance competitive local league tables is explained by Verna:

> Verna: I wanted Saturday school to be fairly independent. I feel if you get a lot of money from people then (laughing) you know
>
> Diane: You'll be tied to what they want
>
> Verna: Yes, some control, some criteria to be met or they'll want the right to send their type of kid to you.

Their 'type of kid' was often those who were excluded or problematic in the mainstream. Both Colibri and Scarlet Ibis had accepted social service referrals, including permanently excluded children, and children who had been emotionally disturbed through traumatic transracial adoption or fostering experiences.

Maxine had been involved in supplementary schooling for 16 years. She gave her own pessimistic version of current policy direction:

> What local authorities are doing is selecting out one school to fund at the expense of the others. It's got nothing to do with the aims and philosophy of supplementary schools and everything to do with pushing local authorities up national league tables that's what we are in danger of becoming, a means to those sort of ends. I can see the dangers, yes, it becomes very obvious once you look.

However there was also evidence of a radical discursive reappropriation of current events in the accounts of Black educators involved in Colibri, the school which was being sponsored by the local authority. They saw themselves as retaining control over policy direction and working from within to co-opt local authority personnel into seeing things more from their perspective. The full-time coordinator at Colibri had recently taken up a prestigious post within the local education authority and was clearly just as committed to changing things from within as she had been from the outside. Similarly Maxine's prognosis of incorporation within mainstream contained transformative possibilities alongside the pessimistic ones that she foresaw.

Conclusion: situating Black female agency

Gurnah suggests the pervasive empirical discourse which seeks to qualify and quantify Black underachievement has obscured the history of Black agency and grassroots activism:

> ... 'facts' about Black oppression, (have) become repetitive or voyeuristic. For even when they give undeniable evidence of what

> that oppression looks like, they simultaneously also present accounts of how Black people in western societies habitually are being degraded and humiliated. What is often missing in their accounts, are corresponding tales of Black people's efforts to improve or reverse their condition. (Gurnah, 1992, p. 91).

In a genealogical analysis of Black female agency within Black supplementary schools it appears it is the mainstream schools that fail Black children rather than Black children who are underachieving. Black women activists, Bryan *et al.* write: 'The education system's success can be measured directly in terms of Black children's failure within it' (1985, p. 58). The story of failure, exclusions, alienation and violence among Black school children made popular by the press have become so consuming that it is now an acceptable 'truth' to think of young Black people only as without hope, underachievers, disconnected, and in disarray. Even the Black community itself appears to be captured by the discourse rather than active within it. By uncovering the subjugated knowledges and hidden histories of these Black supplementary schools, the narratives of Black women educators consistently decentre such 'truths' and reinsert their version of reality: that they invest in education so they can change their lives, and their children's lives.

In creating a sanctuary for the Black child in which he/she is recentred and celebrated, Black women educators reveal the silent, pervasive, seemingly invisible hegemonic project of Whiteness implicit in mainstream schooling. By providing evidence of the possibility of delivering a relevant curriculum with high standards, these schools not only challenge the knowledge claims implicit within the national curriculum, but also subvert the cry of low standards automatically associated with 'other' knowledge or knowledge of the 'other'. Similarly, the supplementary school's childcentred practice and valorising of the parent as 'expert' demonstrates the effectiveness of education when it is negotiated rather than imposed.

Black supplementary schools present the paradox of separate Black provision operating as a mechanism of educational inclusion. There are, as we have discussed earlier, apparent strands of educational conformity within Black supplementary schooling: a buying into the right-wing hegemony of 'back to basics' and 'formal is best'. However, as Kathleen Casey points out, in a racist society the Black person is located very differently in the educational field to the White person. For the Black child to become educated is 'to contradict the whole system of racist signification' (Casey, 1993, p. 123). She conceptualises education as refutation for Black people and writes:

> Central to this complex agenda of aspirations is the notion that knowledge is power, to be wise in 'Black' interpretation is essential to physical and psychic survival; but to succeed at studying 'White' knowledge is to undo the system itself, to refute its (re)production of Black inferiority materially and symbolically. (Casey, 1993, p. 124)

Black supplementary schooling, as a female centred new social movement, works for educational inclusion in order to transform opportunities and so in the process subvert racist expectations and beliefs. The women's strategies for inclusion, emphasis on the formal 3Rs, and dialogue with the mainstream, may appear on the surface conservative and contradictory, in effect they subvert the mainstream discourse on Black underachievement and offer transformative possibilities from the margins. In spite of the educational deprivation the Black communities suffer in the inner city, there is another story to tell, a story revealed through a genealogy of the margins—it is a story of resistance, determination and transcendence.

Notes

Special thanks to the authors and Taylor and Francis for granting permission to reprint this chapter. This research was made possible only by the kind and open participation of all the Black women who were interviewed. Their names, and the names of the schools have been changed.

References

Casey, K. (1993) *I Answer with My Life: Life Histories of Women Teachers Working for Social Change*. New York, Routledge.
Channer, Y. (1995) *I am a Promise: The School Achievement of British African Caribbeans*. London, Trentham Books.
Chevannes, M. & Reeves F. (1987) The Black voluntary school movement: definition, context and prospects, in: B. Troyna (Ed.) *Racial Inequality in Education*. London, Tavistock.
Clark, N. (1982). Dachwyng Saturday School in A. Ohri, B. Manning & P. Curno (Eds) *Community Work and Racism*. London, Routledge Kegan Paul.
Cole, M. & Hill, D. (1995) Games of despair and rhetorics of resistance: postmodernism, education and resistance, *British Journal of sociology of Education*, 16: pp. 165-182.
Connolly, P. (1994) All lads together?: racism, masculinity and multicultural/anti-racist strategies in a primary school, *International Studies in Sociology of Education*, 4: pp. 191-211
Dacosta, C. (1987) Ideology and practice within the Black supplementary school movement. Unpublished PhD thesis, University of Surrey.
David, M., Davies J., Edwards, R., Reay., D. & Standing, K. (1997) Choice within constraints: mothers and schooling, *Gender and Education*, 9, 4: pp.
Dean, M. (1994) *Critical and Effective Histories: Foucault's Methods and Historical Sociology* (London, Routledge).
Department for Education (1992) *Choice and Diversity: A New Framework for Schools*. London, HMSO.
Dhondy, F., Besse, B. & Hassan L. (1982) *The Black Explosion in British Schools*. London, Race Today Publications.
Dove, N. (1993) The emergence of Black supplementary schools: resistance to racism in the United Kingdom, *Urban Education*, 27, January pp. 430-447.
Foucault, M. (1977) *Discipline and Punish*. London, Alien Lane.
Foucault, M. (1980) *Power/Knowledge: selected interviews and other writings*, 1972-77 C. Gordon (Ed.) Brighton, Harvester Press.
Foucault, M., (1981), *The History of Sexuality*, Vol. 1. Harmondsworth, Penguin.
Foucault, M. (1991) Space, knowledge and power, in: P. Rabinow *The Foucault Reader*. London, Penguin.
Frankenberg, R. (1993) *White Women, Race Matters: The Social Construction of Whiteness*. London, Routledge.
Gates, H.L.J.R (1988) *The Signifying Monkey: A Theory of African American Literary Criticism*. New York, Oxford University Press.
Gillborn, D. (1995) *Racism and Antiracism in Real Schools*. Buckingham, Open University Press.

Gillborn, D. & Gipps, C. (1996) *Recent Research on the Achievements of Ethnic Minority Pupils,* OFSTED Reviews of Research. London, HMSO.

Giroux, H. (1994) Living dangerously: identity politics and the new cultural racism, in: H. Giroux & P. McLaren (Eds) *Between Borders: Pedagogy and the Politics of Cultural Studies.* London, Routledge.

Goodson, I. (1995) The story so far: personal knowledge and the political. *Qualitative Studies in Education*, 8: pp. 89-98.

Grace, G. (1978) *Teachers, Ideology and Control.* London, Routledge and Kegan Paul.

Green, A. (1990) *Education and State Formation: The Rise of Educational Systems in England, France and the USA.* Basingstoke, Macmillan.

Gueye, A. (1988) Supplementary Schools in the Black community, *Dragons Teeth*, 29: pp. 2-3.

Gurnah, A. (1992) On the specificity of racism, in: M. Arnot & I. Barton (Eds) *Voicing Concerns: Sociological Perspectives on Contemporary Education Reforms.* Wallingford, Triangle Books.

Hoggart, R. (1957) *The Uses of Literacy.* London, Chatto and Windus.

hooks, b. (1994) *Teaching to Transgress: Education and the Practice of Freedom.* London, Routledge.

Johnson, R. (1979) Really useful knowledge: radical education and working-class culture 1790-1948, in: J. Clarke, G. Critcher & R. Johnson (Eds) *Working Class culture: Studies in History and Theory.* New York, St Martin's Press.

Jones, V.A. (1986) *We are Our Own Educators.* London, Karia Press with the Josina Machel Supplementary School.

King, A. & Reiss, M. (Eds) (1993) *The Multicultural Dimension of the National Curriculum.* London, Falmer Press.

Mac an Ghaill, M. (1991) Black voluntary schools: the 'Invisible' private sector, in: G. WALFORD (Ed.) *Private Schooling: Tradition, Change and Diversity.* London, Paul Chapman.

McLaren, P. (1994) Multiculturalism and the postmodern critique: toward a pedagogy of resistance and Transformation, in: H. Giroux & P. McLaren (Eds) *Between the Borders: Pedagogy and the Politics of Cultural Change.* London, Routledge.

May, Stephen, (1994) *Making Multicultural Education Work.* Clevedon, Multilingual Matters.

Mirza, H.S. (1992) *Young, Female and Black.* London, Routledge.

Mirza: H.S. (1997) Black women in education: a collective movement for social change, in. H.S. Mirza (Ed.) *Black British Feminism: A Reader.* London, Routledge.

Mullard C. (1982) Multicultural education in Britain: from assimilation to cultural pluralism, M.J. Tierney (Ed.) *Race, Migration and Schooling.* London, Holt, Rinehart and Winston)

Reay, D. (1996) Contextualising choice: social power and parental involvement, *British Educational Research Journal* 22: pp. 581-596.

Sawicki, J. (1991) *Disciplining Foucault: Feminism, Power and the Body.* London. Routledge.

Seabrook, I. (1982) *Working-Class Childhood: An Oral History.* London, Victor Gollancz.

Sewell, T. (996) South London supplementary/heritage schools: shifting out of dominance, Kingston University. Paper presented at the British Educational Research Association Conference, Lancaster University, September.

Smart B. (1992) *Modern Conditions, Postmodern Controversies.* London, Routledge.

Solomos, T. & BACK L. (1995) *Race, Politics and Social Change.* London, Routledge.

Steedman, C. (1990) *Childhood, Culture and Class in Britain: Margaret McMillan 1860-1931.* London, Virago.

Stone M. (1981) *The Education of the Black Child: The Myth of Multi-Cultural Education.* London, Fontana Press.

Tomlinson, S. (1984) *Home and School: Multi Cultural Britain.* London, Batsford.

Tomlinson, S. (1985) The 'Black Education' Movement, in: M. Arnot (Ed.) *Race and Gender.* (Oxford, Pergomon Press

Tomlinson, S. & Craft, M. (Eds) (1995) *Ethnic Relations and Schooling: Policy and Practice in the 1990s.* London, Athlone.

Verma, G. Bagley C. (1979) A critical introduction, in: G. Verma & C. Bagley (Ed.) *Race, Education and Identity.* London, Macmillan Press.

Weiner, G. (1994) *Feminism and Education.* Milton Keynes, Open University Press.

Williams, C. (1995) How Black children might survive education, in: M. Griffiths & B. Troyna *Antiracism, Culture and Social Justice in Education.* London, Trentham Books.

Index

A

Africa 9, 14, 16, 20, 21, 22, 24, 25, 26, 27, 28, 29
African 2, 3, 4, 5
African Caribbean 14, 23, 64, 83, 108, 125, 126, 127, 128, 131, 133, 135, 142, 145, 146, 147, 149, 171
American 14, 16, 17, 22, 25, 29, 35, 147, 156

B

Black Unity and Freedom Party 13
  BUFP 9, 10, 11, 12, 13, 14, 15, 17, 19, 20, 21, 22, 23, 36
Black Voice. *See Publications: Black Voice*
BLP 23, 26, 29, 30, 31, 33, 34, 35. *See also* Publications: Bogle L'Ouverture Publications (BLP)
Bogle L'Ouverture Publications. *See Publications: Bogle L'Ouverture Publications (BLP)*

C

childcare 53, 55, 82, 83, 135, 136
childrearing v, *85, 86, 87, 88, 89, 93, 94, 96, 97*
church 11, 13, 22, 23, 54, 62, *95*, 103, 106, 110, 111, 112, 113, 114, 131, 145, 150
citizenship 125, 135, 139, 140, 141, 144, 145, 146, 147
collective action 4, 55, 56, 58, 74, 155
Collins, P 56, *98*
community action 23, 33
community nursery 125, 144, 146
Conservative Party 15
Cottle *39, 42, 43, 44, 46, 49*

D

discrimination 13, 19, 28, 44, 58, 60, 70, 73, 77, 78, 82, *85, 86, 89, 90, 93*, 115, 125, 126, 130

F

feminism 54, 58, 61, 78, 80

G

Generation
  first generation 30, *86, 87, 90, 96*
  second generation *146*
  third generation *146*
George Joseph *11*
Goulbourne 50, 51, 78, 79

H

Hallam, S 148
Harambee 126, 127, 134, 136, 137

M

Marcus Garvey Nursery 126, 127, 130, 136, 147
marginalised 153
McCalla 1, 125, 126, 127, 129, 131, 134, 137, 138, 139, 140, 141, 144, 145, 147
Mirza 4, 6, 101, 113, 114, 116
Multiculturalism 18, 43, 48, 49, 172

N

National Curriculum 3
New Beacon Books (NBB) 21, 23, 25, 26, 31, 32, *33*, 34, *35*, 38
North America 3
nursery workers 136, 139

P

Political Action 38
Publications
    Black Voice 18, 19, 21, 24, 36
    Bogle L'Ouverture Publications (BLP) 23

R

race relations 17, 18, *34*, 38, 46, *86*, *97*, 166
racial 150
racial conflict 40
Reay 4, *90*, *98*, 127, 134, 148
Reynolds *85*, *86*, *88*, *95*, *98*
Rhamie v, 4, 101, 102, 128, 131, 134, 139, 145, 148

S

Schools
    schooling 3, *4*, *6*
    supplementary schooling 4
    supplementary schools 150
Sudbury 50, 77
Supplementary Schooling 150, 157
Supplementary schooling 165, 167
supplementary schooling 150, 153, 155, 157, 159, 160, 162, 163, 164, 165, 167, 169
Susan Hallam 4, 101

T

Trinidad 10–11

U

Universal Coloured Peoples' Alliance (UCPA) 13
USA 5

W

West Indian Standing Conference 12
    WISC 12, *13*, 15